TRANSPORTATION IN EASTERN EUROPE

EMPIRICAL FINDINGS

———

BOGDAN MIECZKOWSKI

EAST EUROPEAN QUARTERLY, BOULDER
DISTRIBUTED BY COLUMBIA UNIVERSITY PRESS
NEW YORK

1978

EAST EUROPEAN MONOGRAPHS, NO. XXXVIII

Bogdan Mieczkowski is Professor of Economics at
Ithaca College

Copyright © 1978 by East European Quarterly
Library of Congress Card Catalogue Number 77-82392
ISBN 0-914710-31-1

Printed in the United States of America

EAST EUROPEAN MONOGRAPHS

The *East European Monographs* comprise scholarly books on the history and civilization of Eastern Europe. They are published by the *East European Quarterly* in the belief that these studies contribute substantially to the knowledge of the area and serve to stimulate scholarship and research.

1. *Political Ideas and the Enlightenment in the Romanian Principalities, 1750-1831.* By Vlad Georgescu. 1971.
2. *America, Italy and the Birth of Yugoslavia, 1917-1919.* By Dragan R. Zivojinovic. 1972.
3. *Jewish Nobles and Geniuses in Modern Hungary.* By William O. McCagg, Jr. 1972.
4. *Mixail Soloxov in Yugoslavia: Reception and Literary Impact.* By Robert F. Price. 1973.
5. *The Historical and National Thought of Nicolae Iorga.* By William O. Oldson. 1973.
6. *Guide to Polish Libraries and Archives.* By Richard C. Lewanski. 1974.
7. *Vienna Broadcasts to Slovakia, 1938-1939: A Case Study in Subversion.* By Henry Delfiner. 1974.
8. *The 1917 Revolution in Latvia.* By Andrew Ezergailis. 1974.
9. *The Ukraine in the United Nations Organization: A Study in Soviet Foreign Policy. 1944-1950.* By Konstantin Sawczuk. 1975.
10. *The Bosnian Church: A New Interpretation.* By John V. A. Fine, Jr. 1975.
11. *Intellectual and Social Developments in the Habsburg Empire from Maria Theresa to World War I.* Edited by Stanley B. Winters and Joseph Held. 1975.
12. *Ljudevit Gaj and the Illyrian Movement.* By Elinor Murray Despalatovic. 1975.
13. *Tolerance and Movements of Religious Dissent in Eastern Europe.* Edited by Bela K. Kiraly. 1975.
14. *The Parish Republic: Hlinka's Slovak People's Party, 1939-1945.* By Yeshayahu Jelinek. 1976.
15. *The Russian Annexation of Bessarabia, 1774-1828.* By George F. Jewsbury. 1976.
16. *Modern Hungarian Historiography.* By Steven Bela Vardy. 1976.
17. *Values and Community in Multi-National Yugoslavia.* By Gary K. Bertsch. 1976.

18. *The Greek Socialist Movement and the First World War: the Road to Unity.* By George B. Leon. 1976.

19. *The Radical Left in the Hungarian Revolution of 1848.* By Laszlo Deme. 1976.

20. *Hungary between Wilson and Lenin: The Hungarian Revolution of 1918–1919 and the Big Three.* By Peter Pastor. 1976.

21. *The Crises of France's East-Central European Diplomacy, 1933–1938.* By Anthony J. Komjathy. 1976.

22. *Polish Politics and National Reform, 1775–1788.* By Daniel Stone. 1976.

23. *The Habsburg Empire in World War I.* Robert A. Kann, Bela K. Kiraly, and Paula S. Fichtner, eds. 1977.

24. *The Slovenes and Yugoslavism, 1890–1914.* By Carole Rogel. 1977.

25. *German-Hungarian Relations and the Swabian Problem.* By Thomas Spira. 1977.

26. *The Metamorphosis of a Social Class in Hungary During the Reign of Young Franz Joseph.* By Peter I. Hidas. 1977.

27. *Tax Reform in Eighteenth Century Lombardy.* By Daniel M. Klang. 1977.

28. *Tradition versus Revolution: Russia and the Balkans in 1917.* By Robert H. Johnston. 1977.

29. *Winter into Spring: The Czechoslovak Press and the Reform Movement 1963–1968.* By Frank L. Kaplan. 1977.

30. *The Catholic Church and the Soviet Government, 1939–1949.* By Dennis J. Dunn. 1977.

31. *The Hungarian Labor Service System, 1939–1945.* By Randolph L. Braham. 1977.

32. *Consciousness and History: Nationalist Critics of Greek Society 1897–1914.* By Gerasimos Augustinos. 1977.

33. *Emigration in Polish Social and Political Thought, 1870–1914.* By Benjamin P. Murdzek. 1977.

34. *Serbian Poetry and Milutin Bojić.* By Mihailo Dordevic. 1977.

35. *The Baranya Dispute 1918–1921: Diplomacy in the Vortex of Ideologies.* By Leslie Charles Tihany. 1978.

36. *The United States in Prague, 1945–1948.* By Walter Ullmann. 1978.

37. *Rush to the Alps: The Evolution of Vacationing in Switzerland.* By Paul P. Bernard. 1978.

38. *Transportation in Eastern Europe: Empirical Findings.* By Bogdan Mieczkowski. 1978

Contents

List of Tables and Figures

List of Abbreviations

AS	*Annuarul Statistic al Republicii Socialiste România*
BRT	Brutto (Gross)Registry Tons
Comecon	Council for Mutual Economic Assistance, CMEA (acronym for)
DN	*Dochód Narodowy Polski*
DOT	Department of Transportation
DWT	Dead-Weight Tons
GDR	German Democratic Republic
GNP	Gross National Product
GUS	Główny Urząd Statystyczny
km	kilometer(s)
MW	megawatts
MWh	megawatt-hours
NRT	Net Registry Tons
OP	Occasional Papers of the Research Project on National Income in East-Central Europe (New York: Columbia University, or Riverside Research Institute)
PAN	Polska Akademia Nauk
pass.	passenger(s)
PK	*Przegląd Komunikacyjny*
PKP	*Przeglád Kolejowy Przewozowy*
PWE	Polskie Wydawnictwo Ekonomiczne
PWN	Polskie Wydawnictwo Naukowe
R&D	Research & Development
RFER	*Radio Free Europe Research*
RFER: BR	*Radio Free Europe Research: Background Report*
RFER: SR	*Radio Free Europe Research: Situation Report*
RS	*Rocznik Statystyczny*
SE	*Statisztikai Évkönyv*
SESEV	*Statisticheskii Ezhegodnik Stran-Chlenov Soveta Ekonomicheskoi Vzaimopomoshchi*
SEzh	*Statisticheskii Ezhegodnik*
SG	*Statistički Godišnjak Jugoslavije*

SGB	*Statisticheski Godisnik na Narodna Republika Bulgaria*
SGPiS	Szkoła Główna Planowania i Statystyki
SJ	*Statistisches Jahrbuch der Deutschen Demokratischen Republik*
SPBH	*Statistical Pocket Book of Hungary*
SR	*Statistická Ročenka Československé Socialisticke Republiky*
STD	*Science, Technology and Development*, U.S. Papers Prepared for the United Nations Conference on the Application of Science and Technology for the Benefit of the Less Developed Areas. Washington, D.C.: U.S. Government Printing Office.
t	ton(s)
WKL	Wydawnictwa Komunikacji i Łączności
ZG	*Życie Gospodarcze*
ZN	*Zeszyty naukowe*
—	(in tables) data nonexistent or negligible
	(in tables) data not available

Preface

One of the least discussed sectors of economic activity is transportation. Yet, with modern-day widespread division of labor and exchange of goods and services, transportation provides the necessary linkage among persons, enterprises, markets, and nations. Without transportation, virtually no specialization in economic activity could take place, our level of living would fall precipitously, and most of our satisfaction stemming from our consumption of services would disappear. Not only would we be unable to travel for business purposes — and incidentally to enjoy the social prestige of some of the means of transport — but we would also be unable to enjoy tourism, specialized services, the adventures and satisfaction of "shopping around," health services dispensed in specialized locations such as spas or some hospitals, the olympics and most other sport competitions, music festivals, conventions, and many others. Without transportation the entire fibre of our modern lives would be destroyed.

The importance of transportation and a virtual absence of comprehensive Western sources on transport in Eastern Europe have prompted me to write a basic study of transport in that area. The study is by choice limited, and it omits several important aspects of transport, among them technology, morphology, and the quality of transport in Eastern Europe. On the other hand, it contains much information hitherto unavailable in the West and some information that so far has been inaccessible or dispersed. On one level, the study transcends its narrow subject matter: its implications extend beyond the sphere of transport, and the interested reader will learn from it much about the functioning of Soviet-type economies and about the wider setting and problems of transport. The study also has a great deal to say to all those theorists and men of action who are contemplating programs of centralized planning for their national transport systems.

The study aims at an interested reader who is not an expert in the theoretical aspects of transport. Those aspects are largely omitted here, and the main focus is on how the transport sector in Eastern Europe actually functions. The theory of transport can be conveniently found in books already published in the West, and the theoretical analysis of transport found in East European sources can add nothing or, at best, only marginally to Western literature on the subject. Such an omission on my part brings, therefore, into sharper focus the specific contribution of this book and allows the reader to concentrate on the assessment of transport in Eastern Europe. The major contribution of this book is contained in chapters 3–5 on the planning of transport in Eastern Europe, its statistical growth, and the cost of transport in Eastern Europe. Chapters 2 and 6 provide original information on the setting of the study and on the international implications of transport in Eastern Europe. Major conclusions and projections into the future are found in chapter 7.

The present study is "a first" on the subject in the English language. A similar study exists in German, but it is already dated and is less comprehensive. The increasing importance of transport in Eastern Europe as well as the increasing importance of Eastern Europe itself render this study particularly topical. In an era of rapprochement and détente, furthermore, it is most timely and appropriate. As economic relations between East and West quicken, it seems reasonable to expect the general public as well as policy-makers to become aware of the physical means that enable East-West commerce to take place and people to associate with each other. A study of transport forms the cornerstone of this awareness.

The preparation of any larger study brings with it debts of gratitude. This work has been no exception — to my deep satisfaction from the strengthening of professional as well as personal friendships. Thad P. Alton, Gregor Lazarcik, and Adam Rudzki gave me advice and access to sources at their disposal. Z. T. Mieczkowski of the University of Manitoba, Elisabeth M. Bass, and Frank Bandor shared their sources with me. Po-Chih Lee, Senior Economist at Bell Canada, helped with the regression analysis found in the last section of chapter 4. Encouragement and constructive criticism are gratefully acknowledged from several colleagues and friends, especially Andrew Ezergailis, Frank Musgrave, and William E. Terwilliger of Ithaca College, and Marek A. Rudzki of the Planning Department of the Port Authority of New York. Zbigniew Siemienski, from whom I learned much as a student, gave me stimulation and his kind attention. Roland Gibson of the State University of New York at Potsdam helped in editing the manuscript. William E. Freeman did a superb job of final technical editing of the manuscript. I would also like to express my deep gratitude and acknowledge my indebtedness to the many librarians from whom I have so liberally received assistance ever since the start of my university studies. Although such assistance is often unappreciated and seldom adequately acknowledged, I wish to state that this and my earlier books and papers, like all others, could not have been brought to a successful conclusion without the understanding and unfailing cooperation of innumerable librarians, who are in the best sense of the phrase "our custodians of books."

My wife Seiko participated in the writing and revising of each chapter and gave me encouragement, help, and loyal faith. It is to her that I gratefully dedicate this book.

I

Introduction

Importance of Transport

The transport system may be likened to the blood circulation system in a living organism.[1] Without it the organism dies. Without transport a modern economy, based on division of labor and large markets, cannot survive either. Conversely, the more efficient the transport system, the wider the scope for division of labor, the more highly developed the economy can become. Thus economic development, as shown for example, by Great Britain since the 1820s and by Japan since the 1870s, depends on improvement in the transport network within the country and in transport links with the outside world. In fact, the volume of goods transported tends to increase at a higher rate than does the gross national product (GNP),[2] placing strains on the transport system and requiring it greatly to increase its efficiency as well as expand its network (see chapter 4). With the increase in per capita income, the demand for transport services to the population also grows at a rate higher than that of personal per capita income. To the extent that growth of freight traffic may tend to impede in some cases the growth of passenger traffic, as in the case of freight vs. passenger train scheduling, or in the case of rush-hour highway and street transport, this two-pronged development of transport creates its own problems.

It is difficult to overestimate the importance of transport for economic development of a country (Owen 1964: 1–21), for regional development and increasing the flexibility in the location of industries, for the smooth functioning of industries, for the distribution of agricultural and industrial products throughout the economy, and for binding an economy through international trade to the economies of other countries by widening the scope of the law of comparative advantage. From the long historical perspective, the wheel was man's greatest invention. Transportation caused common cultural and language groups to develop, and it now pervades all facets of individual and societal life (Underwood 1972: 1; Güttler 1971: 258; U.S. Congress, House, 1959: xvii; Norton 1971: 3-4). Alfred Marshall, the founder of neo-classical economics, attributed to transportation utmost importance (Marshall 1920: 423). It has been now widely recognized that transportation is a major sector of a modern economy, and that it significantly influences the dynamics of economic development (U.S. DOT 1972: vii; Mott 1963: 3).

It seems indisputable that the structure of freight transport is a telling indicator of the directions of a country's economic development and capacities. This concerns both the broad commodity division, such as coal, ores, metals and metal products, and oil, as well as inter-regional transport linkages. A study of transport reveals the regional distribution of economic activity in a country, location of main focal points for foreign trade, the main flows of goods, the inter-regional input-output relations, and the relative economic importance of different regions. Growth of freight transport indicates the changing degree of geographical division of labor, and provides a measure of economic growth of the country. Information on passenger transport yields location of the main urban centers and their relative importance, location of tourist centers, gives an indicator of changing levels of living and changing forms of satisfaction of the need for transport, as do also the shifts from public transport to private transport, or from railroad to bus transport. An analysis of transport statistics may indicate the existence and degree of success of given localization policies, policies to stimulate the economic life in some regions, policies to encourage and possibly to subsidize certain sectors of economic activity (for instance through lower rates on transport of certain commodities or from certain regions), and social policies (for instance through reduction of fares for certain categories of people, for certain specified purpose of travel, or for certain direction of travel). Consequently, a study of transport reveals the most important economic information about a country and the main vectors of its growth. The present book can be regarded only as the beginning of such an analysis for Eastern Europe, providing, as it does, the economic setting of transport in that region.

The degree of socialization of transport provides an insight into the prevalent political ideology in a country. The relative importance of public and private transport provides a clue to the social philosophy and the values and priorities of planners or, more generally, of economic and political decision-makers. The development of different transport modes and their technical endowment tells a lot about the technological stage achieved by a country. Thus a bicycle economy, like that of China, differs qualitatively from a scooter economy, like that of Italy in the 1950s. A railroad economy, like that of the Soviet Union, differs from one that relies heavily on highway transportation, like that of the United States. Even shifts from railway to road transport, such as have been taking place in Eastern Europe, show changes taking place in the spread of industry and of access to transportation. Thus political, philosophical, and economic factors interact on transport, just as transport interacts with the functioning of the economy as a whole (cf. Wolfe 1963: 8-14).

The present study stresses some of the above implications of transport. There are, however, other, partly noneconomic, implications of transport that will not be adequately explored in this volume. Among them are the strategic implications; implications for domestic locational policy of industrial development; implications for potential foreign investors; discussion of facilities for tourist travel; influence on social change and hence also the political implications of transport; transport as a case study of (a) economic development, (b) technological development, (c) organizational achievements; the impact on consumer welfare and on national wellbeing; the legal institutions set up in connection with transport; relation between fluctuations in the demand for transport and fluctuations in the overall economic activity; price elasticity of demand for transport; price competitiveness of the different modes of transport; and labor problems related to transport. It is hoped that some of these topics may be developed at a later date.

Importance of the Present Study

Importance of the subject matter lends importance to the study that treats such subject matter. The present study does not, however, rest only on this tautology. Its main, and separate, claim for attention is the fact of its uniqueness in the literature, for no similar study has been so far undertaken. There are several studies on transport in the Soviet Union, and they are cited in later chapters. The nearest geographical coverage is contained in a German study by Werner Gumpel (1967), but that study is less comprehensive, available only in German, and is by now slightly dated. However, as a pioneering effort, it may be highly recommended. Another useful West German study, by Horst Demmler (1967), covers only transport policy in East Germany.

Current studies on regional economics, geography, and location of industry in Eastern Europe largely abstract from transport problems. A recent collection of essays on geographical problems of Eastern

Europe (Hoffman 1971) is typical in this respect (cf. Brown 1971: 214–15; Wilson 1971). Studies of planning are usually just as oblivious to transport problems; unfortunately, the exceptions are usually superficial (cf. Fisher 1971: 325, 333–34).

The present study brings together observations from the whole area of Eastern Europe for the period after World War II. It is based on statistical material not easily available, or not available at all, in English. Parts of it are descriptive, and parts are quantitative. The present author aimed at a systematic evaluation of the transport system in Eastern Europe as a whole, while at the same time providing information about the individual countries of the area. The author has tried at all times to be as informative as possible so that the present study can be largely used in place of primary statistical information and, where that is impossible, so that it can point out extant sources to researchers.

As an economist, the present author was largely unconcerned with noneconomic implications of the study, some of which have been mentioned above. On the basis of this study, however, many such non-economic implications can be drawn and developed.

The present study incorporates also some independent estimates, made by Western researchers including the present author, of the contribution of the transport sector to the national incomes of the countries of Eastern Europe. Those estimates are not widely available, and hence their dissemination seemed worthwhile. Soviet-type economies, e.g., those of Eastern Europe with the exception of Yugoslavia, suffer from at least sectional unreliability of their statistics, thus making independent checks important as a means of increasing the integrity and reliability of information. This problem was discussed in the author's recent book (Mieczkowski 1975: ch. 3).

The diversity of languages in Eastern Europe makes a comprehensive study in English singularly important; few readers can be expected to have a working knowledge of several of them at the same time. The author's hope has been, therefore, not only to make an original contribution to Western knowledge about transport in Eastern Europe, but also to bring together existing, but not readily accessible, information and place it at the disposal of the reader.

Transport makes up an important proportion of domestic GNP in Eastern Europe. Thus in Poland transport and communications taken together constituted at market prices 5.2, 5.6, and 5.7 percent of domestic GNP in 1954, 1955, and 1956, respectively (Alton 1965: 56–58). In Czechoslovakia. transport and communications taken together at factor cost constituted 11.4, 10.8, 10.2, and 10.1 percent of domestic GNP in 1947, 1948, 1955, and 1956, respectively (Alton 1962: 60). In Hungary, transport and communications taken together constituted 5.8 percent of GNP in current market prices in 1955, and between 10.2 and 11.4 percent of GNP at factor cost (Alton *et al.* 1963: 64, 76). For a comparison, in the West transport accounts for 20 percent or more of the costs of material GNP (Norton 1971: 4).

The secretiveness of communist countries about some aspects of their economies makes the study of their transport systems more important since transport provides the crucial links between all sectors of the economy, whether shrouded in secrecy or not. This does not necessarily mean that a study of communist transport systems will reveal the hidden aspects of the operation of those systems. It implies only a tendency toward better knowledge about the operation of such systems, a step toward fuller information about Eastern European economies as a whole and about their transport systems in particular.

The picture that emerges from the present study is a composite one. Some details are missing from some East European economic systems and are filled in by available details from other systems, adding up to a fuller picture than would be possible on the basis of data for a one-country study. East Germany seems to have engendered the largest volume of information, partly as the result of West German research. The least amount of information was available from the southern tier of Eastern Europe. The sources of the present study are largely official national statistical yearbooks or similar official publications. A large amount of data was obtained from journal and newspaper articles, some from Western sources.

Postwar Eastern Europe inherited a relatively well developed railway network from the prewar period, but its highway network was, except for East Germany and partly Czechoslovakia, very inadequate, even with respect to the immediate needs of postwar reconstruction. Rolling stock was greatly depleted and highly inadequate. Autarkic tendencies, traditional for the Soviet Union, made for a relative initial slackening of the demand on sea transport and to a lesser extent on inland waterways transport, and contributed to the smallness of the demand to develop air transport.

East European transport thereafter seems to have experienced a dynamic growth, an improvement in its composition by modes, and an improvement in quality, both from the technical point of view and from the point of view of convenience to its users. However, as the result of neglect of transport relative to other sectors of the economies

of Eastern Europe, transport seems also to operate under considerable
pressures on its capacity, which makes it more costly to operate than it
otherwise might have been. Complaints about transport bottlenecks
are frequent in Eastern Europe (e.g., Fabirkiewicz 1975), indicating
that the problem is an acute one. The impression left is that, for all its
rising performance, transport constitutes a drag on the economic
growth of the area, and that given a faster growth of that sector the
economies of Eastern Europe would have been able to develop faster
than they have — if only fractionally. The main reasons for the inadequate performance of transport, in view of the needs, seem to be most
of all insufficient past investments,[3] failures in the organizational
structure of transport, inability to utilize the most modern technology
extant, and "the economic and social depreciation of the occupation of
railroad workers" (Szeliga 1975: 4) that gave rise to some labor
problems on the railroads (Szymanska 1976: 3).

Terminology and Scope of the Study

The term *transport* may be defined as that economic activity that
moves persons or goods from one place to another. In its broadest
sense this encompasses all such movement, whether within or between
buildings, plants or places. When the conveyance takes place between
plants or places the transport becomes a clearly independent activity
(Pegrum 1973: 3). The present study treats transport in the latter,
narrower, sense.

Transport can be divided into two main categories, passenger transport and freight transport. Both categories will be treated here, with
emphasis on the economically more important freight transport. Passenger transport is important for economic welfare, social cohesion,
and cultural development, but freight transport provides a measure of
a country's economic potential. Passenger transport can be subdivided
into urban and interurban transport. Freight transport is basically
interurban, although urban deliveries are included in ton-kilometer
statistics. No clear distinction is made in freight transport between
urban and interurban. Or, transport can be divided into domestic and
foreign.

Transport statistics are usually divided into statistics that provide
quantities transported in tons, passengers, or any other physical units,
and statistics that provide information on transport performance in
ton/kilometers (t/km) or passenger/kilometers (pass/km). The latter
measure more closely approximates the indicator of net value added
by the transport sector, or its contribution to GNP.

The modes of transport covered are railways, road transport, water transport, pipelines, and air transport (see chapter 2). Technical and administrative problems connected with each of those modes will be discussed in the present study as background to the economic performance of transport in Eastern Europe. Some modes of transport will not be treated here (other than intraplant transport, as indicated above): namely, transmission of electric current, however distant, transport of gas through gas mains, of water and of sewage within urban areas (although transport of gas, when taking place between localities, will be included under our definition of transport), and belt-transmission (conveyance) of raw materials between quarries or mines and processing plants (cf. Madeyski 1971: 12–13, 53). Horse-driven transport will also be largely disregarded, as will be transport performed within farms, cable-car transport, and ski lifts (cf. Piskozub 1975: 36–42).

Within road transport, the proportion performed within the enterprise is substantially higher in Eastern Europe than in the West. Thus in East Germany, it represented 55.5 percent of motor transport in 1957; by 1964 it declined to 45.1 percent. Some enterprise transport is long-distance, presumably between plants belonging to the same enterprise (Demmler 1967: 92). This high proportion of intraenterprise haulage in road transport is due mainly to the relative underdevelopment of road transport in Eastern Europe, as indicated by the decline in the said proportion between 1957 and 1964, during which time road transport in general had a chance to develop.

The term *East Europe* is used here to cover all European centrally planned economies other than the Soviet Union, namely, Poland, East Germany, Czechoslovakia, Hungary, Romania, Bulgaria, Yugoslavia, and Albania. The term *Soviet-type economies* is used to cover all these countries except Yugoslavia. The countries of Eastern Europe are interesting in part because there is greater systemic diversity within the supposedly monolithic bloc of communist countries than in either of the two leading communist powers, the Soviet Union and China. From the point of view of planning and the planning system, the price system, national institutions, ideology, and other aspects — among them transportation — the countries of Eastern Europe present an absorbing laboratory that provides an insight into the currently possible deviations within the bloc of communist nations, and into different solutions of economic problems. Diversity in Eastern Europe and its influence on the Soviet Union was stressed during the Conference on the Influence of East Europe and Western Areas of the USSR on Soviet Society held at the University of Michigan in 1970. According to the conference, that influence has existed in terms of political innovation, the demonstration effect of economic reforms, multiple variants of socialist planning, seminal impact on social science, and influence in literature (Szporluk 1976: 1–146). From these differences and mutual interactions a consensus is likely to emerge in the future, and for this reason the last chapter contains some projections into the future of transportation in Eastern Europe.

The term *communist* is used to denote under the formal rule of the Communist Party, not the final, communist stage of the Marxian vision of socialism, where, in the utopian ideological view, from everybody would be taken according to his (Marx would have added "or her" by now) ability, and to everybody would be given according to his needs. In this sense of the term, the East European countries are "communist," which does not imply any particular preferences on the part of the population but recognizes only the locus of governmental power.

The period chosen for the study, 1945–1975, includes the early postwar years, during which the power of the Communist Party was not absolute in Poland, Czechoslovakia, and Hungary. Communist influence was, however, already strong, mainly because of the presence of Soviet troops in those countries after their liberation from German occupation. The early postwar period witnessed the introduction of central planning, preference for production of producer goods, emphasis on social consumption and predominance of communist propaganda. Reconstruction, however, had first priority during that period. From 1947–1948 Communist Party rule in those countries became unrestricted, and it became the despotic, superauthoritarian stalinist type until 1954–1956 in Poland and Hungary, and until later in other East European countries. At some periods, Soviet dominance over the area had to be enforced with Soviet troops — at which time transport played an important role in the implementation of Soviet policies, as in 1956 in Hungary and in 1968 in Czechoslovakia — while troop movements in other East European countries helped prevent them from falling out of the communist orbit, as they did in Poland in 1956. Transport has also played an important role in integrating the East European countries within Comecon, the communist trading bloc established in 1949 and given a more important role in 1956. Comecon (an acronym for the Council for Mutual Economic Assistance) now includes the USSR, Mongolia, and Cuba, as well as the East European countries with the exception of Albania. Yugoslavia is an associate member.

Another East European organization, the Warsaw Pact, or Pact for Mutual Assistance and Unified Command, signed on May 14, 1955, depends greatly on the transport network. Annual maneuvers of the Warsaw Pact countries, held in different member countries, tend to emphasize that dependence, and Soviet troops kept in Eastern Europe to guard transport lines underscore the connection between transport and Soviet politics (cf. Korbonski 1969: 10, 23).

Extrapolations and prognoses may be attempted on the basis of this study. Regardless of whether such crystal-ball gazing is correct, it is hoped that the present study will contribute to a better understanding of both the past and the future and to a realistic assessment of the present.

II

Geographic and Economic Determinants of Transport in Eastern Europe

East European Economic Geography and Transport

East Europe is not a geographically uniform region. Its northern flank — Poland and East Germany — is part of the North European plain and has the West Coast–Temperate Marine climate with mild winters (cf. Renner et al. 1953: 167–190). Topographically, it is a lowland without major obstruction to transport and with rivers traversing the area in a northerly direction. Its northern border is the Baltic Sea, which provides access to sea transport, while its southern border is the Carpathian, Sudeten, and Ore Mountains (the latter two are easily traversible by transport lines, including the Elbe River and a proposed Oder–Danube canal; see Kolaczkowski 1974: 10).

The middle part of East Europe lies in the Danube basin and consists of two landlocked countries — Czechoslovakia and Hungary — and Romania, although important industrial regions of northern Czechoslovakia lie in the Elbe watershed and although northern Yugoslavia and northern Bulgaria (included in the southern flank of East Europe) lie in the Danube watershed. The climate of this region tends to be more continental (except for western Czechoslovakia) and belongs to the Humid Continental–Long Summer type. This part of East Europe has mountainous or hilly regions in the north, in particular the Carpathians and Transylvanian Alps, and the Danube lowlands in its southern reaches. While railroads traverse this region in all directions, there is a tendency for the main streams of traffic to go east and west, except for traditional Czechoslovak routes north to Germany and the Baltic sea and south to Vienna. Two of the three countries of this area are landlocked (Czechoslovakia and Hungary); the third, Romania, has access only to the Black Sea and thus is somewhat isolated from the main world shipping routes.

The southern flank of East Europe consists of Bulgaria, Albania, and Yugoslavia — the basic Balkan region. Its climate is mainly Medi-

terranean, but in its northern part, in the Danube watershed, a Humid
Continental climate prevails. It is, except for the northern Danube
plain, a mountainous and rugged area with few navigable rivers and
with considerable obstacles to transport. The main traffic routes run
along the coastlines and to the capitals; but new highways, especially
in Yugoslavia, tend to make all parts of the area more accessible.
Winter transport tends to be severely hampered in this region of East
Europe.

This division of East Europe explains the order of presentation
chosen for the present study, namely, from Poland (sometimes for
comparative purposes, from the USSR) to Yugoslavia. Albania, for
which statistical coverage is scanty, is for the most part left out.

Unlike the Middle East, the Caribbean, or Singapore, East Europe
does not lie on important world trade routes. Almost all of the movement of goods and people between East Europe and the outside is
generated by East European relations with the outside world, and only
a very small proportion of transport is of transit, or entrepôt, character. Because of this, the volume of transport is below what it otherwise
might be. However, if the Soviet Union utilizes the period of détente
more dynamically and builds up its trade with the West, then externally created demands on East European transport may well receive
a new stimulus.

It may be noted that postwar political realities in Eastern Europe
have tended to slow the growth of transport between Eastern Europe
as a whole and the outside world. The political and military hegemony
of the Soviet Union has directed the foreign trade of East European
countries eastward; and since the 1940s the USSR has become by far
the most important foreign trade partner for all East European countries except Yugoslavia, where the political anathema cast on it by
Stalin in 1948 helped to reduce Soviet economic influence. Despite
their seeming political uniformity, however, the East European countries reveal variations that influence the volume of goods transported
between them and the outside world. Romania has, in this respect,
been the maverick of the communist world, increasing its trade with
the noncommunist world to about two-thirds of its total trade. Hungary, during the period of the New Economic Mechanism starting
before 1968 (see Mieczkowski 1975: 222–23), also enlarged its economic relations with the noncommunist world, although relatively less
than Romania. Poland turned to large credit-financed imports from
the West following the rejection of Stalinism in October 1956 and
again following the ouster of the Gomułka regime in December 1970.

Yugoslavia permanently turned its eyes westward following its exclusion from the Cominform in 1948. East Germany preserves a special relationship in trade with West Germany, which is both quantitatively and qualitatively important for East Germany. Therefore, the degree of reliance on transport between individual East European countries and the outside world differs considerably, despite the seemingly monolithic character of communist rule in East Europe.

A factor that tends to limit transport between East Europe and the outside world and among the countries of Eastern Europe is the autarkic tendency of central planners in all Soviet-type economies. For reasons ranging from the convenience of internal balancing in economic planning and from balance of payments considerations to xenophobia and nationalism, the planners of Eastern Europe show a preference for securing domestic supplies rather than imports — the result is to reduce the relative volume of goods transported in international trade. Since the issuance of passports is rigidly controlled (except in Yugoslavia) and since preference is shown to travel within the communist area, international passenger transport tends to be reduced more so between individual East European countries and the West than among those countries.

The economic map of East Europe divides the area basically into two parts, namely, the more developed north (Poland, East Germany, Czechoslovakia, and Hungary) and the less developed south (Romania, Bulgaria, Albania, and Yugoslavia). Table 2.1 gives relevant information for all countries covered here. Poland has the largest area (see col. 1), followed by Yugoslavia, Romania, Czechoslovakia, Bulgaria, East Germany, and Hungary. Albania is quite small. Poland also has the largest population, followed by Yugoslavia, Romania, East Germany, Czechoslovakia, Hungary, and Bulgaria (see col. 2). Albania is again inconspicuous. Population density (see col. 3) is clearly highest in the economically more advanced northern group of countries. But Poland's share of population employed in agriculture and forestry is on the level of the less industrialized southern countries (see col. 4), although the share of agriculture and forestry in its national income is somewhat lower (col. 6).

Industrial production per capita is, in descending order: East Germany, Czechoslovakia, Hungary, Poland, Romania, and Bulgaria (Bozyk 1974: 28). The absolute level of national income is, in descending order: Poland, East Germany, Czechoslovakia, Romania, Hungary, and Bulgaria. For per capita national income, the countries are ordered as East Germany, Czechoslovakia, Poland, Hungary, Bulgaria, and Romania (Bozyk 1974: 25). These orderings again reflect the twofold division of East Europe.

The same twofold division of East Europe is apparent from column 6 of table 2.1, which shows that the relative contribution of agriculture and forestry to the national income of individual countries has been highest in Bulgaria, Romania, and Yugoslavia. Since agriculture implies the production of more goods within the household and since industrialization implies division of labor and exchange, the countries that rely more on agriculture are likely to impose less demand on transport. Column 7 indicates the changes in the demand for transport that have probably resulted from recent growth of industrial production in East Europe. These rates have been quite high and relatively more so in the less developed countries of the area (except for Poland, which went through a period of accelerated growth in the early 1970s). Column 8 shows the relative economic importance of individual countries in East Europe in terms of their estimated Gross Domestic Product expressed in U.S. dollars. Column 9 indicates the relative level of living in terms of Gross Domestic Product per capita.

Column 10 reveals that East Europe (except for Yugoslavia and Albania), like the Soviet Union with its 77 percent share of railroad in transport performance, is by and large a "railroad economy" region (cf. Williams 1962: 1–3). Yugoslavia and Bulgaria show a heavy dependence on trucks (53 and 35 percent respectively), presumably because of topographic obstacles to the operation of railroads. Hungary's 24 percent share in transport performance by trucks in 1972 was in third place.

Geography also influences transport through the location of major centers of economic activity, particularly through the location of industrial centers. Development of new centers, such as Titograd in Yugoslavia or Nowa Huta in Poland, necessitates construction of new transport links. Expansion of existing centers necessitates increase in the capacity of existing transport links. The main industrial centers (including their environs) in East Europe are:

Poland:	The Silesian region, Warsaw-Łodz, Poznan, Gdansk-Gdynia, Krakow, Kielce, Wrocław
East Germany:	Leipzig, Dresden, Karl-Marx-Stadt, Berlin (East), Magdeburg, Halle, Chemnitz
Czechoslovakia:	Plzen, Ostrava, Prague, Bratislava, and the Ore and Sudeten Mountains region
Hungary:	Budapest, Miskolc, Pecs
Romania:	Bucharest-Ploesti, Cluj

TABLE 2.1
Basic Geographic and Economic Information about the Countries of East Europe

	Area (square km) (1)	Population in 1973 (thousand) (2)	Population density (number of persons per square km) (3)	Percentage of the labor force in 1972 in: agriculture and forestry (4)	Percentage of the labor force in 1972 in: industry (5)
Poland	312,677	33,363	107	38.6	27.6
East Germany	108,178	17,043	157	12.0	42.3
Czechoslovakia	127,877	14,578	114	16.7	38.4
Hungary	93,000	10,430	112	25.0	35.3
Romania	237,500	20,828	88	44.2	26.1
Bulgaria	110,549	8,620	78	32.8	31.6
Albania	28,700	2,350	82	–	–
Yugoslavia	255,804	20,940	82	44.6	17.7

	Share of agriculture and forestry in national income in 1967 (6)	Average rate of growth of industrial production in constant prices 1971-73 (7)	Estimated Gross Domestic Product (billion US$ in 1963 average prices in 1967) (8)	GDP per capita in 1967 (US$ per capita) (9)	Share of railroads in national transport performance (t/km in percent) (10)
Poland	19.1	9.9	30.70	961	77[od]
East Germany	13.9	6.3	25.21	1,476	70[bd]
Czechoslovakia	11.8[a]	6.6	20.33	1,421	73[bd]
Hungary	20.2[a]	6.6	10.07	984	85[de]
Romania	27.8[a]	12.9	13.94	723	68[bd]
Bulgaria	30.4[a]	9.7	7.62	917	59[c]
Albania	–	–	–	–	–
Yugoslavia	20.5	8.3	–	–	36[b]

a only agriculture   b 1972   c 1971   d including pipelines   e 1969

Sources: RS 1974: 47, 66, 636, 647, 658, 702;
SJ 1973: 3, 4;
SR 1974: 23, 74;
AS 1974: 5, 9;
SEzh 1971: 3;
SG 1974: 88, 103;
Zacher 1974: 162;
United Nations, Economic Survey of Europe in 1969, part 1, p. 9.

Bulgaria: Sofia, Plovdiv
Yugoslavia: Belgrad, Ljubljana, Zagreb, Sarajevo, Skoplje
Albania: Tirana, Korce

Thus, in all the East European countries, major industrial centers are found in the capitals together with administrative and major population centers — historically located on trade routes — which tends to increase the demand for transport on routes linking the capitals with the rest of the East European countries and creates a tendency toward transport routes radiating from the capital and extending toward the provinces. The stronger this tendency, the smaller the number and importance of other industrial centers in the country, as in Romania. It should be noted, though, that efforts are being made to distribute manufacturing activity more evenly throughout the countries of Eastern Europe, which — when successful — will result in a more rectangular arrangement of transport networks and a tendency for fewer demands on that network.

Mining creates a demand for transport that is well distributed in time, though not in space. The main mining areas in East Europe are determined by the geographical location of mineral deposits.

Poland: Upper Silesia (coal, iron ore, lead, zinc), eastern Lublin region (newly developing coal basin), southwest Poland (copper), southwest border with East Germany (brown coal), Kielce region (sulphur), Wałbrzych (coal), Jasło-Krosno (oil).

East Germany: Harz (zinc, uranium), southeastern region (brown coal).

Czechoslovakia: Ostrava region (coal), Plzen (coal), northwest region (coal), widely distributed iron ore deposits, Ore Mountains (uranium), Kosice (magnesium).

Hungary: Suneg-Tapolca (bauxite), Pecs (coal), Dorog (brown coal), Pecs (uranium), Miskolc (iron ore).

Romania: Ploesti (oil), Copsa Mica (natural gas), Eastern Carpathians (copper, zinc, manganese).

Bulgaria: Plachkovtsi (coal), Rudozem-Madan (lead, zinc), Varna (manganese).

Yugoslavia: Slovenia (iron ore, bauxite, lead, zinc), Vares (iron ore), Vojvodina region (oil), Plevlja (brown coal), along the Adriatic coast (bauxite), central Yugoslavia (iron ore), eastern Yugoslavia (chromium, lead, copper).[1]

Agricultural activity creates a highly seasonal demand for transport, peaking at harvest time in late summer and fall and continuing at a substantially lower level in other seasons with the hauling of fertilizer, machinery, spare sparts, construction materials, and other agricultural inputs. Unlike mining, agriculture in East Europe is widely distributed, with the main production areas situated in the alluvial lowlands, river basins, valleys, and plains.

Several general observations can be made about this locational information. Manufacturing, mining, and agriculture are not distributed evenly throughout Eastern Europe, thus giving rise to transport needs different from the simple exchange of goods produced under conditions of specialization. In Poland and East Germany, much mining and manufacturing is carried on in the southern part of the country, and hence the important transport links are with the northern part, both for domestic and foreign markets. In Czechoslovakia, the western — Czech — part of the country is the more industrialized, and important mining activities are located in the Czech part of the Silesian basin. Similar uneven distribution of economic activities characterizes other countries of Eastern Europe.

In each country there are distinct industrialized regions, just as there are several relatively backward, or at least primarily agricultural, regions. Some locational decisions for manufacturing have been made for political, rather than economic and geographic, reasons, as was the case with Nowa Huta steel works near Kraków and the Żeran automobile factory near Warsaw. Thus a given location of economic activity cannot necessarily be presumed to minimize costs, including transport costs.

As documented by a leading British expert on East European geography and industrial location, two conflicting trends have been apparent in planned industrial location during the postwar era in Eastern Europe. One of them has been the dispersal of industry away from the traditional industrial regions, while the other has been further concentration of plants in those regions. Figure 2.1 shows both trends. The shaded areas show prewar concentration of industry, including the most important historically, the "industrial triangle" between Halle in East Germany, Łódź in Poland, and Budapest in Hungary. That area held 75 percent of the region's industry in 1939, but this declined to 50 percent by the late 1960s. The number of industrial jobs in the "industrial triangle" increased from 5.9 to 6.7 million in the same period, while some 6 million new mine and factory jobs have been provided in areas outside the triangle (Hamilton 1971: 179). The con-

FIGURE 2.1
Distribution of Major Industrial Plants Constructed or Reconstructed in Eastern Europe During 1944–69

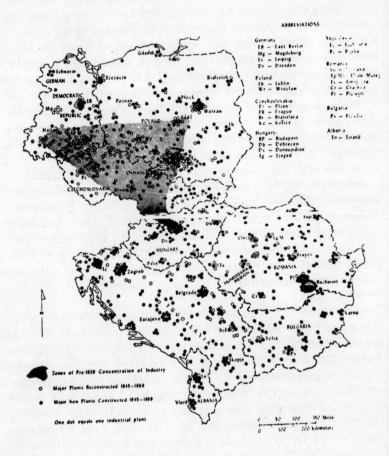

Source: Hamilton 1971: 180–81 (Reprinted by permission of the publisher)

centration of additional capacity in existing industrial centers has tended to lower transport costs, but at the same time it has tended to localize the benefits of industrialization. The dispersal of industry into new areas, on the other hand, while it has increased the social costs of transport, has provided jobs in regions where demographic pressures and unemployment or underemployment have tended to be high; it has served social policy by providing a wider geographical basis for the take-off into industrialization; and it has had some desirable political side-effects. The dispersal of industry has been a more prevalent feature in postwar planned economic development and planned industrial location. It has reduced interregional inequalities in the distribution of income (Koropeckyj 1977), and it has tended to strain the demand on the transport systems.

Figure 2.1 shows that the concentration in the traditional industrial zones continued on in the postwar period. It also shows that planned dispersal of industrial activity was considerable, but that much of it tended to cluster around new industrial centers. The dispersal trend has thus not been all-pervasive and has so far left some areas underdeveloped, such as some northern voyvodships in Poland.

Except for the four countries of the northern tier, transport links with the industrialized countries of Western Europe are relatively long. The best solution of the problem of lengthy transport links in foreign trade seems to be a heavy reliance on mutual East European trade and development, not adequately exploited by the East European countries.

Partly because of divergent historical experience and partly because of geographical differences, the East European countries do not constitute an area of uniform transport systems (cf. Rachev 1971; Bras 1975). Each country has its own particular problems, although the general solutions sought and the direction of further evolution seem to be similar in all: higher relative rate of growth of road transport, the spread of more efficient motive power, the introduction of containerization and other labor-saving innovations.

Geographic and Demographic Dimensions of Transport Statistics in Eastern Europe

The northwestern areas of East Europe have a better transport network than do its eastern and southern areas. The density of transport has two dimensions. The geographic dimension relates the average number of kilometers of length of the transport network of a given mode to a unit of area — usually 100 square kilometers. The demographic dimension relates the average number of kilometers of length of transport network of a given mode to a unit of population — usually 10,000 people. These two relations can be expressed by the following formulas:

$$I_g = 1/a \qquad \text{and} \qquad I_d = 1/p$$

where: I_g = geographic indicator of transport density.
I_d = demographic indicator of transport density.
l = total length of the network of a given transport mode.
a = area of the country, in 100 square kilometers.
p = population of the country, in 10,000 people.

The first indicator shows the geographical accessibility of a given mode of transport and is particularly useful in analyzing conditions of freight transport. The second indicator shows the accessibility of transport to the population and is particularly useful in assessing the availability of passenger transport, although population multiplied by average production per capita also gives an indication of the demand for freight, as does population multiplied by average per capita income.

Due to geographic and economic differences among the regions of a country, a synthetic indicator, I_s, based on concepts included in the preceding two equations may be expressed by the formula:

$$I_s = 1/\sqrt[3]{ap}$$

Finally, an analytical indicator of density in transport network I_a, may be used as the synthetic indicator is. It may be expressed by the formula:

$$I_a = 1/\sqrt[3]{apQ}$$

where Q = indicator of the economic development of a given region, expressed at one's discretion in terms of value of production, value of industrial production per capita, etc. (cf. Madeyski, Lissowska, and Marzec 1971: 69-70).

The geographic and the demographic indicators can be expressed in the form of their reciprocals, namely, in terms of the number of square kilometers of territory per one kilometer of transport network, and in terms of the number of inhabitants per one kilometer of transport network. Such forms show more clearly the hinterland or the support that a selected mode of transport gives to a geographic or demographic entity. The geographic and the demographic indicators of transport density for the East European countries are shown in table 2.2 (cf. Gunther 1965: 118-32).

Comparisons among countries have to be made cautiously, though. There are qualitative differences among transport lines, e.g., between single- and double-track railway lines, between highways and roads of different surface, and between rivers of different depth. Different countries may include different kinds of routes in the length of their transport network. Even the same kind of route, e.g., hard-surfaced highway, may be vastly different in quality (concrete, asphalt, crushed stone, or macadam) and width. With these cautionary remarks in mind, we can make the following observations from table 2.2.

The geographic density of the railroad network (I_g) reveals the existence of two groups of countries. One, embracing East Germany, Czechoslovakia, Hungary, and Poland (in decreasing order), has a density of transport network from 13.3 to 8.5 kilometers per 100 square kilometers. The other, embracing Romania, Yugoslavia, and Bulgaria, has a density from 4.6 to 3.8. A similar, but lesser, difference shows up in demographic density of the railroad network (I_d), which for the first group of countries varies from 9.1 for Czechoslovakia to 8.0 kilometers per 10 thousand inhabitants for Poland, while for the second group of countries, it varies from 5.3 to 5.1. Highway network density is more difficult to compare due to varying standards adopted in national statistics; but Czechoslovakia seems to have the best highways and bus services. The density of other modes of transport is substantially smaller, which shows up dramatically in the last two columns of table 2.2.

To summarize table 2.2 in descriptive terms, in Romania all transport infrastructure has shown considerable growth and improvement (Keefe 1972: 43-48). The same can be said about Bulgaria (Keefe 1974: 59-63; Rangeloff 1957: 372-83). Albania has only limited railway mileage (Skendi 1956: 245-47) — by 1970 there were only about 135 miles of completed lines (Keefe 1971: 46) — although additional mileage is in the planning stage (Chekrezi 1971: 184). Albania's road system is rather primitive (Skendi 1956: 240-45; Keefe 1971: 45), and a French traveler in 1964 described Tirana as a capital without cars (Mahuzier 1965: 133). Among the southern countries, Yugoslavia has made perhaps the most valiant effort to improve its transport system from its backward state in the 1950s (Neuberger 1957: 370-85).

On the other hand, transport infrastructures of the countries of northern Eastern Europe are superior to those in Southeastern Europe. Poland has a relatively well developed system (Rudzki 1957: 406-23; Keefe 1973: 44-47), as do East Germany (Keefe 1972a: 26-30), Czechoslovakia (Mares 1957: 392-414; Keefe 1972b: 26-30), and Hungary (Keefe 1973a: 48-54; Racz 1957: 316-33; Czere 1966: 201-12).

The following comparisons can be made with countries outside the East European area (for 1973) (*RS 1975:* 613, 614): For the railroad

TABLE 2.2

Geographic and Demographic Density of Transport Network in East Europe in 1973

	Length of network, thousand of km (l)	Km of network per 100 square km of area (I_g)	Km of network per 10 thousand inhabitants (I_d)	Average number of square km of area per 1 km of network	Average number of inhabitants per 1 km of network
Poland:					
Railroads[a]	26.6	8.5	8.0	11.8	1,255
Highways:					
hard surface	137.8	44.1	41.3	2.3	242
bus lines	97.2	31.1	29.1	3.2	343
Inland waterways:					
navigable	6.9	2.2	2.1	45.3	4,839
for shipping	4.6	1.5	1.4	68.4	7,296
Airline transport[b]	3.1	1.0	.9	100.3	10,704
Pipelines	1.6	.5	.5	201.2	21,469
East Germany:[c]					
Railroads	14.4	13.3	8.4	7.5	1,185
Highways:					
aggregate	45.6	42.1	26.7	2.4	374
state	12.4	11.4	7.3	8.7	1,378
Inland waterways	2.5	2.4	1.5	42.5	6,694
Pipelines	.7	.7	.4	152.4	24,004

Czechoslovakia:

Railroads[a]	13.3	10.4	9.1	9.6	1,097
Bus lines	234.2	183.1	160.6	.5	62
Inland waterways	4.1	3.2	2.8	31.0	3,532
Air transport[b]	5.6	4.4	3.9	22.7	2,591

Hungary:[c]

Railroads	8.6	9.2	8.3	10.8	1,207
Highways	29.7	31.9	28.6	3.1	350
Inland waterways	1.6	1.7	1.5	58.1	6,488
Pipelines	2.9	3.1	2.8	32.1	3,580

Romania:

Railroads[a]	11.0	4.6	5.3	21.6	1,890
Highway	76.8	32.3	36.9	3.1	271
modernized highway	12.3	5.2	5.9	19.2	1,687

Bulgaria:[d]

Railroads[a]	4.2[d]	3.8	5.1	26.3	1,961
Air transport[b]	3.2[d]	2.9	2.9	34.1	2,536

Yugoslavia:

Railroads[a]	10.4	4.1	5.1	24.6	1,974
Road: class I-IV	97.8	38.2	47.7	2.6	210
Class I-III	10.1	17.8	22.2	5.6	451

a aggregate, standard and narrow gauge   b domestic   c 1972   d 1970

Sources: Calculated on the basis of *RS 1974*: 47, 66, 381; *SJ 1973*: 3, 4, 234; *SR 1974*: 23, 74, 369; *SPBH 1973*: 45, 189; *AS 1974*: 5, 9, 277; *SEzh 1971*: 3, 155, 160; *SG 1974*: 88, 103, 225, 231, 233.

network, the geographic indicator of transport density (I_g) is higher in Poland, East Germany, Czechoslovakia, and Hungary than in most Western countries, except for Belgium (13.3) and West Germany (13.0). Other I_g values are, for instance, as follows: Austria — 7.8, Denmark — 5.8, France — 6.3, Holland — 6.9, Great Britain — 7.5, Italy — 6.7, Japan — 7.0, United States — 3.6. In countries with difficult terrain and a large area, the I_g indicator is quite low, as for example Canada — 0.7; and the Soviet Union — 0.6.

The demographic indicator of rail transport density (I_d) for Poland, East Germany, Czechoslovakia, and Hungary is comparable to that for Austria (8.7) and lower than that for Canada (32.9), the United States (15.8), and Sweden (14.9). It is higher than in most other developed countries, as for instance Belgium — 4.1, Denmark — 5.0, France — 6.0, Great Britain — 3.1, Italy — 3.7, Greece — 2.9, and Japan — 2.4. Thus the railroad network in northern Eastern Europe seems quite adequate.

For the highway network, the geographic indicator of transport density (I_g) — compared with some reservations — is for the four countries of northern Eastern Europe higher than for Austria, France, and Sweden, but lower than for Japan, the United States, and Holland. Even for Romania it is much higher than for the Soviet Union.

The demographic indicator (I_d) for highways (calculated on the basis of *RS 1975:* 549, 614) seems to be similar for the four countries of northern Eastern Europe to that for Austria (43.9), West Germany (43.3), Belgium (24.6), Spain (42.1), but is smaller than for Italy (52.5), Great Britain (61.0), Sweden (119.8), and the United States (242.7). It is much higher than for the USSR (5.5). It should be noted that the quality of the highway network in Eastern Europe seems substantially below that in most other industrialized countries. (For further international comparisons see Owen 1964: 216-17).

Since transport lines by themselves do not assure accessibility (e.g., trunk lines offer only minimum accessibility), another indicator has to be added: relative endowment with transport termini, stops, etc., which are covered by the generic term *transport points*. As in the case of the length of the network, the density of transport points can be measured by two basic formulas:

$$I_{gg} = t/a \qquad \text{and} \quad I_{dd} = t/p$$

where: I_{gg} = indicator of the geographical density of transport points.

t = aggregate number of transport points in the network of a given transport mode.

a = area of the country, in 1,000 square km.

I_{dd} = indicator of the demographic density of transport points.

p = population of the country, in 100,000 people.

(Note that variables a and p have larger numerical values than in the preceding equations.)

The reciprocals of those two indicators show the average hinterland of a transport point and the average number of people who have to rely on a transport point respectively. Table 2.3 shows the density of transport points in Poland in 1963. The highest density is indicated by transport points in highway bus transportation; the smallest is, predictably, in air transport.

Indicators of the density of transport points are more difficult to interpret than those of transport network because of the enormous qualitative differences between transport points and because of some necessarily arbitrary statistics-gathering decisions. For instance, loading operations on the railway can be performed on any siding, but table 2.3 obviously excludes makeshift arrangements; bus passengers can gain access to transport routes at request stops, but, again, table 2.3 obviously excludes those. There is also a qualitative difference between the central railroad station in the capital city or any large city, and a village station in the provinces, with perhaps two trains servicing it per day. Such considerations also make intercountry comparisons more dubious; different coverage and different standards may appear in different countries' statistics on transport points.

The accessibility of transport is determined partly by the density of the network, partly by the density of transport points, and partly by the spatial arrangement of the network. The latter can be basically rectangular, one that covers its area with a grid that decreases distances to the given network, or it can be radial, one that stresses the importance of a transport center. The basic arrangement in East Europe is rectangular, particularly in the areas with better transport, as in western Poland, East Germany, or Czechoslovakia (cf. Fiedorowicz 1976: 19). Fig. 2.2 shows the arrangement of the main railroad lines and their relative importance in Poland. The radial spatial arrangement, called "concentric" in Eastern Europe, predominates in aerial transport, which characteristically connects the capital with the main economic and population centers of the country. Figure 2.3 shows, as an example, the domestic network of the Polish airline Lot.

TABLE 2.3

Density of Transport Points in Poland in 1963

	Number of transport points (t)	Density of transport points per 1,000 square km (I_{gg})	Density of transport points per 100,000 people ($_{dd}$)	Average area of hinterland of a transport point in square km	Average number of 1,000 people per passenger transport point
Railroad: freight[a]	3,452	11.05	11.12	90.5	–
passenger	3,036	9.71	9.81	102.9	10.2
Road: by bus[b]	24,200	77.44	78.21	12.9	1.3
Inland waterways: freight	30	.096	.097	10,416.7	–
passenger	100	.320	.323	3,125.2	309.4
Air transport	7	.022	.023	44,642.8	4,420.0

a   includes enterprise loading facilities

b   road freight transport has been disregarded

c   some stops of river craft not included

Source: Tarski 1968: 107.

FIGURE 2.2
Spatial Arrangement of Railroad Mainlines in Poland

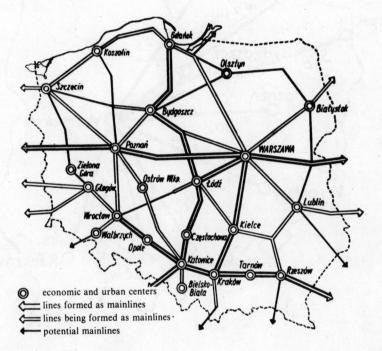

Source: Fiodorowicz 1974: 78

FIGURE 2.3
Domestic Airlinks in Poland in 1973

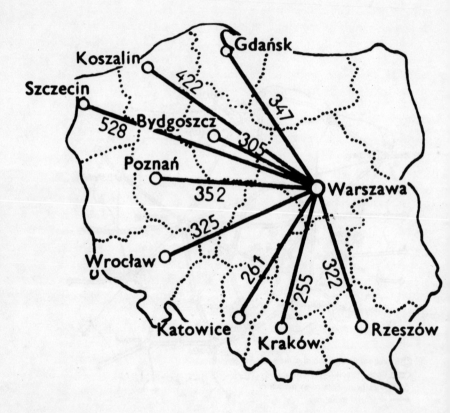

Source: *Rocznik Statystyczny Transportu 1974:* insert facing p. 160

The arrangement of transport routes tends to be rectangular in the northwestern part of East Europe, where better transport links exist. This is at least partly because the relatively higher development of that region has created multiple industrial and urban centers equivalent in economic importance to the capitals. Geographically, the North European plain is also amenable to more even development of transport. Finally, political factors are relevant: the division of Berlin has tended to reduce its economic importance in East Germany, while in Czechoslovakia Prague and Bratislava are political centers for the Czechs and the Slovaks, respectively. In Southeastern Europe, the radial arrangement is relatively more pronounced because the capital plays a relatively more important role in countries of that area.

Fig. 2.4 shows the main international railroad routes in Eastern Europe, while fig. 2.5 shows the regular domestic air routes in Eastern Europe in 1959. The rail routes tend to be more rectangular, while the air routes tend to be more radial, except for Bulgaria (see Berezowski 1975: 286–317). .

The indicators of static traffic density (passengers or tons transported per kilometer of roadway) and dynamic traffic density (passenger/kilometers or ton/kilometers per kilometer of roadway) may also be calculated. Comparisons between East and West Germany reveal substantial similarities in the trends of those indicators. On the railroad, static passenger traffic density tended to decline, while static freight density tended to increase in both countries. Dynamic passenger traffic density on the railroad, after experiencing an early increase, tended to fall in both countries after 1955–1957, while dynamic freight traffic density rose in both countries (Günther 1965: 287–93). Thus the similarity of general economic developments and trends seemed to exert a stronger influence on these indicators than did the differences in those countries' economic systems.

Within a given spatial arrangement of transport routes, one can encounter routes that are approximately straight-line connections between main transport points and routes that meander (usually for geographical reasons, but sometimes for political, demographic, or economic reasons), and that thus unnecessarily or spuriously increase the length of the network and the indicators of its density. In this connection a useful coefficient may be added to our previous indexes, namely, the coefficient of lengthening (circuitry factor) of a transport route:

$$L_1 = l/s \ . \ 100$$

FIGURE 2.4

Main International Railroad Routes in Eastern Europe

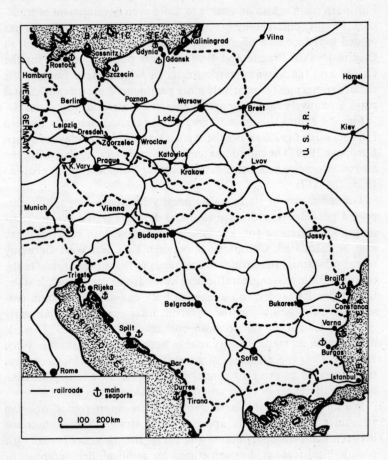

Source: adapted from Berezowski 1962: 127

FIGURE 2.5
Regular Domestic Air Routes in Eastern Europe in 1959

Source: adapted from Berezowski 1962: 184

where: L_1 = coefficient of lengthening

         l = actual length of a transport route

         s = straight-line distance (or geographic distance).

A different coefficient of lengthening, expressed in terms of percentage lengthening of a transport route, takes the form:

$$L_d = (l - s)/s \ . \ 100$$

We can compare, with a view toward reducing costs of transport, the coefficients of lengthening L_1 for different modes of transport between the same transport points; to do so, the relative coefficient of lengthening is used:

$$L_{1_{mn}} = L_{1_m}/L_{1_n} = l_m/l_n$$

where: $L_{1_{mn}}$ = relative coefficient of lengthening

         m and n = different transport modes.

Table 2.4 shows the coefficients of lengthening for different transport modes in Poland. The coefficient of lengthening is larger than the average shown in this table when calculated for most routes between cities other than Warsaw (cf. Madeyski, Lissowska and Marzec 1971: 71), which seems to confirm the rule that the less important a route is, the larger the coefficient of lengthening. The railroad route between Warsaw and Bialystok is almost a perfect straight line. Most railroad routes are slightly longer than highway connections. Inland waterway links tend to be substantially longer than highway or railroad routes between the same cities. In southeastern Europe, where the terrain is more difficult, the coefficient of lengthening of surface modes of transport is likely to be greater than in Poland and East Germany.

Other Geographical and Economic Considerations

The rapid tempo of industrialization and development of raw materials has produced new demands on the transport network in Eastern Europe. New economic activity was sometimes located without regard for the existing transport network, as with the new coal field near Lublin, Poland, and with other mining areas; on the other hand, it was sometimes decided with existing transport links taken into account, as with the Nowa Huta steel complex near Krakow, Poland. Even in the latter case, however, new capacities had to be built into the existing transport network (cf. Gumpel 1967: 33–34).

Increased specialization and division of labor provide another stimulus to transport. If each area of the country were to strive for self-sufficiency, the need for transport would be minimized, and transport would be necessary only between economic units situated in the immediate vicinity. Economic specialization leads, therefore, to transport between enterprises, while geographical specialization extends the distance over which goods are transported.

Since industrialization and economic development raise per capita incomes, there is an impact on the demand for freight and passenger transport. With rising productivity, each member of the labor force tends to produce more goods, and thus — given the size of the labor force and the degree of division of labor — more goods need to be transported. Each person in the country, having on the average a higher disposable income, consumes more and thus needs more goods transported to him or her. In addition, this representative member of the population, who now has a higher income, demands relatively more services (in accordance with Engel's law), including transport. Hence, greater demand for passenger transport tends to be built up, too. In conformity with this tendency the number of journeys made by an average inhabitant in Poland is expected to more than double between 1970 and 1990 (Madeyski, Lissowska, and Morawski 1975a: 114).

Two other developments devolve on the last point. The first is that the labor force participation rate, or the average number of those who actually enter the labor force from among those in the work age, tends to rise with economic development. This is because new jobs open up for labor, because they are more accessible, and because of social amenities such as kindergartens and day schools, on the one hand, and because of activization of women, their rising economic and professional ambitions, and their greater ability to leave home for outside work (due to falling net reproduction rates and to an increase in labor-saving household devices). This trend has been observed in all East European countries; in some, e.g., East Germany and Czechoslovakia (Mieczkowski 1975: 198, 251–53), it explains the major portion of the rise in the labor force. The effect of rising labor force participation rates is to enhance the tendency for per capita incomes to rise, and hence for demands on transport to increase.

The second development is that an increased labor force necessitates development of transportation to work-places, mainly urban transport, but also highway and railway transport. As new urban centers develop, they require development of public transport; and as old centers grow, they require extension of the old means of transport (e.g., extension of bus lines and opening up of new ones) and construction of new ones, such as subways. Suburban commuter traffic is

TABLE 2.4

Coefficients of Lengthening for Routes Linking Warsaw with Voyvodship Centers

From Warsaw to:	Kilometers Automobile roads:			Railroads:		
	s	l_h	L_{lh}	l_r	L_{lr}	L_{rth}
Bialystok	174	196	112.6	174	100.0	88.8
Bydgoszcz	226	259	114.6	284	125.6	109.6
Gdansk	298	343	115.3	324	108.6	94.5
Katowice	263	292	111.0	316	120.2	108.3
Kielce	156	176	112.8	193	123.7	109.7
Koszalin	389	431	110.8	523	134.4	121.3
Krakow	255	293	120.5	325	133.8	111.0
Lublin	151	163	107.9	170	112.6	104.4
Lodz	121	132	110.0	138	115.0	104.5
Olsztyn	175	217	124.0	228	130.3	105.1
Opole	258	309	111.2	323	116.2	104.5
Poznan	283	303	107.1	308	108.7	101.7
Rzeszow	240	297	124.0	370	154.2	124.7
Szczecin	452	520	114.8	518	114.5	99.6
Wroclaw	304	347	114.1	403	132.6	116.2
Zielona Gora	280	433	113.9	473	124.5	109.4
Average	259	294	113.5	317	122.4	107.8

s straight line distance
l_h highway distance in km
L_{lh} coefficient of lengthening of highway transport
l_r shortest distance by rail
L_{lr} coefficient of lengthening of railroad transport
L_{rth} relative coefficient of lengthening of railroad in relation to highway

From Warsaw to:

	Inland waterways:				Air connections:	
	l_w	L_{lw}	L_{lwh}	L_{lwr}	l_a	L_{la}
Bialystok	–	–	–	–	–	–
Bydgoszcz	260	115.0	100.4	91.5	–	–
Gdansk	396	132.6	115.4	122.2	338	113.2
Katowice	627	238.8	214.7	198.4	–	–
Kielce	–	–	–	–	–	–
Koszalin	–	–	–	–	–	–
Krakow	423	174.3	144.4	130.1	263	108.2
Lublin	–	–	–	–	–	–
Lodz	–	–	–	–	137	113.1
Olsztyn	–	–	–	–	–	–
Opole	1,142	410.8	369.6	353.6	–	–
Poznan	656	232.2	216.5	212.9	346	122.1
Rzeszow	–	–	–	–	315	131.4
Szczecin	677	149.8	130.2	130.7	552	122.2
Wroclaw	1,042	343.0	300.0	258.5	323	106.1
Zielona Gora	865	227.6	199.8	182.9	–	–
Average	676	261.0	229.9	213.3	325	125.5

Source: Tarski 1968: 120-1

l_w distance by inland waterway
l_a distance by air transport
L_{la} coefficient of lengthening of air transport
L_{lw} coefficient of lengthening of transport by inland waterway
L_{lwh} relative coefficient of lengthening of inland waterways in relation to highway
L_{lwr} relative coefficient of lengthening of inland waterways in relation to railroad

increased by the typical East European housing difficulties in the cities, because of which some members of the labor force have to live far from their places of work, and by the creation of a new social class — commuting peasant-workers — who sometimes live up to 100 kilometers from their place of work. Suburban transport is plagued by delays (Dzieciolowski 1975: 7; cf. Mrzyglad 1962: 114–17).

Since East European countries have been abandoning the Stalinist policy of economic autarky and have been increasing their foreign trade turnover, new demands for long-distance — partly seaborne — transport have been created. In the East European context, foreign trade relations create an additional demand for transit services through Poland between the USSR and East Germany and between Czechoslovakia and the port of Szczecin; through East Germany between Poland and West Germany; through Hungary between Romania and Austria and between the USSR and Yugoslavia; and through Yugoslavia from Hungary. Since foreign tourism has also become a major source of foreign exchange, especially in Yugoslavia and Bulgaria, new demands have been created for improved highways, railroads, and air connections. Transit and tourist transport services may give rise to some competition among the socialist countries of Eastern Europe.

In a wider geographic and political context, transport and the main transport routes have been instrumental both in placing Eastern Europe under communist control and in unifying it within the Soviet bloc. During the 1944–1945 campaign, Soviet armies moved westward in their successive offensives along the North European Plain through Poland, East Germany, and Czechoslovakia, and from the Ukraine and the Black Sea along the Danube plains through Romania, Bulgaria, Hungary, and Czechoslovakia (and linking with Yugoslavia). The Western allies made political concessions at Teheran (December 1943), Yalta (February 1945), and Potsdam (July 1945) that effectively consolidated Soviet gains. Geography combined with military strategy and politics to create the postwar East European bloc as a political entity. Later, this entity was linked by transport, as will be shown in chapter 6, into an economic unit within Comecon (cf. Wolfe 1963: 15–43, 70, and passim).

Finally, several military considerations are connected with both geography and economics, and they exert considerable influence on transport in East Europe (cf. Gumpel 1967: 40–42; Martin and Harding 1976: 4–5; Harbeson 1959: 1–20). Individual bilateral agreements between the Warsaw Pact countries and the Soviet Union specify the right of Soviet troops to use those countries' transport infrastructure. Coordination in such use of transport takes place through the Comecon Transport Commission in Warsaw.[2] Transport routes, especially those that run east and west (see fig. 2.1), are developed with strategic considerations in mind, and an excess capacity and fuel reserves are maintained in case of a military emergency (Gumpel 1967: 40–42). Development of defense industry and the location of this industry contribute to the specific demands made on transport. It should be noted that transport facilities can be used for military as well as for civilian purposes, even though the military has partly developed its own specific means of transport (Malek 1975: 113). Only urban and suburban transport have no direct recognizable military use, except as means of transport for individual military personnel.

Maintenance of strategic reserves in transport, as well as current use of transport modes for purposes connected with the defense establishment, imposes economic opportunity costs on the national economies of the East European countries. While such costs in themselves do not set the East European countries apart from others in a defense-conscious world, the relative size of such costs with respect to GNP may be, and apparently is, larger than in noncommunist countries, indicating a relatively larger economic sacrifice.

Some Additional Demographic Dimensions by Mode of Transport

The relative development of different modes of transport varies among the East European countries, partly as the result of geography (e.g., lack of railway development in Albania), partly as the result of the general stage of economic development of a country (e.g., the relative backwardness of road transport in Romania), and partly as the result of planned decisions (e.g., the relative backwardness of individual transport by car in East Europe). It may therefore be illuminating to provide some information on the relative dimensions of transport services by individual modes.

First, let us present some comparative information about the railroad. Table 2.5 gives 1965 data for passenger and freight transport on standard- and narrow-gauge railroad. The table shows that West Germany led in the number of passengers and passenger/kilometers transported, while Poland led the East European countries in both respect. There is a clearer distinction between Western and Eastern European countries in the average distance traveled by passengers (col. 3): West European passengers made longer average trips. There is

TABLE 2.5
Passenger and Freight Transport on Railroads in 1965[a]

	Number of passengers transported (thousand)	Pass/km transported (million)	Average distance traveled by passengers (km)	Average number of trips per capita	Average length of transport of one ton (commercial) (km)	Per capita loading on national network (tons)
Poland	971,538	34,318	35.3	30.8	238.5	9.6
East Germany	684,213	17,446	25.5	40.2	164.8	12.1
Czechoslovakia	634,018	21,636	34.1	44.8	242.6	13.6
West Germany	1,070,248	38,419	35.9	18.9	192.0	4.4
France	619,693	38,281	61.8	12.6	270.4	4.5
Italy	320,892	26,502	82.6	6.2	307.4	.7

a   standard and narrow gauge

Source: Bac 1969: 185.

also a clear distinction in the average number of per capita trips by rail (col. 4): East European countries showed a marked superiority. The lower indicators for the West European countries were due to greater availability of alternative transport, mainly in the form of private cars and buses.

In freight transport by rail, the mean length of transport of one ton was highest in Italy and France, average in Czechoslovakia and Poland, and lowest for the two Germanies. A more pronounced East-West distinction appears in the last column of the table, where the number of tons per capita loaded on the railroad was quite high in Eastern Europe and much lower in Western Europe, again because alternative modes of transport were available.

Table 2.6, col. 1, shows that in Western Europe modes of transport other than the railroad were, indeed, relatively more available. Poland and Czechoslovakia showed the greatest relative reliance on railroad transport. The remaining columns of table 2.6 show that Poland, as representative of the East European countries, used its railroad capacity, both in passenger and in freight transport, more intensively than did the Western European countries. This was apparently done at the cost of greater discomfort to passengers and more bottlenecks and pressure on users of freight transport. There was substantially less pressure on West European railroads.

Table 2.7 focuses on comparative conditions of passenger transport. In general, the East European countries show a greater absolute reliance on public transport than do the West European countries (cols. 1 and 2) as the result of appreciably greater availability of private passenger cars in Western Europe (col. 4). Poland shows a smaller number of passenger/kilometers per capita by bus than do the other three East European countries shown, due to lesser availability of buses and due to its somewhat lower per capita income than in the other three countries. The relatively low per capita income in Italy also shows up in the bus and overall passenger transport in that country. The Yugoslav figure for bus transport is quite high, but then Yugoslavia shows a relatively high reliance on bus transport due to its topography (see col. 3).

It can also be noted that the share of passenger transport by bus is lower in Eastern Europe than in Western Europe. Yugoslavia, as already mentioned, is a significant exception, while Czechoslovakia has achieved the West European proportion. Even so, the share of road transport increased notably in Eastern Europe during the post-war period. For instance, in Hungary the share of passengers trans-

TABLE 2.6
Comparative Railroad Performance in 1965

	Share of railroad in total tons transported (percent)	Number of passengers per seat on the railroad	Number of pass/km per seat (thousand)	t/km transported per freight car (thousand)	t/km transported per ton of railroad capacity (thousand)
Poland	35	1,440	52.0	424.6	18.0
Czechoslovakia	25	. .	. .	. .	7.7
West Germany	17	744	27.6	192.0	8.9
France	16	476	29.6	214.0	5.9
Italy	. . .	451	37.2	142.0	5.9

Source: Bac 1969: 185-8.

TABLE 2.7
Some Comparative Conditions of Passenger Transport in 1970

	Number of pass/km by bus per capita	Number of per capita pass/km by all public transport	Share of bus transport (percent)	Number of cars[a] per 1,000 inhabitants
Poland	894	2,026	44.1	14.7
East Germany	1,013	2,049	49.4	68.0
Czechoslovakia	1,493	2,699	55.3	53.4
Hungary	1,161	2,742	42.3	23.2
Yugoslavia	995	1,528	65.1	35.1
West Germany	750	1,388	54.0	234.1
Holland	730	1,345	54.3	192.0
Belgium	964	1,746	55.2	212.9
Great Britain	985	1,531	64.3	208.2
Italy	573	1,223	46.9	190.2

a   all cars, not just private

Source: Gis and Sierakiewicz 1973: 26-28.

ported by road rose from 12.8 percent in 1950 to 47.5 percent in 1966, and the share of passenger/kilometers traveled by road rose from 5.6 percent in 1950 to 25.9 percent in 1966 and to more by 1970, as shown in table 2.7 (Wojterkowski 1968b: 265). Similar changes took place in Poland (Wojterkowski 1968a: 368). In Western Europe, Italy is an exception: its share of transport by bus is similar to that in Eastern Europe (col. 3) (cf. Kuzienkowski 1975: 4).

Col. 4 reveals that Eastern Europe has relatively few cars. Among the East European countries, East Germany leads in this respect, followed by Czechoslovakia. Other East European countries have relatively fewer cars. These comparisons again indicate the preference of East European planners for public transport, as against individual transport by car, whether privately owned or not.[3]

On the whole, the three tables presented in this section show a comparative emphasis in Eastern Europe on railway transport, probably an excessive utilization of rolling stock, and a meager endowment with individual means of transport. The aggregate quantitative performance of the transport sectors in Eastern Europe is substantial, but transport does not seem to offer adequate convenience to its users.

National Planning of Transportation

The Framework of Transport Planning in Eastern Europe

Socialist societies claim that planning is one of the advantages they can offer in the management of scarce resources. "Planning is an attempt, by centralizing the management of the allocation of resources sufficiently, to take into account social costs and social benefits which would be irrelevant to the calculations of the decentralized decision maker" (Sirkin 1968: 45).[1] Under central planning as it exists in Eastern Europe, all major economic decisions are completely centralized under a system usually referred to as a command economy. Such a system suffers, according to Oleg Zinam, from three main drawbacks:

1. It is impossible to construct a simple maximizing behavior model for it. There are multifarious and often conflicting incentives and constraints, conflicting interests and severe limitations on freedom of managerial action.

2. "[P]olitical, economic and ideological elements are so inextricably intertwined that no attempts to separate economic from non-economic factors promise success. To get meaningful results, one must either analyze the whole package, or give up the effort."

3. The quality, dependability, and availability of information is poor, and the empirical basis for any theory of a command economy is thereby inadequate. One reason for this is that the "tenets of Marxian theology inhibit the freedom of inquiry in economic theory" (Zinam 1969: 33–34). Endogenous problems with data gathering and ideological commitment to the success of socialism — if not in reality, then at least on paper — are also undoubtedly responsible for the drawbacks of statistical coverage in a command economy.

In the field of transport, Zinam's second observation may be supported by the following statements taken from an East German source: Transport in Eastern Europe is an "important instrument of power" of the central state administration. "The transport policy of the GDR is an intimate part of the aggregate policy of worker and peasant power. . . . The transport policy serves . . . to bring about the victory of socialism in the GDR." With specific reference to transport planning, the same author stated that because of the bond between workers, peasants, and the working intelligentsia, "the complex development of different transport services can be realized through socialist transport policy" (Lindner 1962: 14-15). The above quotations not only claim that socialist planning is inherently superior, but they also indicate the primacy of politics in planning. The latter may have led to economic errors, but the Marxian view of transport as a service industry and hence as partly unproductive may also have led to errors. It may be doubted whether serious and uncorrectable mistakes had been made in transport planning for these reasons, but there may have been some (cf. Demmler 1967: 11 and ch. 1; Michalski 1975: 41).

It is beyond doubt, however, that planning for increased production in the sectors that concentrate on material production determines the demand for transport services; clearly, productive inputs and outputs have to be transported to and from enterprises. The relationship between the growth of, e.g., industrial production or GNP and the demand for transport services is, however, not entirely determined by shifts of production between plants and regions of a country, changing sources of raw materials, changing composition of inputs and thus of their geographical origin, changing composition of output and thus of its geographical destination, changing factor productivity, changing technology, and changing substitutability of different modes of transport (cf. Demmler 1967: 109-10). In addition, the relationship between the growth of output of goods and that of transport is complicated by the fact that output is calculated as a monetary value and in the socialist countries is subject to various statistical manipulations — such as double-counting — that are designed to overstate its growth (see Mieczkowski 1975: ch. 3), while transport is expressed in physical terms — tons or ton-kilometers — which are much less liable to statistical overestimation (cf. Demmler 1967: 110-11). Planning of transport services has to rely consequently on a sample of physical output plans for the most important users of transport services (Demmler 1967: 112), as will be shown below. This interrelation between transport planning and general planning has been stressed even more strongly in a Western source: "the transportation study is an integral part of the overall planning process, and cannot adequately be considered in isolation." (Bruton 1970: 22).

Despite these drawbacks, reduced somewhat in importance by the

1970s, planning continues in command economies, and transport planning in particular yields certain advantages, though at a cost that may, in the final macroeconomic analysis, be excessive. Planning comes close to accurate forecasting, and it includes detailed indicators for the shipping enterprises as well as for the transport modes. On the railroad detailed norms are used for car handling, consolidation of shipments and other ways of increasing the efficiency in the use of the infrastructure. Cross haulage and excessive hauls can be eliminated through proper plan analysis (Williams 1962: 75). Such a procedure — though intensive in resource use for planning — tends to maximize the utilization of the means of transport (cf. Khachaturov 1952: 113).

Werner Gumpel, on the basis of Soviet and East European examples, denied that planning has an important practical role. He mentioned "problems of absence of planning" and concluded that in general and in regional transport planning the planned element is actually small and is tautological in the sense of simply acting according to a plan. Gumpel suggested the term *improvisation economy* as more descriptive of East European practice (Gumpel 1967: 48). In his view, market economies have been ahead of planned economies in transport planning because of documented "substantial deficiencies" in the East European transport planning. That planning is not comprehensive and consequently it fails to allocate efficiently transport work among different modes, to utilize interfaces, and to eliminate what I describe in chapter 5 as irrational transport. Gumpel was also highly critical of the "planning chaos" in Soviet transport. The transport plan does not correctly reflect transport needs because enterprises and industries "pad" their requirements, which produces false estimates of investment needs and which harms some enterprise and some social needs as the result of unequal "padding" and disproportional allocations. This state of affairs is not noticeably improved by the rigidity imposed by planning over short-run solutions that cannot be easily adjusted at short notice. The result is considerable social waste (Gumpel 1967: 55-56, 58).

The basic assumption in the communist approach to the transport sector is its obligatory service character, that is, it is subordinate to such considerations as capacity, convenience of workers, and absence of Sunday work (cf. Demmler 1967: 84, 101-102; *ZG* 1975, no. 27, pp. 1-2; ibid., 1975, no. 47, p. 16; Zbierajewski 1975: 5). The basic functions of different modes of transport are their complementarity, modernization, specialization, maximization of service, and lowering of unit costs (cf. Madeyski 1971: 42-43). Both these elements, i.e., the assumption of the subordinate character of transport and the concept of the basic functions of transport, exert a deep imprint on the planning of transport.

The planning process determines the future demand for transport as well as transport capacity from the points of view of volume, regional distribution, and distribution in time (Tismer 1963: 92–97; cf. Institut Kompleksnykh Transportnykh Problem 1968: 17). It is, of course, helpful that transport in Eastern Europe is socialized, but this fact does not make it very different from most other countries. Railroads were under state ownership in Eastern Europe before World War II just as they are at present in Western Europe. Other transport modes are largely, but not wholly, under state ownership, as shown in the example of East Germany in Table 3.1 (cf. Günther 1965: 228, 247–50, 257).

This predominance of socialized ownership makes planning easier: planners can issue direct orders to transport organizations (as well as to their socialized customers) and can back up those orders by a system of close scrutiny and personal responsibility of the officials in charge of given enterprises (cf. Demmler 1967: 18). Wide socialization also makes possible an integral planning coordinating the work of different transport modes so as to maximize productive efficiency and to mini- mize the social costs (cf. Lissowska 1971; and Khachaturov 1959: 286–88; United Nations 1967: 11–13; Andruszkiewicz 1975a: 91–99).

The secondary aim of planning is to reduce fluctuations in service caused by seasonal and other factors. The coefficient of fluctuation (not otherwise defined) on East German railroads declined from 10.8 percent in 1957, to 10.3 percent in 1958, to 9.2 percent in 1960, and to 6.6 percent in 1962. The same coefficient fell also during the same period in all other modes of transport (*Ökonomik der Arbeit* 1965: 40). Fluctuations in transport are also avoided in the short-period by planning for the full use of transport capacity during Sundays and holidays, as, e.g., in inland transport (Demmler 1967: 101–102).

Central planning has undoubtedly contributed to the predominance of the railroad in Eastern Europe, since planners tend to favor large production units both as more convenient to manage and control and as more apt to satisfy the planners' need for conspicuous success, or for impressive success indicators, which is not necessarily the same thing. In the railroad, the planners found a ready large-scale form of organization particularly responsive to central administration and central planning. Moreover, as productive enterprises tended to be- come larger under the sponsorship of central planners, they also

TABLE 3.1

Nationalization of Transport in East Germany, 1950-60

(percentages)

	Railroad	Sea Transport	Motor Transport	Inland Waterways	Total
1950	100		21.7	28.5	66.6
1955	100		49.2	52.4	76.4
1958	100		65.7	51.4	81.9
1960	100		75.6	53.0	86.3

Source: Lindner 1962: 18.

TABLE 3.2

Percentage Distribution of Performance in Socialized Freight Transport as Between Transport Modes in Poland

A. Quantities transported (percentages based on tons):

	Railroad	Road (motor)	Inland waterways	Sea	Civilian air transport	Pipelines	Road (horsedrawn)
1949	93.6	4.4	.7	1.3	—	—	..
1950	91.6[a]	..	.7	1.4	—	—	..
1955	80.1	17.8	1.1	1.0	—	—	..
1960	84.1	13.2	.9	1.8	—	—	..
1960[b]	39.9	56.7	.4	.8	—	—	2.2
1965	36.3	60.6	.5	1.2	—	.7	.6
1970	29.6	66.9	.7	1.4	—	1.2	.2
1973	24.2	72.6	.6	1.3	—	1.3	.1
1975	20.3	76.3	.7	1.3	—	1.3	.1

B. Performance (percentages based on ton/kilometers):

1949	82.5	.3	.8	16.3	—	—
1950	78.6[a]	..	.6	20.3	—	—
1955	74.5	1.7	1.1	22.7	—	—
1960	65.5	1.4	.9	32.2	—	—
1960[b]	61.6	5.3	.8	32.2	—	—
1965	53.9	5.6	.9	37.5	2.1	—
1970	43.0	6.8	1.0	46.2	3.0	—
1973	38.6	8.1	.6	49.4	3.3	—
1975	33.8	8.5	.5	53.9	3.3	—

a   not full coverage   b   start of a new, more comprehensive series

Sources: Calculated on the basis of RS 1960: 260; RS 1962: 253; RS 1974: 385; RS 1975: 316.

tended to gain their own access to the railway network by means of their own sidings, thus making transport by rail that much more economical (cf. Demmler 1967: 72; Mieczkowski 1975: ch. 4).

As a result, rail transport has traditionally played a dominant role in Eastern Europe, whose economies, with the exception of Albania, may be called railroad economies. Out of the total *domestic* transport services performed, the railroad accounted in 1958 for 89.9 percent in the Soviet Union, for 96.6 percent in Poland, for 81.6 percent in East Germany (in 1964), for 89.8 percent in Czechoslovakia, and for 84.9 percent in Hungary (Demmler 1967: 70–71). As shown in table 3.2, this high percentage has recently tended to decrease, partly in recognition of the railroad's cost disadvantage in short-distance transport; but the railroad still carries a disproportionate share of domestic traffic. In comparison, only 40.6 percent of domestic traffic was carried by railroad in West Germany in 1964 (Demmler 1967: 70; for the U.S. cf. Kneafsey 1975: 118). This subject will be explored in detail in chapter 4 below.

It should be stressed that the socialists are hardly bashful about their claims concerning transport planning. For example, T. S. Khachaturov wrote that Soviet economists proved that planning of the national economy, transport, regional distribution of production, and efficient use of the infrastructure can result in rapid increase of transport performance. Infrastructure and the amount of equipment have grown slower in the Soviet Union than did the volume of transport. Socialist ownership of the means of production made possible the integration of Soviet transport into a single system (Khachaturov 1965: 189–90).

Similarly, Karl Hofmann (1960: 42), in East Germany, claimed that under socialism a rational distribution of transport among transport modes is achieved. A special ideological halo is thus attached to circumstances of transport under socialism, making it radically different from and superior to transport conditions under capitalism (cf. Hofmann 1960: 53, 117; Galitskii 1950: 111; Galitskii 1956: 58–59).

The countries of Eastern Europe formulated the principle of desirability of overall transport planning even in the early postwar period. In Poland this view was expounded in 1947 in the form of a request that a uniform transport system be created to cover the whole country, "making up a unity logically and rationally formed, welded organizationally, and functioning in accordance with the real state, economic, and social needs. . ." (Madeyski 1971: 21–22). The paramount importance of transport for economic and political development was already clearly understood, and it was resolved to use transport for the fulfillment of communist goals.

Long-range Plans

Planning in transport has different time periods. Long-range (perspectivistic) planning has to do with periods of over ten years and concentrates on future investment priorities (Michalski 1975: 38). Multi-year planning spans the period of the Five-Year Plans and conforms to those plans. Annual planning covers subperiods of the Five-Year Plans and gives transport organizations their concrete service tasks; this planning is also called "technical and exploitative" planning, indicating its direct applicability to the work of transport enterprises. Operative planning is subdivided into quarterly and monthly plans (Liberadzki 1971: 176–77).

The subordinate character of transport is directly reflected in one of the two main functions of the long-range (perspectivistic) plan: (1) determination of the rate and directions of the economic development of the country; and (2) determination of the main investment needs in the long run (Liberadzki 1971: 178). It is apparent that the economic development of the country defines the tasks of transport and helps to determine the investment needs in that area. Similarly, operative plans are based on figures showing the tasks of individual producers in the economy and hence on their needs for transport services (Liberadzki 1971: 178).

Long-range plans for transport are prepared by transport sections of special commissions for long-range plans, commissions formed of planners, scholars, and executives. The work of the transport sections is necessarily circumscribed by the work of other sections, and the validity of long-range transport plans depends on the validity of overall long-range planning. The time span of such planning, usually fifteen years, seems to preclude precise indicators, except to pinpoint investment projects that are likely to prove necessary by the end of the period.

Multi-Year Plans

Multi-year plans for transport are derived from plans based on directives of the Communist Party leadership and the Council of Ministers. As stated above, transport plans use the method of sampling the main users of transport services with regard to their material production (the Germans use the term *Hauptkettenglied*). Horst Demmler (1967: 113–14) described a more complicated procedure in which the key branches of the economy yield, by way of technical and economic coefficients, the indicators of growth for the whole economy. From those, production/transport ratios based on past experiences provide the indicators of transport needs (cf. chapter 4).

Just as in the Soviet Union, a distinction has to be made between tariff distance in transport *(Versandweite)* and actual distance traveled *(Transportweite)* (cf. Williams 1962: 33–39). The former is the shortest distance between the point of loading and the destination. The latter is the actual distance covered. Characteristically, actual distance traveled is longer than tariff distance. The average tariff distance is used in calculations of future transport needs in view of the multi-year plans and in view of the distribution of that average distance between various commodities covered by the plans. One can appreciate that shifts in the relative importance of various commodities produced cause variations in transport needs owing to differences in their average tariff distances (Demmler 1967: 115–16; Hofmann 1960: 62). In Poland the actual distance traveled is taken into account in measures of transport performance and may be actually used for planning purposes (Michalski 1975: 64).

The goals for each individual means of transport are then derived from the calculation of the volume of transport for individual goods and their average distance traveled (see Günther 1965: 158) and on the basis of "the socialist principles of distribution of consignments of goods as between different modes of transport" (Demmler 1967: 116). The historical distribution of transport performance among individual transport modes is shown in tables 3.2 to 3.7.

In table 3.3, the distribution of quantity transported shows the relative increase in short-haul traffic by road and in plant motor traffic and the decline in the relative importance of the railroad. The distribution of transport performance shows an even steeper decline in the relative importance of the railroad and the dramatic emergence of long-distance sea transport, even to the extent of distorting the relative domestic importance of other transport modes.

It is interesting to note that the average tariff distance for different goods transported in East Germany tended to increase during the 1950s, probably indicating a wider geographical distribution of productive capacities as the result of national economic planning (Hofmann 1960: 63). International comparisons show that the length of hauls depends on the size of the country, the United States and the USSR showing the greatest average length of hauls.

Furthermore, the average transport distance for East Germany as a

TABLE 3.3

Percentage Distribution of Freight Transport Performance among Transport Modes in East Germany

A. Quantities transported (percentages based on tons):

	Railroad	Road	Inland waterways	Sea	Civilian aircraft	Pipelines	Plant Motor Transport
1949	60.1	17.9	4.5	–	–	–	17.6
1950	65.9	19.6	4.4	–	–	–	19.0
1955	53.3	17.9	3.3	0	–	–	25.5
1960	45.5	25.2	2.4	.3	0	–	26.6
1965	41.4	26.4	1.9	1.0	0	.6	28.6
1970	34.4	23.6	1.8	1.1	0	2.0	37.1
1972	32.8	22.9	1.6	1.2	0	2.5	39.7
1974	32.5	20.1	1.7	1.3	0	3.0	41.4

B. Performance (percentages based on t/km):

	Railroad	Road	Inland waterways	Sea	Civilian aircraft	Pipelines	Plant Motor Transport
1949	81.8	5.5	7.4	–	–	–	5.3
1950	81.0	5.2	8.5	–	–	–	5.2
1955	81.2	4.8	7.0	1.5	–	–	5.5
1960	64.9	5.2	4.4	20.8	0	–	4.7
1965	49.5	5.1	2.8	38.4	0	.1	4.1
1970	32.4	4.8	1.8	54.5	0	1.7	4.7
1972	33.2	5.0	1.7	52.6	0	2.3	5.1
1974	33.4	4.9	1.6	52.0	0	2.6	5.4

Source: *SJ 1973*: 235-36; *SJ 1975*: 221-22.

TABLE 3.4

Percentage Distribution of Freight Transport
Performance among Transport Modes in Czechoslovakia

A. Quantities transported (percentages based on tons):

	Railroad	Road	Inland waterways	Sea	Air	Pipelines
1950	88.0	10.8	1.2	..	..	–
1955	64.2	34.5	1.3	–	..	–
1960	58.9	39.9	1.1	.1	–	–
1965	51.3	45.9	1.0	.2	–	1.6
1970	49.2	46.9	.9	.2	–	2.8
1973	46.4	49.8	.9	.2	–	2.8
1975	45.5	50.8	1.0	.2	–	2.5

B. Performance (percentages based on t/km):

	Railroad	Road	Inland waterways	Sea	Air	Pipelines
1950	95.0	1.1	3.9	..	..	–
1955	86.9	2.8	4.1	6.2	..	–
1960	80.0	4.1	3.3	12.6	–	–
1965	76.8	4.8	2.9	11.2	–	4.3
1970	71.6	5.7	2.9	12.3	–	7.5
1973	69.2	6.6	2.6	12.9	–	8.6
1975	70.4	8.2	2.9	13.5	.1	4.9

Sources: Calculated on the basis of *SR 1962:* 287, 293, 295, 296; *SR 1974:* 369, 375, 377, 378, 381; *SR 1975:* 383, 389, 391, 392, 395; *SESEV 1976:* 269-70, 276-77.

TABLE 3.5

Percentage Distribution of Freight Transport
Performance among Transport Modes in Hungary

A. Quantities transported (percentages based on tons):

	Railroad	Road	Inland waterways	Pipelines
1950	79.4	13.0	2.1	1.0
1960	47.8	36.3	1.2	.6
1965	44.6	46.8	1.0	1.8
1970	41.3	51.9	1.1	3.3
1973	40.0	53.4	1.1	4.4
1975	19.9	75.5	1.9	2.8

B. Performance (percentages based on t/km):

1950	88.9	1.5	8.8	.5
1960	85.0	5.7	8.3	.4
1965	81.7	8.0	8.0	2.1
1970	74.9	10.8	10.3	3.9
1973	65.9	11.0	15.9	7.1
1975	59.4	22.0	10.7	7.8

Sources: *SPBH 1963:* 80; *SPBH 1973:* 190; *SPBH 1974:* 176; *SE 1975:* 235.

TABLE 3.6
Percentage Distribution of Freight Transport
Performance among Transport Modes in Romania

A. Quantities transported (percentages based on tons):

	Railroad	Road	River	Sea	Air	Pipelines
1950	91.3	2.7	2.9	.5	–	2.6
1955	84.1	10.4	2.3	.3	–	2.9
1960	54.7	39.9	1.4	.1	–	3.9
1965	44.5	51.0	1.1	.5	–	2.9
1970	39.8	55.8	1.0	1.0	–	2.6
1973	38.8	56.8	.9	.9	–	2.5
1975	33.8	62.1	.9	1.0	–	2.2

B. Performance (percentages based on t/km):

	Railroad	Road	River	Sea	Air	Pipelines
1950	83.4	.5	7.3	6.7	–	2.1
1955	87.7	1.6	3.9	4.2	–	2.6
1960	83.6	4.0	3.6	4.5	–	4.3
1965	70.2	5.7	2.8	18.9	–	2.4
1970	51.2	5.5	1.4	39.9	–	2.0
1973	53.2	5.6	1.6	37.3	–	2.3
1975	44.6	6.4	1.4	45.6	–	2.0

Sources: *AS 1974:* 280-81; *AS 1976:* 342-43.

TABLE 3.7

Percentage Distribution of Freight Transport Performance among Transport Modes in Bulgaria

A. Quantities transported (percentages based on tons):

	Railroad	Road	Inland waterways	Sea	Air
1952	45.6	51.6	1.7	1.1	—
1960	22.7	75.8	.9	.6	—
1970	11.8	85.1	.6	2.5	—
1975	24.2	68.5	1.4	5.9	—

B. Performance (percentages based on t/km):

	Railroad	Road	Inland waterways	Sea	Air
1952	73.8	7.8	6.5	11.9	—
1960	57.3	16.7	5.1	20.9	—
1970	22.2	12.6	2.9	62.3	—
1975	25.4	9.2	3.5	61.9	—

Sources: Calculated from *SEzh 1971*: 154; *SESEV 1976*: 269-70, 276-77.

whole increased between 1947 and 1959 from 128 km to 150 km, and
the average tariff distance increased from 118 km to 141 km (Hofmann
1960: 62). The spatial spread of economic activity in East Germany is
evident here.

Tables 3.2 and 3.4–3.7 show close similarities to what table 3.3
shows for East Germany. In table 3.5, for example, the railroad's share
of quantities transported in Hungary in 1950 was about 10 percentage
points lower than its share in transport performance. In 1972 this
difference increased to about 30 percentage points, indicating a relative increase in distances transported. The services of road transport
increased greatly during the same period, showing its considerable
growth relative to other transport modes. The same was true of pipeline transport. (Romania, many of whose pipelines were built before
the period shown in table 3.6, did not conform to this trend.) Maritime
countries such as Poland, East Germany, Romania, and Bulgaria
show a rapid relative growth of transport by sea in terms of transport
performance; here, the longer distances of sea transport are a decisive
factor. As in Western Europe (Bayliss 1965: 126), the average distance
covered in railroad transport was longer than in road transport.

Transport by passenger car, not shown in tables 3.2–3.7, has
recently shown a relative increase in importance. It has been estimated
in Poland that passenger cars trailed buses in transport performance
until at least 1965, but that there were more passenger/kilometers in
passenger cars than in buses by 1970 (Malek, Grzywacz, and Zymela
1973: 391).

Multi-year plans for transport also include investment plans covering new equipment (e.g., diesel locomotives) and new plant (e.g.,
construction of new transshipment points, electrification of new lines,
construction of repair works). Investment in transport had high
priority during early postwar reconstruction; but in the 1950s, it
received low priority, and stress was put on maximum utilization of
existing capacity. Investment plans will be discussed in a separate
section below.

In the planning of road transport for long-range and multi-year
periods, several methods are used. (1) The *indicative method,* which
concentrates on the expected growth of demand for transport and the
expected increase in the efficiency of existing equipment; comparison
of the two magnitudes so derived indicates the need for additional
equipment. (2) The *method of extrapolation,* which projects the same
(herein lies its weakness) growth tendencies in transport that existed in
the past. (3) The *regression line method,* which studies econometric

relations between independent variables such as the aggregate amount of production and the demand for transport services. A correlation coefficient of not less than 0.8 allows use of a regression line to anticipate future changes in the demand for transport. (4) The *elasticity of demand method,* which yields percentage changes in the demand for transport on the basis of individual variables summed up to give the aggregate change in the demand for transport (Lissowska 1971a: 148–51).

Annual Plans

Transport performance depends on the demand for its services, which in turn derives from the production record. In this section, we will abstract from passenger transport, which will be covered in a separate section. The main focus will therefore be on the ways of estimating the demand for transport services in freight transportation.

As already stated, transport plays a subordinate role in the centrally planned economy. There is no indication in the planning process that the managers of transport organizations can pick and choose whom, how, and when they are going to serve. Given reasonable demands on them, demands spread out in time, they accept it as their duty to satisfy their customers — a duty that seems to possess a stronger element of compulsion than seems true for enterprises in the sphere of material production.

There are two mutually supplementary types of planning procedures designed to produce annual transport plans, and their discussion here follows closely an excellent analysis by Horst Demmler (1967: 117–151). They are: (1) the method of proportions of dispatching (shipments), and (2) the methods of regional balances of material production and use. A third method, that of transport contracts, will be discussed in the section on operative planning.

1. *The method of proportions of dispatching* is based on past proportions between dispatching (hauls) and production; these are sometimes called "coefficients of transportability" (Khachaturov 1965: 191). For instance, a production of 50 million tons of coal has always resulted in the shipment of 45 million tons of coal, then the shipment coefficient becomes 0.9. The coefficient of transportability (or the coefficient of haulage) may be defined by the formula

$$T_c = q_{tr}/q_{pr}$$

where T_c = coefficient of transportability

q_{tr} = the tonnage transported

q_{pr} = the tonnage produced (Hofmann 1960: 122; Tarski 1968: 52-53).

Should the coefficient be more than unity, it would indicate that part of the goods in question was transported more than once, as was true in Poland in the case of cement in 1955 (Tarski 1968: 53).

When this coefficient of transportability is multiplied by the planned production quantities of a given year, the product shows the quantity to be transported during the year in question (Hofmann 1960: 123). If the planners expect the coefficient of transportability to change as a result of a change in location of productive enterprises or as a result of a change in the percentage of the local use of the product, then the coefficient is changed accordingly to reflect such planned developments. Table 3.8 shows the coefficients of transportability of several goods that are of more importance in bulk shipments in Poland; table 3.9 shows the same for East Germany.

This procedure results in the derivation of the quantity of goods to be transported in a given year and can be used in conjunction with input-output analysis. In order to obtain plan figures for transport performance in ton/kilometers, the quantities of individual goods to be transported in a given year have to be multiplied by the average distance over which they have been transported according to past experience. (For calculation of the average distance of haul, see Galitskii 1956: 36.) The aggregate of these products provides a fairly reliable estimate of future demand for transport services, since possible changes in the values determining it can be easily taken into account in the calculations.

There are several disadvantages to the method of proportions of dispatching. (1) Some products produced during the preceding plan period will be transported in the given period, while some products produced in that period will be transported in the following period. The proportions of these residuals may vary between plan periods owing to uneven distribution of production in time (cf. Feld 1965: 65). (2) The distribution of transport of a given product between different transport modes may change, producing bottlenecks and excess capacities in the modes so affected. It is unlikely, however, that substantial shifts will occur on this account between individual years, and over the longer run such shifts can be taken care of in the process of annual planning. (3) The distribution of production in time over the given year (as well as the precise distribution of shipments between the transport modes) are not given in the annual plan. Such data can be produced only in the operative plan discussed in the following section. (4) In order to be fully binding and comprehensive, the transport plan based on this method would have to go into further detail on indi-

TABLE 3.8
Coefficients of Transportability on Standard-Gauge Railroad in Poland

	1955	1960	1965	1970	1972
Bituminous coal	.85	.88	.89	.90	.91
Cement	1.02	.82	.82	.74	.79
Grains	.35	.43	.49	.38	.36
Potatoes	.06	.05	.06	.04	.04
Sugar beets	.63	.59	.48	.24	.23

Source: Michalski 1975: 60.

TABLE 3.9

Coefficients of Transportability of Several Bulk Goods Sent by Railroad in East Germany

	1955	1956	1957	1958
Coal and coke	.32	.32	.33	.33
Iron ore	.72	.63	.63	.64
Metals	.82	.78	.79	.80
Cement	.96	.94	.87	.81
Potatoes	.14	.09	.09	.10
Grain, legumes, oleaginous plants	.28	.29	.25	.20
Sugar beets	.55	.53	.53	.56

Source: Hofmann 1960: 122.

vidual transport by enterprises, by modes, in time, by distance, and by junctions through which the different hauls have to pass (cf. Hofmann 1960: 127). Generating these details would require a veritable army of planners, and the famous tongue-in-cheek estimate by the Soviet cybernetist V. M. Glushkov that planning would, on the basis of past trends and in not too long a time, occupy the entire adult population of the Soviet Union would come true in Eastern Europe (Levine 1967: 114). In practice, therefore, the method of proportions of dispatching can serve only as a general indicator of the future demand for transport services; the particulars of that demand are filled in by operative planning — through transport contracts entered into by those directly concerned in the transport process, thus avoiding the specter Glushkov raised.

The advantage of the method of proportions of dispatching is that it gives an indication of the future demand for transport services even in the early stages of mapping the annual plans. It provides early warning signs of possible bottlenecks and may be extended to provide general transport indicators for individual sectors and branches of the economy. It enables individual transport modes to prepare themselves in advance for changes in the future demand for their services and thus to anticipate future transport contracts well before they are entered into in the process of operative planning. In itself, however, the method is insufficient: it fails to provide day-to-day directives for different modes of transport, directives that would optimally spread out in time the job to be done and that would distribute the tasks adequately among transport modes.

A more general measure is the synthetic indicator of transportability, which is defined as the relation between the total amount of freight transported (in tons) and total production (also in tons). There are obvious difficulties in so quantifying and in meaningfully relating the volume of transport and especially the volume of production. A Polish attempt to do so resulted in estimates of the synthetic indicator for Poland of 2.422 in 1955, 2.561 in 1956, 2.444 in 1957, 2.435 in 1958, 2.405 in 1959, and 2.334 in 1960 (Tarski 1968: 58). The same indicator for the Soviet Union in 1963 amounted to 3.04 (Tarski 1968: 58n).

The denominator of the synthetic indicator of transportability may be the national income in money terms at constant prices rather than physical estimates of aggregate production. This indicator shows in Poland a reduction from 2.11 in 1955 to 1.83 in 1967 (Tarski 1968: 60).

The numerator of the synthetic indicator may be the performance figure of ton/kilometers instead of tons; this establishes the relationship between transport performance per unit of national income. This form of the synthetic indicator has shown an upward tendency in Poland: from .263 in 1955 to .305 in 1967 (Tarski 1968: 62).

A related measure is the coefficient of elasticity of transport, which shows the relationship between the relative change in transport performance and the relative change in national income:

$$E = \Delta q/q/\Delta NI/NI$$

where E = coefficient of elasticity of transport
    q = transport performance in t/km
    NI = national income.

In Poland this coefficient was 1.24 for the period 1955-1967, indicating a faster growth in the transport sector than in the growth of the economy as a whole (Tarski 1968: 63). Given the value of the coefficient of elasticity and given the planned increase in national income, planners can calculate the needed increase in transport performance.

Finally, Hungarian planning produced the concept of a synthetic indicator of transport performance, one that points to a functional relationship between the demand for transport and several factors:

$$I_{tr} = c \; I_T^{\alpha_1} \; I_{tt}^{\alpha_2} \; I_{mi}^{\alpha_3} \; I_w^{\alpha_4} \; I_{rr}^{\alpha_5} \; I_t^{\alpha_6} \; I_r^{\alpha_7}$$

where: I_{tr} = transport performance in t/km
    c = a constant
    I_T = GNP
    I_{tt} = territorial distribution of production
    I_{mi} = material intensity of production
    I_w = share of material production in GNP
    I_{rr} = the level of real rates for transport services
    I_t = level of technology in the transport sector
    I_r = level of rationalization of transport (added to the formula by Tarski 1968: 78)
    α = partial coefficients of the elasticity of demand for transport services.

This indicator does not seem to be, as yet, adapted to precise planning, but it is an approach to the definition of the multiple relationships that influence and determine the demand for transport (cf. Tarski 1968: 78-79). The author of this indicator also came out in favor of a cybernetically administered transport system (Kádas 1970).

2. *The method of regional balances* of material output and use stresses the demand on transport links and thus seems particularly responsive to the nature of transport services. It is also regarded as particularly suited to the socialist economy (Galitskii 1956: 39).

In the regional balances method, each district prepares data on aggregate inventories at the start of the planned year, on the planned use and planned output of materials, and on the planned inventories at the end of that year. When the algebraic sum of planned output, less planned use, less year-end inventories, plus beginning-of-the-year inventories for a district is positive, then the district is a net surplus one and has a positive transport balance. If it is negative, the district is a net user of goods (or, to borrow a term from international economics, it is a net importer), or a deficit district, and it has a negative transport balance. The task of the planner is, then, to match the output of, and the demand for, individual goods as between districts — the intra-district transport of those goods being more easily and automatically arranged. Thus, surplus districts are paired with deficit districts in such a way as to minimize claims on transport services and to avoid, if possible, movement of empty cars. What seems particularly adapted to the planning of transport is that the planners prepare geographical flow charts of individual goods to provide visual control over the demands on the means of transport and over possible ways of minimizing the streams of transport services. The flow charts show the average number of ton/kilometers per kilometer of road used by the given mode of transport (cf. Hofmann 1960: 96, for an example of such a flow chart; Khanukov 1965: 114–17).

Instead of flow charts, input-output tables can be prepared for the interdistrict flow of goods: the dispatch district is listed in the first column and read along the horizontal lines, and the receiving districts are read in the columns. Such a sender-receiver table can be drawn up according to districts or according to cities or stations and can be prepared on an annual, quarterly, or monthly basis. The table may be reduced to a number of the most important bulk goods; for some purposes, it can contain individual goods (cf. Hofmann 1960: 97–106). A similar, separate chart can be made for shipping and receiving goods to and from abroad (cf. Hofmann 1960: 106–107). Finally, the table can include the routes taken by goods from one place to another; in this form, it can be converted into a flow chart. Such a chart can then be used to make through-flow charts for individual transport centers to help in the organization of shuttling, reloading, refrigeration service, and storage (cf. Demmler 1967: 146–48).

The regional balances method is supposed to cut down on unnecessary movement of the means of transport and to help minimize the social costs of transportation. However, as noted by Demmler, problems of planning of transport provide an outstanding illustration of

Hayek's thesis that a demonstration such as Oskar Lange's — that the economic problems of central planning are theoretically solvable — does not of itself prove much, since the practical application of such a theoretical solution is highly questionable (Hayek 1956: 207-14). According to Demmler (1967: 140-41), the method of regional balances, while theoretically rational, presents in practice insurmountable difficulties. The parameters do not remain constant in time, relationships between them change from month to month, and central planning becomes pragmatically impossible.

But variability of parameter functions is only part of the problem encountered in the method of regional balances. When one realizes that quality and assortment differences make for special and differentiated demands on the means of transport, the method of regional balances becomes extraordinarily complex. To use Demmler's examples (1967: 141), simple coordination between coal-surplus and coal-deficit districts hardly does justice to the actual problem of providing coal, since its qualities differ according to the particular use to which coal may be put. Coking coal, coal for the chemical industry, briquettes, and coal for household use are in effect different commodities, not even near substitutes for one another. Similarly, wood should be differentiated into mine timber, construction wood of different kinds, pulp wood, wood for making of boxes, and the like. With this need for differentiation, the method of regional balances remains, in practice, applicable to only a few simple bulk raw materials undifferentiated by their nature, e.g., iron ore.

Furthermore, it is argued that, in practice, determination of senders and receivers of goods does not in itself determine the route to be taken (that route being at least partly influenced by the existence of other on-the-way dispatches and deliveries). Besides, and partly in connection with this point, the method of regional balances does not provide any information about intradistrict movement of goods and omits some goods the transport of which might influence both the interdistrict routes and the use of transport equipment. For these reasons, the regional balances method has been criticized in East Germany as not as well suited to it as it is to the Soviet Union (Demmler 1967: 141).

Annual plans for road transport by and large use the balances method that compares transport tasks with transport capacity. Transport tasks are defined regionally, as in the case of the railroad, but not necessarily using the same territorial coverage; they include the length of hauls and their directions as well as the composition of freight with regard to its transportability in each region and subregion. Similar information is needed in planning passenger road transport.

Since full investigation into highway transport needs is very time-consuming, substitute planning is used in practice (Lissowska 1971a: 151–52). It is based on transport applications and transport contracts prepared in advance by the users of transport facilities and categorized according to organizational forms of road transport. The freight tonnage is shown on those applications and contracts according to the main freight classifications. Those transport needs that do not have to be applied for in advance are estimated on the basis of past experience. This method is less than adequate for planning because it does not contain enough information (e.g., about the territorial distribution of transport needs), because it does not allow correction by transport planners, and because it does not offer an opportunity to check on plan fulfillment (Lissowska 1971a: 152). It also has to be combined with calculations that change transport needs (expressed in tons) into transport performance (expressed in ton/kilometers). (Several formulas used for such recalculation are shown in Lissowska 1971a: 153–59.)

Operative plans

Operative planning, introduced in Eastern Europe during the early 1950s (in Poland in May 1951), correlates the productive tasks of various sectors with those of transport enterprises and ensures fulfillment of the overall economic plan. It is divided into quarterly and monthly plans (formerly, there were also five-day plans) adapted to seasonal fluctuations in traffic. The plans are divided according to the various means of transport, with monthly (formerly, five-day) plans being tantamount to final orders to the transport enterprises (Rudzki 1954a: 10–11; Rudzki 1957: 422).

Generally, operative transport planning starts with productive enterprises filing their production and transport plans with their associations at least forty-five days before the start of each quarter. Plans then go to the ministries concerned, from there to the State Planning Commission and to the Ministry of Transport (cf. Rudzki 1954a: 11). Quarterly loading plans are prepared by senders, who then send them to their administrative superiors (associations, central administrations, etc.), who, in turn, compare those plans with the production and purchasing plans of the producing enterprises and request corrections of the loading plans when necessary (Liberadzki 1971: 182; Michalski 1975: 191). Monthly plans include loading norms and a special part for loading during weekends and holidays — designed to make better use of those days (Liberadzki 1971: 184).

Because the method of proportions of dispatching and the method of regional balances used in annual plans are so indeterminate (discussed in the preceding section) and because they are not binding on users of transport services, operative planning relies on a supplementary *method of transport contracts.* According to Demmler (1967: 120–21), "without the system of transport contracts the planning of traffic could be only a [general] framework planning." And, the system of transport contracts is "the means with the help of which one can actually produce an operative plan." It is not a concretization of the annual plan, but it is in itself a specific form of planning and plan fulfillment (Demmler 1967: 121).

In this connection, Osmar Spitzner asserted in the legal journal of East Germany that the general economic plan states only the proportions of production and distribution. However, since it does not comprehensively organize production and distribution, economic contracts are necessary to express more concretely social obligations of enterprises. The contract system is, therefore, a directive and distinctive form of planning, and is not merely a continuation of the general plan (Spitzner 1961: 1689–90).

Hofmann described the short-run plan of haulage as "absolutely necessary." Both the East German railroad and the shipping by water use monthly operative plans (Hofmann 1960: 128; cf. Galitskii 1956: 77–82).

In the contract method of transport planning, all enterprises that supply each other with some goods have to enter into contractual relations in advance of a plan period. These contracts, when applying to shipments above a specified minimum weight, oblige both the supplier and the recipient of the commodities to enter, also before the start of the plan period, into a separate contract with the applicable transport service. The minimum quantities that oblige shippers and receivers to make such contracts differ between transport modes and between senders and receivers of goods. Thus, in East Germany, they are for senders 1,200 tons per year for the railroad and 2,000 tons per year for inland waterway transort. For the receivers, they are 6,000 tons per year for the railroad and 100,000 tons per year for inland waterway transport. For transport by truck, there are apparently no minimum quantities in East Germany (Demmler 1967: 121–24; cf. Michalski 1975: 191–94). The annual contracts specify distribution of consignments within the year by quarters and, in the case of road transport, by month (Demmler 1967: 124).

The disadvantages of the currently used operative planning have been summarized as:

1. It leads to a dispersion of effort since all hauls have to be reported. About half the transport users in East Germany show an average demand for cars of less than ten double-axle cars per month, and they use only about 4 percent of transport capacity.

2. Directional information about haulage is inadequately processed. While senders of more than 800 tons per month give in their operative plans the location of the recipient and while others give the railroad office of the recipient, these data are not prepared for the whole railroad network because such preparation would require too much time.

3. Information is inadequately transmitted by the transport offices.

4. Cooperation of local administration in the preparation of operative plans is inadequate (Hofmann 1960: 130–31).

5. On the East German railroad, the responsibility for transport is cut up among a number of different bureaus and branches without adequate communication among them (cf. Hofmann 1960: 132–39).

6. Planning of the interregional movement of goods contains the seeds of too many possible variants. Thus, given just thirty suppliers and 100 recipients of a given product, there are some three million mathematically possible variants for the distribution of goods between senders and receivers. "It is impossible to consider all of these variants in order to select the best of them." (Feld 1965: 65). Linear programming is used to help in meeting this problem.

Since transport users want to ensure themselves adequate services when they need them and since the supply of transport services is limited, the tendency on their part has been to exaggerate their transport needs. In practice, then, the contract method becomes a rationing method with a permanent tug of war between the users and the planners. It seems that eventually such a system might be replaced by price direction; but prices in Soviet-type economies are notoriously distant from scarcity prices, and planners tend to keep them that way. It may be doubted, therefore, whether a fundamental change will take place in the present system of rationing through contracts (cf. Demmler 1967: 125–27).

As with his proposal in connection with the method of regional balances, Hofmann (1960: 139–68) advocated that the planning system in transport change over to one of "streams of goods"; this would give a better indication of capacity, needs, and both the geographical and the time sequence of the disposition of goods. The streams of goods can be shown either in tabular input-output form divided into senders and receivers (an example of such a table is found in Hofmann 1960: 146), or by goods, or as a general overview in the form of a map showing the density of traffic (an example is found in Hofmann 1960: 147), a map that can be divided into two-directional lines of streams (example in Hofmann 1960: 150). The key importance in this planning would be accorded to planned flows through transport junctions (example in Hofmann 1960: 151, reproduced in Demmler 1967: 148). Such flow-plans can be made both in operative terms and in terms of annual and multi-year plans (Hofmann 1960: 163-68).

That transport often plays a subordinate role is also revealed in the fact that individual enterprises have to accommodate themselves to transport availabilities. They cannot choose what type of railway wagons they may use; that decision is made by the railroad. Such an approach makes fulfillment of transport plans more flexible by accommodating the impact of the changing demand for transport services. Furthermore, in the operative plans, very strict time schedules are imposed for loading and unloading of wagons, their length depending on (1) loading or unloading, (2) number of wagons to be handled, (3) type of goods, (4) position of goods in transit, and (5) season of the year (in the case of refrigerated products). It may be easily imagined that the bureaucratic effort involved in such planning is prodigious, but positive results are obtained: the average turnaround time of railroad cars is shortened. In East Germany that turnaround time decreased from 4.12 days in 1951 to 3.49 days in 1964 with a coincidental increase in the average length of the journey (Demmler 1967: 85-86; for comparative statistics see Günther 1965: 164, 235) and then rose to 3.92 days in 1972 (*SJ* 1973: 238; Günther 1965: 202). In Great Britain average wagon turnaround time decreased to 11.0 in 1970 (Thompson and Hunter 1973: 184). Even if transport enterprises have the decisive voice on the mode of services that will be rendered, transport as an economic activity is placed in a subordinate position: in the final analysis, it accepts the terms imposed by planners. This is even more so than for directly producing (material) sectors of the economy.

Operative plans in road transport are made on a quarterly, monthly, ten-day, and daily basis. They embody specific loading and route orders, and their goal is to select the proper vehicle for the task at hand, to select the optimal route, and to specify the daily tasks. The criteria for planning may be to minimize empty runs, minimize the work necessary to perform given tasks, or to minimize aggregate costs (Lissowska 1971a: 159-60).

In road transport, the general direction of motor transport was established in East Germany shortly after the war when socialized transport enterprises were subordinated to a centralized administration (Demmler 1967: 93–94). Private transport was directed by motor transport collectives (Demmler 1967: 94). In 1954 the organization of transport was reformed: transport direction and planning was decentralized into regional directorates covering both socialized and private transport (Demmler 1967: 94–95). The transport orders — which have to be made out before the consignment is made — provide (as on the railroad) taut time limits on the loading, unloading, and movement of trucks. If deadlines are exceeded, an additional payment is exacted (Demmler 1967: 96–97).

The organization of road transport is partly decentralized throughout Eastern Europe not only due to these regional directorates but especially because a large share of it is carried by the productive enterprises' own transport. Official effort has gone toward a reduction of the share of enterprise transport in transport performance of 71.5 percent in the Soviet Union (in 1963), 47.8 percent in Poland (in 1971), 48.2 percent in East Germany (in 1969), and a high percentage in Czechoslovakia (Malek, Grzywacz, and Zymela 1973: 201–11). Efforts to concentrate transport services in specialized commercial transport enterprises are officially regarded as part of the rationalization of the East European economies; but it appears that the interest of enterprises in securing a dependable — i.e., dependent — source of transport services within their own organizations is a serious obstacle to centralization. Judging by capitalist experience, deconcentration of highway transport is the preferred and more efficient solution of road transport, although associations of truckers in the West also help to bring them some advantages of centralization (cf. Malek, Grzywacz, and Zymela 1973: 199–200). In Western Europe the share of the enterprises' own transport in the road haulage industry was comparable to that in Eastern Europe; in terms of transport performance, it varied between 42.3 percent in Italy in 1958 and 68.2 percent in Belgium in 1960. The share of enterprise truck ownership was higher, varying between 68.2 percent in the Netherlands in 1956 and 93.0 percent in France in 1958, which indicates lower-than-average use factor in such transport (see Bayliss 1965: 31). Transport by the enterprise's own trucks may in certain instances be more expensive than commercial (for "hire or reward") transport, as seems to be indicated by the experience in Holland (Bayliss 1965: 30–32, 119–20).

In inland water transport, East Germany first founded a work cooperative for inland transport, which was replaced in 1949 by the German Ship and Transloading Center and in 1957 by the socialized enterprise of German Inland Shipping (responsible only for centralized traffic; other transport functions are decentralized [Demmler 1967: 100]).

In connection with operative plans, mention should be made of the dispatcher *(speditor)* and his role in Eastern Europe. He combines the role of the transport broker (who acts on behalf of the supplier of the transport service) and the role of the *speditor* (who acts on behalf of the transport user). He came to handle the actual administration of the transport process: i.e., organization of the consignments so as to satisfy the needs of the recipients and to make optimal use of existing transport capacity (Malek, Grzywacz, and Zymela 1973: 70; Neider 1976: 29–30).

Planning of Passenger Transport

The demand for passenger transport cannot be planned strictly and precisely because planners have no direct means of determining it. In practice, therefore, demand is estimated on the basis of the following determinants: (1) change in the size of the population; (2) average distance traveled; (3) change in the money income of the population; (4) change in the number of employed in individual districts, and change in commercial intercourse between different localities; and (5) expected change in vacation traffic (cf. Demmler 1967: 151–52; Galitskii 1956: 84–89; Galitskii 1950: 74–79). An important limiting factor is freight traffic plans, which tend to be given first priority (cf. Galitskii 1956: 84). Planners distinguish long-distance transport of passengers, intradistrict transport, and commuting or suburban transport (Galitskii 1956: 84). This distinction helps provide the right kind of railroad cars, since long-distance traffic requires a higher proportion of sleeping cars. Commuting traffic is influenced by the emergence of industrial centers and by the availability of housing (cf. Galitskii 1956: 84; Litterer-Marwege 1967: 226–33; Leszczycki and Lijewski 1972: 109–17; Maleszewska 1976; Rajkiewicz 1976; Podogrodzka 1977). A disproportionately large share of suburban passenger transport belongs to large urban centers (cf. Galitskii 1950: 75; for Western planning, cf. Bruton 1970: 65–70, 78–94).

The change in population size can be incorporated into the planning of passenger transport by means of the demographic indicator of passenger travel. Its formula is:

$$I_{dem} = pass./pop.$$

where I_{dem} = demographic indicator of passenger travel
    pass. = number of passengers
    pop. = population of the country (Tarski 1968: 48; Michalski
        1975: 58-60).

The indicator greatly depends on the level of living of the population; this level is showing an upward tendency. Other factors that may influence the demographic indicator are proportion of the population in the labor force, geographical location of industry, the opening up of new transport routes or of new modes of transport, increases in the number of holidays, changes in the availability of housing in industrial urban areas, and changes in the policy on reduced-fare tickets. The demographic indicator of travel grew fairly steadily in Poland from 27.6 in 1950 to 64.5 in 1967 (Tarski 1968: 49). It grew particularly stronger for passenger bus travel (Malek, Grzywacz, and Zymela 1973: 36). Table 3.10 shows the dynamics of the demographic indicator in Eastern Europe for all long-distance transport (i.e., except urban transport) and separately for highway passenger transport (cf. Günther 1965: 209-13). Eastern Europe can be divided into three groups of countries according to their demographic indicator of passenger travel. The first group consists of East Germany and Czechoslovakia and shows high indicators at the start of the period covered in table 3.10, with Czechoslovakia showing a very high demographic indicator of the density of highway travel. In both countries the indicator for highway travel rises relatively faster than the indicator of aggregate travel. The second group of countries — Poland and Hungary — shows intermediate demographic indicators of passenger travel. It shows a higher rate of growth of the indicators than the first group; this is easier to achieve because of the lower starting level, especially in the case of highway travel. Finally, the third group of countries — Romania, Bulgaria, and Yugoslavia — shows very low demographic indicators of passenger travel at the beginning of the period and a rapid rate of growth. In this group a particularly high rate of growth was achieved by the indicator for highway travel. As the result of these disparate tendencies in the three groups of countries, the proportionate gap between them has narrowed during the period shown, but their differences remain prominent.

The demographic indicator can also be used to derive the expected growth of freight movement (Tarski 1968: 48-49), but its usefulness in this respect seems limited, since freight traffic is directly a function of economic, rather than demographic, variables.

TABLE 3.10
Demographic Indicators (dem) of Passenger Travel in Eastern Europe, 1950-1973

	Poland		East Germany		Czechoslovakia		Hungary	
	Aggregate I_{dem}^a	Road I_{dem}^a	Aggregate I_{dem}	Road I_{dem}	Aggregate I_{dem}	Road I_{dem}	Aggregate I_{dem}	Road I_{dem}
1950	27.6	4.7[b]	124.0	6.0	..	..	..	..
1955	39.7	5.5	171.5	18.7	..	..	..	..
1960	38.5	11.1	209.2	38.7	128.1	85.7	72.8	23.7
1965	56.3	26.1	206.9	54.2	159.9	115.3	90.0	36.8
1970	74.6	42.1	204.4	64.9	157.9	119.7	97.3	45.9
1973	90.3	57.4	211.9[c]	69.5[c]	159.9	124.7	101.6	53.9

a socialized transport   b 1952   c 1972

	Romania		Bulgaria		Yugoslavia	
	Aggregate I_{dem}	Road I_{dem}	Aggregate I_{dem}	Road I_{dem}	Aggregate I_{dem}	Road I_{dem}
1950	7.9	.7	9.5[b]	2.2[b]	13.4	2.0
1955	15.7	1.1	..	..	11.5	1.9
1960	15.7	3.9	19.5	9.2	17.3	5.5
1965	22.8	8.9	..	..	23.6	11.2
1970	34.1	17.7	52.1	39.4	34.6	26.7
1973	43.3	25.5	..	25.5	42.8	36.0

Sources: Tarski 1968: 49; Malek, Grzywacz, and Zymela 1973: 230; calculated on the basis of: *RS* 1956: 212; *RS* 1974: 66, 67, 386; *SJ* 1973: 3, 237; *SR* 1962: 297; *SR* 1974: 99, 371, 375, 380; *SPBH* 1967: 11; *SPBH* 1974: 45, 180, 181; *AS* 1974: 22, 278-79; *SEzh* 1971: 4, 154; *SG* 1958: 165, 167, 171; *SG* 1962: 172; *SG* 1969: 197, 200, 202, 205; *SG* 1974: 103, 225, 228, 230, 234.

For the general indication of traffic needs, there is another indicator, that of traffic density. Its two alternative formulas are:

$$I_{den1} = pass./1 \qquad \text{and} \qquad I_{den2} = (pass/km)/1$$

where I_{den} = indicator of traffic density

pass. = the number of passengers

1 = length of transport network.

The formulas thus yield either traffic volume per kilometer of transport network or transport performance per kilometer of transport
network, depending on which formula is used. The indicator can also
be used to derive an expected freight indicator. Polish experience
reveals a rise in the indicator of traffic density for both passenger
traffic (from 16.87 in 1955 to 18.50 in 1967) and freight traffic (from
9.29 in 1955 to 11.92 in 1967) (Tarski 1968: 51).

Planners can also use a version of the synthetic indicator of transportability (see above, on proportions of dispatching), which is defined as the relation between the number of passengers or passenger/
kilometers transported in millions, and national income in constant
prices in e.g., billions of monetary units (cf. Tarski 1968: 60–62;
Michalski 1975: 89–90). This measure, like the preceding ones, provides only a general notion of possible future demand for passenger
transport. The form that uses the number of passengers declined in
Poland from 3.98 in 1955 to 3.53 in 1967, and the form that uses
passenger/kilometers declined in the same period from 0.147 to 0.100
(Tarski 1968: 60, 62).

Once the expected amount of passenger transport is determined, the
planners determine passenger train schedules and the number of cars
in each train. In so doing, they calculate average occupancy per axle in
order to determine the utilization of passenger equipment (Galitskii
1956: 87; Galitskii 1950: 78). They also plan for increasing the average
speed of trains and are helped in this respect by the gradual introduction of electric and diesel trains, which are noticeably faster than
steam-locomotive trains, particularly in suburban transport.

Planning of passenger transport includes planning of those investments that are used by travelers (especially passenger stations and all
the facilities in them) and passenger cars. Double-decker cars are used
in some commuter traffic, and the construction of cars is being
improved.

Determination of Needed Transport Capacity

The long-range, multi-year, and annual plans focus basically on
demand for transport services, while the interplay with supply is more

clearly visible in operative planning, since actual transport orders depend on the availability of the means of transport. Both for this reason and in order to arrive at a better idea of investment needs in the transport sector, planners have to determine the needed transport capacity and, by comparing it with existing capacity, to derive the needs for investment in transport equipment.

The forwarding capacity depends on the following factors: (1) the number of transport units and their types; (2) the average turnaround time; (3) the average capacity of the transport units; and (4) the through capacity of the transport routes. The average turnaround time can be calculated from aggregate figures; but for the purposes listed below, it is derived from the average distance over which goods of a given kind are transported, the average speed of transport, and the average time needed for loading and unloading. The average capacity of the transport unit is based on technical data and on past experience; but it is expected that between plan periods, it would show an increase — just as decreases are expected in the turnaround time.

The capacity needed can be calculated as the sum of capacities needed to transport individual goods. These are derived from the production plan in terms of physical weight units. The number of railroad cars or other units of transport can then be derived on the basis of the following formula:

$$\frac{\text{tons to be transported per year} \times \text{turnaround time in days}}{\text{days in the year} \times \text{average capacity of transport units}} = \text{number of transport units needed}$$

For instance, if 18 million tons of coal have to be transported by rail per year, if the average capacity of railroad trucks is twenty tons, if their average turnaround time is four days, and if their life is longer than a year,[2] then the number of railroad trucks needed can be derived as follows:

$$\frac{18,000,000 \text{ tons} \times 4 \text{ days}}{365 \text{ days} \times 20 \text{ tons}} = \text{ca. } 10,000 \text{ trucks}$$

The number of units needed for particular uses is aggregated, and to it are added the "nonworking units," comprising units used for intra-enterprise transport, units in repair and in outfitting, and national units in foreign countries less foreign units available for domestic transport (Demmler 1967: 153).

On the railroad, one can also calculate the number of locomotives needed using technological and economic parameters, in particular, the number of ton/kilometers per locomotive based on past experience. Similar calculations yield the number of passenger cars needed by the railroad.

To the difference between needed capacity and available capacity the planners have to add the number of units needed for normal replacement of superannuated capacity. During tight planning periods (and taut planning seems to be the rule in Soviet-type economies), the replacement need absorbs the discrepancies generated in the planning process; the usual result is obsolescence of the transport stock in Eastern Europe (cf. Khachaturov 1952: 127–32).

In order to assure themselves of the needed supply of new transport units, planners tend to favor domestic rather than foreign production, as in the case of railroad car production in Poland, East Germany, Czechoslovakia, and Hungary, truck production in the same countries, bus production, some aircraft production, and shipbuilding in Poland. When, for economic or geographical reasons, it is impossible to secure a 100 percent domestic supply, the planners try to make sure of foreign supply and then tend to favor "secure" sources of supply from other centrally planned economies (apart from the understandable political preference in the same direction). For instance, the Soviet Union buys Polish railroad cars and Polish ships, and Poland buys Soviet passenger airplanes. By and large, however, all communist countries tend toward autarky in securing the means of transport, just as is the case in other industrial products in Eastern Europe.

Planning of Investments in Transport

Comparison of existing transport capacity with the calculated need yields investment needs. These may be decreased somewhat by planned improvements in the efficiency of the existing capacity as well as by improvements in the efficiency of equipment to be introduced, and they have to be increased by planned withdrawal of unusable equipment.

In making their investment plans, the planners are faced with several different possibilities. In the West, the decision on which investment to choose is reached with the help of the rate of interest. But planners in Eastern Europe are still by and large barred from using this convenient tool for ideological reasons: Marx associated interest with capitalist exploitation. However, if no interest were used in Eastern Europe, the most capital-intensive methods of production would be attempted, despite a pronounced scarcity of capital in Eastern Europe.[3] But East European planners certainly have come to recognize the problem of allocation of the scarce resource of capital and have followed the Soviet practice of calculating the so-called recoupment (payback) periods for different forms of investment. This practice contrasts vividly with the sophisticated methods of investment appraisal used in the West (cf. Munby 1968: 16), and more will be said about it below.

The need for new equipment tends to be reduced by proper upkeep of existing transport equipment, particularly by repair and overhaul.[4] In socialist practice, two kinds of overhaul are distinguished: current repairs and capital repairs. Repair workshops have to plan the volume of their work ahead of time, and for this an example of planning for repairs of locomotives (Galitskii 1950: 103) seems useful: assume that the plan for freight movement for the coming year necessitates 78 million locomotive/kilometers, and that the norm for the run between capital repairs is 390,000 kilometers and the norm for runs between current repairs is 130,000 kilometers; the demand for repairs will then be derived as follows:

$$\frac{78 \text{ million locomotive/kilometers}}{130 \text{ thousand kilometers}} = 600 \text{ freight locomotives}$$

Out of that number, two-thirds, or 400 locomotives, will be scheduled for current repairs, and one-third, or 200 locomotives, for capital repairs. On that basis, repair workshops will be able to prepare themselves for the volume of work expected during the plan year.

The plan for repairs of railroad cars is based on the accepted length of time between repairs rather than on mileage covered. Thus, for most cars with central beams, capital repairs take place every eight years and current repairs every four years, meaning that they are alternated. For two-axle cars without central beams and with wooden bodies, refrigerated cars, upholstered passenger wagons, sleeping cars, and restaurant cars, capital repairs take place every six years and current repairs every three years. For passenger cars with wooden benches and luggage and mail cars, capital repairs take place every nine years and current repairs every three years (Galitskii 1950: 104; cf. Khachaturov 1952: 216; Michalski 1975: 98–100). The main differences between capital and current repairs lies in their thoroughness and in the fact that during capital repairs parts are exchanged for new ones while during current repairs they are overhauled (cf. Galitskii 1950: 103–104). Capital repairs of trucks and buses are determined by mileage and those of trailers by time (Malek, Grzywacz, and Zymela 1973: 267).

e present author was given examples by an East European rail-
engineer of inadequate repairs done during the Stalinist period,
en railroad crews were wont to make pledges to extend the mileage
d the periods of exploitation without capital repairs. The net result
of such "storming of production" was a wasteful shortening of life of
equipment used and, ultimately, increased dependence on replacement investments. This wasteful *shturmovshchina* has been now
apparently abandoned, thus extending the useful life of capital equipment and tending to decrease the current need for investments for
replacement (cf. Westwood 1963: 21–22).

Investments in transport depend on investments in other sectors of
the economy. First, the output of such investments depends on the
machine industry, precision instruments industry, chemical industry,
lumber industry, and the like, and on their increased capacities.
Second, exploitation of such investments depends on increased capacity created in other industries, as shown, e.g., by the need for
increased generating capacity if railroad lines are to be electrified (cf.
Galitskii 1950: 110). Third, central planners may give lower priority to
investments in transport than to investments in the "productive"
sectors of the economy, and transport may thus take the brunt of any
adjustments needed as the result of failures or stresses in other sectors.

The following categories of investments in transport were listed by
Galitskii (1950: 116–129): new railroad lines, electrification of existing
lines, fuel sector, automatic bloc systems, junctions and terminals,
locomotives, railway cars, railway tracks including bridges, new inland waterways, repair shops, ports and landing piers, cars and trucks,
highways, and the air transport sector. This list obviously misses pipelines, which have become increasingly important since 1950. Galitskii
added to his list the production plan for the industry that produces
transport equipment (1950: 129–131).

The traditional Soviet practice of calculating the recoupment period
can be summarized as follows (Khachaturov 1954: 97–121; Demmler
1967: 1960–965; the explanation below relies heavily on Demmler's
exposition of Khachaturov). Suppose planners want to determine the
desirability of electrifying a line (variant 1) as against introduction of
better steam or diesel locomotives (variant 2). Electrification entails
larger investment outlays, but it lowers the costs of exploitation as
compared with the other alternative. Variants 1 and 2 may be thus
defined by the inequalities:

	Variant 1		Variant 2
Costs of investment	A_1	$>$	A_2
Costs of exploitation	E_1	$<$	E_2

Assume then the following. Investment costs on the construction of the electrified line amount to 90 million rubles, while investment costs of the same line under steam or diesel traction amount to 70 million rubles. Costs of exploitation, including amortization, amount to 2.5 and 5 million rubles, respectively. The formula

$$(A_1 - A_2)/(E_1 - E_2) = t$$

yields the recoupment period, t, which in this case equals eight years. This period is simply the time needed to compensate for the greater investment outlay on electrification.

The reciprocal of the recoupment period, equal to

$$1/t = \delta$$

yields the coefficient of investment effectiveness δ, which can also be calculated as

$$(E_2 - E_1)/(A_1 - A_2) = \delta.$$

The coefficient δ is then compared with the standard coefficient of the effectiveness of investment, or Δ, which is determined by the planners:

$$1/t_o = \Delta$$

It should be noted that in Soviet-type economies the coefficient δ plays the role that marginal efficiency of investment plays in Western economic analysis; the coefficient Δ plays the role of the interest rate. If δ is greater than Δ, then the outlay of capital is considered profitable, just as in comparisons between the marginal efficiency of investment and the rate of interest. Equality between δ and Δ makes the proposed investment just marginal.

The marginality condition can also be expressed by the formula:

$$\Delta(A_1) + E_1 = \Delta(A_2) + E_2$$

Variant 1 would then be profitable if

$$\Delta(A_1) + E_1 < \Delta(A_2) + E_2$$

Khachaturov also provided a method to represent the effectiveness of investment in relation to the volume of transport with the help of figure 3.1, in which the left vertical axis represents annual cost savings and the horizontal axis shows the volume of transport. The curve $E_2 - E_1 = f(F)$ shows the cost savings as a function of changing volume of transport. The curve allows one to read whether, given a certain expected volume of transport and a certain norm for investment effectiveness Δ, a planned investment is profitable. For instance, if a coefficient of investment effectiveness of 0.06 is prescribed as standard, then with a volume of transport of 1,500 this coefficient will not be reached, thus making the proposed investment submarginal. Only a volume of about 1,700 makes the investment marginal.

In an interesting parallel to the reswitching method of calculating

FIGURE 3.1
Assessment of the Effectiveness of Investment in Transport

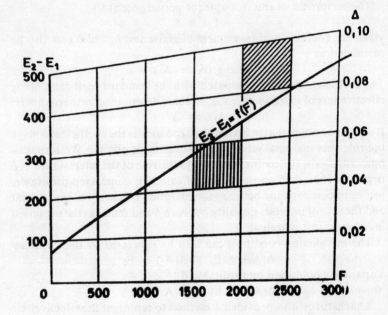

the profitability of investments in the West (cf. Samuelson 1973: 615-16), East European planners can discount the various amounts of investment to be undertaken at different times. In this way a capital outlay made at time t, when divided by $(1 + \Delta)^t$, can be made comparable with other outlays. Demmler (1967: 162) noted the inconsistency: planners here use the rate of interest, but the concept of the recoupment period studiously avoids the same ideologically suspect concept of interest rate.

The East European method of comparing the efficiency of investments, based as it is on the concept of recoupment period, does not lend itself directly to intersectoral comparisons. One of the difficulties inherent in this system is the problem of finding criteria for the determination of the standard coefficient of the effectiveness of investment Δ for different sectors of the economy and for different branches within those sectors. In practice these coefficients are determined at different levels for individual branches, ranging (according to Khachaturov 1954: 111, 118) between 0.05 and 0.20; in railroad transport it amounts to about 0.10 and in road transport to 0.06. Thus, in the final analysis, it is the branch of the transport sector, not the coefficient of investment effectiveness δ, that decides the acceptability of a given investment project.

Two considerations make for the likelihood of undercapitalization of the transport sector under these procedures for investment planning. First, the standard coefficient of investment effectiveness Δ tends to be higher for transport than for other sectors. Second, the use of the recoupment period and the coefficient of investment effectiveness does not allow for optional determination of capital intensity. This second point bears further explanation.

When the following inequality obtains:
$$\Delta(A_1) + E_1 < \Delta(A_2) + E_2$$
then the more capital-intensive variant 1 will be accepted when, as apparently is the case, the operating costs include depreciation allowances (Demmler 1967: 163; Khachaturov 1954: 96ff). Under such conditions, a part of the capital invested in a project flows back every year. In the first year, this part is equal to Δ . A_1, in the second year it is equal to Δ . $A(1 - (1/t))$, and in the last year it is equal to Δ . A/t. On the other hand, however, the inequality $\Delta(A_1) + E_1 < \Delta(A_2) + E_2$ assumes an average interest burden that implies no reduction of the values of investment projects A by past depreciation allowances. The additional capital necessary for the more capital-intensive variant is then brought into calculation in the form of

Δ . A, equal to the average interest cost. However, the average annual interest cost can actually be calculated as approximately (cf. Demmler 1967: 164 n104) equal to

$$(\Delta A + \Delta(A/t))/2 = (\Delta A/2) \ . \ ((t + 1)/t)$$

From this it appears that the annual interest cost for investments with longer duration is only about half as great as postulated by the socialist economists. This fact leads to the conclusion that investment decisions in the transport sector tend to discriminate against investment projects that have a long period of exploitation. They also neglect externalities or spillover effects and thus fail to introduce social benefits into planned decision making.

A note of caution needs to be added. Demmler (1967: 164-65) raised the point that it is not always sufficiently clear whether in all cases in which the coefficient of investment effectiveness is used the depreciation allowances are actually included in the costs of operation. When those allowances are not so included, the previously explained situation is reversed, and the interest burden becomes too small; the smaller it is, the shorter the life of the capital object. Instead of the condition $\Delta(A_1) + E_1 < \Delta(A_2) + E_2$, we would now have the inequality:

$$A_1 \ . \ \Delta((1 + \Delta)^t/(1 + \Delta)^{t-1}) + E_1 <$$
$$A_2 \ . \ \Delta((1 + \Delta)^t/(1 + \Delta)^{t-1}) + E_2$$

or:

$$(E_2 - E_1)/(A_1 - A_2) > \Delta((1 + \Delta)^t/(1 + \Delta)^{t-1})$$

The latter inequality replaces the previous formal condition of:

$$(E_2 - E_1)/(A_1 - A_2) > \Delta$$

One should observe that the expression $\Delta((1 + \Delta)^t/(1 + \Delta)^{t-1})$ is larger than Δ as long as t is smaller than infinity.

A different and administratively functional formula has recently been introduced in East Europe to calculate the indicator of the effectiveness of investments in transport (adapted from Tarski 1968: 250):

$$E = ((1/T)(J + C)^b)/\Delta_Q$$

where: E = indicator of the effectiveness of investment

  T = marginal time of return (amortization) of investment outlays

  J = investment outlays and the quantity of those outlays frozen in construction-in-progress (to calculate this there are special official instructions, cf. Komisja Planowania 1962: pt. 2, 14, 18, cited by Tarski 1968: 250)

  C = aggregate annual cost of transport

  b = coefficient that corrects for the influence of the period of exploitation of the capital on the economic effectiveness of the given investment variant

ΔQ = annual production effect, taken as constant throughout the period of exploitation of capital.

The value of factor T can be changed and differs among countries, amounting in Poland (in 1968) to 6 and in the USSR to 10. Factor J is comprehensive and includes all direct and indirect investments undertaken in connection with the choice of a given mode of transport or a given means of transport. The annual production effect ΔQ is expressed in terms of physical performance or physical amount transported.

The application of the formula has produced some controversy. The value of T of 6, as accepted in Poland, is considered too small. The assumption of a twenty-year lifespan of capital goods is considered too short. Finally, it is conceded that economic or noneconomic criteria other than the indicator E may be used to decide on the form and direction of investments, e.g., the country's location policy, balance of payments considerations, tourism, and defense (cf. Tarski 1968: 251-52). The formula, however, is subject to improvements and manipulation, and, while not exclusive as a determinant of investment, it may shed some light on the advisability of different investment projects and on the minimum effectiveness of investments, however arbitrarily defined.

A similar formula is used on the Polish railroads to calculate the effectiveness of investments (adapted from Michalski 1975: 120, with explanation of factors as above):

$$E = (((1/T)J + C)b + r)/\Delta Q$$

where r = average annual value of raw materials used plus average annual cost of repairs.

We should note as a postcript to this section that other plans in transport — not discussed here — cover the labor force in transport, use of materials, and the finances necessary to conduct transport operations (cf. Gumpel 1967: 53-54). These plans are subsidiary to the main transport activity and may be conveniently left out of the present discussion.

General Evaluation of Transport Planning

The aim of the centrally planned system of transport is to assure maximization of economic operation in a planned, ex ante sense and in a rational way that takes all available alternatives into account. The system tries to minimize social costs and to maximize social benefits.

Coordination between the sectors of material production and transport is the key to this planning process, while passenger transport seems to be based on assumptions of a certain growth determined basically on the political level and connected with general policy toward consumers.

The centrally planned transport system aims also at promoting economic growth (on existing lines) and development (with changing importance of different sectors) of individual countries — as well as of the Comecon region as a whole — and, in particular, at a balanced development of different regions and of transport links between them so as to coordinate production and territorial input-output relations and to maximize the development of the country concerned.

Finally, under socialism, where there is no "destructive competition" for profit, the conditions for close cooperation between different transport modes are met (cf. Hofmann 1960: 117). Planning for such cooperation places transport under socialism in an avowedly advantageous position.

However, several problems in the planning of transport tend to hamper attainment of the above goals and advantages.

1. There seems to be no overall coordinated planning of transport in Eastern Europe. This was acknowledged with reference to the Soviet Union by the Soviet Minister of Transport in 1965 (Beshchev 1965: 11, quoted in Gumpel 1967: 46–47). There is no adequate and meaningful calculation of social costs; and, indeed, such a calculation may be in practice impossible, given the rigidity of the price system and the complications introduced into it by a system of subsidies, differential turnover taxes, and positive and negative budget differences. Planlessness goes to the extent of locating plants apparently without any regard for transport costs.

An interesting step toward coordination of different transport modes was undertaken in Bulgaria in 1974 with the creation of a National Transport Complex — a new form of unified management that is expected to use the planning-programming approach in coordinating intermodal transport in the country. The National Transport Complex is under the control of the Ministry of Transport and is governed by a council consisting of members of the Ministry's collegium and representatives from other ministries, public organizations, districts that have an important transport sector, scientific workers, and others. The main functions of the National Transport Complex seem to be intermodal coordination of transport and an overall improvement of transport facilities. The first general impression of the new complex is that it is based on a relatively flexible economic system but that a cumbersome administrative apparatus may hamper its efficiency, which will inevitably depend largely on the proper organization of the necessary cooperation with other branches of the economy. As past experience shows, bureaucratic rivalries usually make this difficult to achieve (RFER: Bulgaria, January 17, 1974: 3–5).

2. Transport plans are basically expressed in terms of physical quantities. Such terms are not suited to comparisons of relative efficiencies, and they lead to uneconomic distribution of freight among transport modes. Financial plans are derived from plans expressed in physical quantities; they are their passive shadows, not a basis for decision making. In this way, there is no planned economic coordination of transport; rather, there is only ex ante administration of transport (cf. Demmler 1967: 167–69).

3. Regional planning and location also seem inadequate. Larger cities, especially the capitals of countries, show inordinate growth of population and industrial plants, but small localities tend to hibernate permanently without an adequate industrial infrastructure. Some regions remain stubbornly underdeveloped, e.g., part of northern Poland (the Koszalin and the Olsztyn voyvodships). These diverse growth rates create tremendous pressures and demands on the transport systems in some regions and within the largest cities, while the transport network in other areas remains underdeveloped (cf. Gumpel 1967: 47–48; 58–59).

4. Transport is a handmaiden of the "material" sectors of the economy. Fluctuations in those sectors are transmitted with a multiplied force to the transport sector, and the existence of such fluctuations (Zielinski 1973: 35–48; Mieczkowski 1967; Pajak 1975: 18) exacerbates the problems that face planners of transport. The planned system in East Europe has been dubbed the "economy of improvisations," and specific mention has been made of "plan vacuum" filled with figures from the preceding period rather than with planned determinants of desired future economic activity (Gumpel 1967: 48).

5. Comecon has so far failed to produce a rational plan for long-term development of transport within its area. So far, only partial coordination has been attempted as well as organizational and technological cooperation and joint work on individual projects (Gumpel 1967: 49). It may be that preoccupation with forceful industrialization through national plans has prevented individual members of Comecon from paying attention to intraregional coordination of transport;

urgent investment needs and bottlenecks may have been their primary concern. It may be that the state administrative bureaucracies developed their own autarkic nationalisms and group interests inimical to those of far-reaching cooperation or to unification of planning effort (cf. Brzeski 1974: 191).

6. One gets the impression that transport decisions are made primarily on the basis of past usage: a cost-benefit calculus is difficult in East European economies, and it seems hardly to have been started or attempted. Under such conditions, growth of transport tends to be "more of the same"type of growth rather than a dynamic development in search of new solutions, greater efficiency, and new technologies. Planners tend to choose the safe procedure of operating within the realm of the known, the tried, and the accepted. This deprives planning of its basic conceptual advantage. In fact, according to one expert, transport planning in the West shows decided superiority over East European planning (Gumpel 1967: 49; cf. Hay 1973: 145–153; Gajda 1975: 58; Lissowska and Bauer 1975: 68).

Even so, a recent study of West European and U.S. trucking regulations (made for the American Enterprise Institute and the Hoover Institution) concluded that regulation — which is an aspect of planning — when practiced in the West creates monopolies and oligopolies, raises freight rates, increases average cost of operation, fails to increase profits by promoting inefficiency, reduces quality of service, and does not succeed in protecting the market position of competing modes, in this case of the railroad (Moore 1976: 139–48).

7. Different values of the standard coefficient of effectiveness of investment Δ in different branches of the economy result in a suboptimization of economic solutions for the economy as a whole. Not only is the ideological phobia of the rate of interest at fault here. It seems that the primary cause of such suboptimization is the basic conflict between a desire to find objective criteria for investment decisions on the one hand, and, on the other, to reserve for the planners their assumed and cherished right to determine the flow of investments to various branches of the economy according to their own scheme of priorities. Transport planning (and its use of different values for the coefficient Δ) illustrates the planners' insistence on exercising their subjective evaluation of different branches of the economy, their importance, and their future contribution to the growth of the country. This factor may be one of the reasons behind the falling effectiveness of investments for the USSR economy as a whole (Khachaturov 1964: 110).

8. As noted above, not all of the possible alternative solutions in transport can be taken into account in practice.

East European countries have recognized some of these disadvantages and have at least verbally committed themselves to their correction. However, attempts at correction may actually not go very far. Thus, the Comecon Commission for Transport is concerned only with "methodological, and organizational and technical questions of complex character." These questions include, among others, the producing of "current materials for coordination of the long-term development plans for transport on the basis of which representatives of the members of Comecon and of the Commission prepare current tasks for the quantum of goods to be transported and for the main directions of the technological development of all transport modes." (Gavrilov 1964: 18, cited after Gumpel 1967: 50). This is hardly a sweeping manifesto for comprehensive region-wide planning.

On the national level, efforts are being made to rationalize the price structures in the transport sector. These will be discussed in chapter 5. We can note here that those efforts are far from adequate for the task at hand. Furthermore, the verbal commitment to rationalization of transport management has not seemed to carry adequate weight in reality. The most commonly used term seems to be *integration,* which signifies a desire to distribute transport tasks among transport modes in a way that would minimize social costs of transport performance and would ensure transport performance in accordance with needs. The solutions vary among countries, depending largely on their prevailing general economic model, which in order of increasing centralization is as follows: Yugoslavia, Hungary, Bulgaria, Poland, East Germany, Romania, and Czechoslovakia (cf. Steplowski 1975: 102–24; Madeyski, Lissowska, and Morawski 1975a: 115–23). All systems, however, use the basically nonparametric method of transport planning (Steplowski 1975: 157) as represented here.

There are various subsidiary plans in transport in addition to the basic planning outlined above, including technical and economic planning — planning of technological improvements, planning of the work of the rolling stock, planning of raw materials supplies and reserves; planning of employment, training of personnel, planning of wages, planning of costs, and financial planning (see Michalski 1975: chs. 3–13; Malek, Grzywacz, and Zymela 1973: ch. 5).

The effort expended in this complex planning is indeed prodigious; but at the same time such extensive planning seems to curb the haphazard and arbitrary decision making that seemed dominant during the Stalinist period. It thus tends to decrease the force of the political factor in transportation. General scientific rules have been developed and followed from about 1955, and the expertise on all levels of transport has improved. Many of these rules have been derived from the West and have contributed to increased professionalism in East European transport. However, at least on paper, the rules for planning in Eastern Europe seem to be unnecessarily rigid and inflexible while at the same time omitting several important factors from their scope. It seems as if the East European countries have moved from the dominance of political factors to the opposite extreme of imposing rigid and exclusive formulas and rules and leaving out judgmental considerations, hunches, flexibility, and pure common sense. While it seems less undesirable than the former extreme, this attitude may involve costs of its own to the present and future functioning of transport in Eastern Europe.

Finally, the empirical results of East European planning of transport within individual countries do not seem to have been very successful in eliminating waste. Unnecessary haulage takes place on a staggering scale, and cost consciousness reveals extensive blind spots. These problems are discussed below, in the last section of chapter 5, under the rubric of "irrational transport."

Statistical Growth of Transport in Eastern Europe since World War II

One of the proofs of planning performance, though not necessarily the most important one, is the growth of what is being planned. The growth of transport may be of course partly unplanned and has to be set against the needs for transport and against its potential growth. Some comparative evaluation of transport performance will be made in chapter 5 in terms of the cost of growth of transport. The present chapter concentrates on the bare statistical growth in transport services in Eastern Europe.

Official vs. Independently Calculated Indexes: Differences and Methodology

Aggregate measures of growth in Soviet-type economies, as well as any measure provided officially in terms of value, tend to be unreliable. Unexplained retroactive changes are sometimes introduced into the data, and the quality of official estimates is sometimes exceedingly murky.[1]

The omission of passenger transport from some official measures of growth or from measures for some periods creates further difficulty. It is by now a tradition in the West to duplicate communist statistics by independent derivation of aggregated growth series on the basis of physical output data. Such procedure, described with reference to transport in Lazarcik (1965: 1–5), and in Korbonski and Wittich (1967: 1–8), usually results (for an exception see Lazarcik and Wynnyczuk 1968: 13) in figures lower than official growth rates. The causes of differences between official and independently calculated indexes may not be accidental, but they are difficult to discern, as stated in an independent study on the Polish index of transport that embodies work by the present author:

> The official indexes represent net value added estimates at constant prices . . . probably elaborated to a large extent on the basis of enterprise reports on their constant-price output and costs, and thus

vitiated by all the well-known factors affecting statistical data in the Soviet-type economies which are linked with plan fulfillment reports. Part of the discrepancy, of course, may be due to the normal differences between a true value-added index and an output index with constant value-added weights, and part to the differences in the price weights used. On the whole, however, many of the year-to-year growth rates shown in the Polish estimates, in particular — but not exclusively — in the early years, appear simply to be unacceptable on the basis of the output data which are available, even with the most generous assumptions as to the effect of the above factors. In that sense, then, our index for the period 1949–65 appears unqualifiedly as a better measure of growth in this sector. [Korbonski and Wittich 1967: 16–17]

The formal difference in the derivation of the official and the independently calculated indexes is that the official index is basically a value-added index, while the calculated index is an index of physical output. The value-added index may reflect artificial price relationships created by systems of subsidies and unproportionate taxes, although the problem of price changes is largely (though not entirely) solved by the use of constant prices. These constant prices do not reflect, however, factor cost relationships for reasons just stated. Where distortions are greatest, as in the housing sector, this fact necessitates recalculation of the contribution of the sector at factor cost for purposes of independent assessment (see e.g., Alton et al. 1965: 67–85).

The formula used for independent calculation of the index numbers of output in transport, and for the derived net value added is:

$$Q_{ol} = (\Sigma^{q}_{l} \cdot {}^{p}a)/(\Sigma^{q}_{o} \cdot {}^{p}a)$$

or:

$$Q_{ol} = ((\Sigma(q_{l}/q_{o}))(q_{o} \cdot p_{a}))/(\Sigma(q_{o} \cdot p_{a}))$$

where Q_{ol} is the physical volume (or quantity) index; q_{o} and q_{l} are quantities of a product or service produced in the base year and given year, respectively; p_{a} is the price or weight of the product or service in the year chosen for weights (cf. Lazarcik 1965: 5).

The physical output series represent in most cases the annual performance of a mode of transport in the form of ton/kilometers and passenger/kilometers performed during given years except for local, as in urban, private, or intraenterprise transport. In the case of such exceptions, series of passengers transported (e.g., by urban transport) are used, or employment series, or the number of transport vehicles.

The price weights used in the independent calculations are in terms of estimates of net value added by different services in a given year, usually a year chosen around the middle year of the period under study. The resulting series "are, of course, not true net value added indexes since no attempt could be made to measure the change over time in the real volume of inputs in relation to that of output" (Korbonski and Wittich 1967: 5). However, it should be pointed out that alternative calculations employing different weights (e.g., weights reflecting gross value added, or weights in terms of the sales value of output [*produkt globalny* in Poland], or weights with different years used as the basis for weighting) produce only minor differences from the index that uses the net value added as weights. Such an index can thus be regarded as a correct reflection of the contribution of the transport sector to the net national product (cf. Korbonski and Wittich 1967: 5-6).

Statistical Setting of Transport in Eastern Europe

In order to provide the setting of transport in the East European economies, we can use some of the independent calculations provided by Alton (1974). They involve changes in the sectoral accounts of the East European countries but lump together, as do the official statistics, transport with communications. However, since transport constituted about 85 percent of the joint net value added of transport and communications in Poland (Korbonski and Wittich 1967: 6), 85 percent in Czechoslovakia (Lazarcik 1965: 5), 87 percent in Hungary (Czirjak 1965: 11, 13), and 95 percent in Bulgaria (Lazarcik and Wynnyczuk 1968: 29, in 1965), data pertaining to that joint sector may be taken as broadly indicative of the transport sector.

Changes in the share of employment in transport and communications in total employment are shown in table 4.1. In all countries shown, the tendency has been for the share of employment in transport and communications to increase, indicating the growth of that sector's importance — at least in terms of employment. On the other hand, the tendency for the growth in the share of employment in transport in aggregate employment is contrary to the experience of most industrialized countries. Over the period 1950-1964 the share of employment in transport in aggregate employment outside agriculture and forestry declined in the United States from 7.7 to 5.8 percent, in France from 10.5 to 8.2 percent, in Great Britain from 9.1 to 7.5 percent, and in West Germany from 7.7 to 7.3 percent. In contrast, in most East European countries the same share rose during this period: in Poland

TABLE 4.1

Changes in Employment in Transport and Communications as Percent of Total Employment, 1950-72

	1950	1960	1970	1972
Poland	4.6	5.4	6.4	6.5
East Germany	7.0[a]	7.2	7.5	7.5
Czechoslovakia	4.9	5.8	6.6	6.7
Hungary	4.2	6.8	7.5	7.6
Romania	2.2	2.8	4.3	4.4
Bulgaria	1.5[b]	4.1	6.0	6.0
Yugoslavia	2.0[a]	2.6	3.3[c]	6.9

a 1952   b 1948   c 1967

Sources: Alton 1974: 263; Alton 1970: 59; *SG 1974*: 117.

from 10.2 to 10.3 percent, in East Germany from 6.8 to 7.1 percent, in Hungary from 8.5 to 9.4 percent, in Romania from 8.4 to 8.7 percent, and in Bulgaria from 6.3 to 9.5 percent. Only in Czechoslovakia did this share decline: by a mere one-tenth of one percent, from 8.5 to 8.4 percent. It declined by more in the Soviet Union, from 13.1 to 12.4 percent, the latter figure still representing a comparatively high proportion (Grzywacz 1969: 257). This comparison between West and East European trends implies that either labor productivity in transport in Eastern Europe lagged considerably behind that of Western Europe, more than it did in other sectors, presumably as the result of relatively backward transport technology, or that the proportion of volume transported to GNP outside agriculture and forestry rose in Eastern Europe relative to that in the West, or both. In either case the tendency for the share of employment in transport to rise in Eastern Europe and fall in the advanced countries of the West seems to indicate inefficiency in the transport sectors of the East European economies. It may be added that the recent explosive increase in labor productivity in aggregate Polish transport — by 7.1 percent in 1972 (over 1971), by 6.0 percent in 1973, and by 10.8 percent in 1974 (Tokarski 1975: 3) — indicates the existence of perceptible prior inefficiencies in the transport sector in that country and, by analogy, in the other East European countries. In Bulgaria labor productivity on the railroad increased between 1965 and 1968 by 11.6 percent, a somewhat disappointing figure (Barbov 1969: 467). Labor productivity in Eastern Europe may have grown by less than was possible at least partly because of high labor turnover on the railroad (for the Polish case, see Szymanska 1976: 3; for the Czechoslovak case, see RFER: SR, May 12, 1976: 6, 8).

Table 4.2 shows official indexes of fixed capital in transport and communications. Growth of capital tended to be stronger in the less developed countries of Romania and Bulgaria, but in all East European countries it showed a rapid rate of increase. In view of our previous remarks on table 4.1, one may conclude that capital accumulation in transport apparently tended to be largely of the extensive type, rather than of the labor-saving intensive type. However, the investment effort in Eastern Europe was considerable, with an especially high increase chalked up during the 1965–1972 period. This strong investment effort has continued in the more recent period.

Table 4.3 shows annual rates of increase in labor productivity in transport and communications in Eastern Europe. Three groups of countries are distinguishable in that table: (1) those with rising rates of

TABLE 4.2

Official Indexes of Fixed Capital in Transport and Communications, 1950-1972
(1950 = 100)

	1960	1965	1972
Poland[a]	100	117	162
East Germany[a]	100	121	144
Czechoslovakia	139	163	200
Hungary	120	140	177
Romania	131	177	307
Bulgaria[b]	130	159	256

a   1960 = 100   b   1952 = 100

Source: Alton 1974: 280.

TABLE 4.3

Average Annual Rates of Growth of Labor Productivity in Transport and Communications, 1960-1972

(in constant prices; percentages)

	1960-65	1965-70	1967-72	1960-72
Poland	2.7	2.9	4.9	3.4
East Germany	2.8	3.7	4.5	3.6
Czechoslovakia	2.2	0	1.9	1.3
Hungary	2.8	1.0	.9	2.0
Romania	4.2	6.7	4.3	5.1
Bulgaria	8.9	6.0	4.8	6.6

Source: Alton 1974: 279.

labor productivity, including Poland and East Germany, (2) those with decreasing increments of labor productivity, including Czechoslovakia, Hungary, and Bulgaria, and (3) Romania, where increments of labor productivity remained constant between the 1960-1965 and 1967-1972 periods.

Table 4.4 shows average rates of growth in the contribution of transport and communications to GNP of the East European countries. When compared with the growth rates of the total GNP, the growth rates of transport and communications are almost uniformly higher, except in Czechoslovakia and Hungary during 1965-1972. This indicates that the contribution of transport and communications to GNP was higher than the average for all sectors of the East European economies.[2] However, it does not indicate that the efficiency of transport was higher, nor does it imply that more genuine transport needs were being satisfied.

On the whole, tables 4.1-4.4 depict an appreciable relative and absolute growth of transport and communications, and by this proxy of transport itself, in employment, labor productivity, capital, and contribution to GNP. We may conclude that transport has been a highly dynamic sector in Eastern Europe and that the growth of the economies of that region has been accompanied by a strong, although not necessarily efficient, expansion of the transport sector.

Independently Calculated Indexes:
Results

Official statistics in Eastern Europe provide a wealth of information about transport, as in Polish published data: length of the transportation network for different transport modes, growth of gross production, gross production, costs and net production figures, employment in transport, wage fund and wages, growth of net production in transport, investments, capital engaged in transport, value of services, quantity transported (in tons and in passengers) and performance in transport (in ton/kilometers and passenger/kilometers), length of the railroad lines by voyvodships, shipments by rail of the main bulk commodities, transport by rail by foreign or domestic direction, rail transport of passengers by kinds of tickets and by length of journey, highways by kind and by voyvodships, number of different means of highway transportation, highway transport of goods by kind of enterprise and by kind of means, growth of the number of buses (interurban) and their performance, information about air transport, inland waterways, sea transport, and ports, and some economic and technical

TABLE 4.4

Average Annual Rates of Growth of the Contribution of Transport and Communications to GNP of the East European Countries, and of GNP, 1960-1972

(at constant prices; percentages)

A. Transport and communications:

	1960-65	1965-70	1967-72	1970-72
Poland	6.6	6.1	7.8	6.8
East Germany	3.2	4.1	5.7	4.0
Czechoslovakia	4.8	2.8	3.9	3.7
Hungary	4.6	1.7	2.1	2.9
Romania	9.2	9.7	7.5	8.9
Bulgaria	9.9	10.4	8.6	9.8

B. GNP:

	1960-65	1965-70	1967-72	1970-72
Poland	4.1	4.1	4.6	4.6
East Germany	2.9	3.4	3.5	3.4
Czechoslovakia	2.0	4.8	4.6	3.9
Hungary	4.2	4.3	4.4	4.2
Romania	5.0	6.0	7.0	6.3
Bulgaria	6.3	6.6	6.2	6.6

Source: Alton 1974: 274.

indicators of transport performance (see *RS 1974:* 381–99). A general empirical study such as this cannot possibly reproduce all that information for the East European countries. Instead, it concentrates on statistics of aggregate output. Shares of different transport modes were provided in tables 3.2–3.7.

We will concentrate here on aggregate series of value added in transport compared to the national product series and on the changing composition of transport. We will rely on independently calculated indexes that, in our judgment, more correctly reflect the actual contribution of transport to the economic activity of East European countries. Intercountry comparisons will also be attempted.

Since the present study is independent also in the sense of not being part of a larger, all-sector study, we will use index numbers rather than value figures to give a meaningful idea of the growth of the transport sector in individual countries regardless of their size and their monetary unit.

Table 4.5 shows the calculated indexes for the transport sector's net value added in Poland. The derivation of the calculated index for 1937–1965 is described in detail in Korbonski and Wittich (1967). The index numbers for 1964–1965 have been recalculated here in view of new information, and the author's index for 1965–1973 has been grafted to the old one at 1965. (For international comparisons see United Nations, *Statistical Yearbooks* and *Monthly Bulletin of Statistics.*)

Table 4.6 shows the value series for national income, net value added in industry, agriculture, and construction, and the foreign trade turnover in Poland, all taken from official statistics. These series are based on value figures in constant prices. Table 4.7 shows Polish official series of physical output covering production of coal, steel, cement, and four main cereals; they represent, respectively, changes in physical output in mining and industry, construction, and agriculture. Neither of these two tables is dealt with here; they serve only to provide data for the regression analysis in the last section of the present chapter.

Table 4.5 is largely based on this author's original index, which was incorporated into Korbonski and Wittich (1967) and improved by them. Their figures for 1964 and 1965 have been changed in accordance with new information on physical performance series. A more comprehensive "version A" of that index was used here. From 1964 on, the pipeline transport begun in that year was added to the railroad transport by dividing pipeline ton-kilometers by four and by adding

TABLE 4.5
Calculated Index of Transport in Poland, 1937-1973

	Component Indexes		Index of Aggregate Transport
	Freight	Passenger	
1937	40.0	22.1	33.6
1946	30.8	36.7	32.9
1947	34.7	43.8	37.9
1948	48.3	51.0	49.3
1949	56.8	54.5	56.0
1950	62.2	66.9	63.9
1951	75.6	77.6	76.3
1952	82.8	91.7	86.0
1953	90.3	90.9	90.5
1954	84.9	92.7	87.7
1955	91.2	96.6	93.1
1956	100.0	100.0	100.0
1957	103.3	106.0	104.3
1958	111.4	109.4	110.7
1959	117.1	108.7	114.1
1960	126.5	106.0	119.2
1961	134.1	111.5	126.0
1962	144.9	118.2	135.4
1963	155.5	125.9	144.9
1964	159.8	138.7	152.2
1965	168.8	147.6	161.2
1966	212.6	158.6	193.2
1967	233.0	166.8	209.2
1968	268.1	172.0	233.2
1969	292.7	182.6	253.1
1970	330.9	191.1	280.6
1971	380.8	204.7	317.4
1972	465.2	225.0	378.8
1973	509.9	244.4	414.4
Weights	64.34	35.66	100.00

Sources: Tables 4.10 and 4.11.

TABLE 4.6

Indexes of the Official Value Series of Polish National Income, Net Value Added in Industry, Agriculture and Construction, and Foreign Trade Turnover, 1947-1973

	National Income 1950 = 100	Industry	Net Value Added in: Agriculture 1950 = 100	Construction	Foreign Trade Turnover[a] 1950 = 100
1947	57	51.6	66.0	32.2	46.3
1948	74	69.2	83.2	45.2	71.9
1949	87	84.7	89.8	70.1	88.3
1950	100	100.0	100.0	100.0	100.0
1951	108	115.2	98.7	124.3	107.4
1952	114	131.2	98.0	145.7	106.6
1953	126	148.6	103.3	166.5	114.1
1954	139	162.5	102.5	166.6	121.8
1955	151	177.8	106.0	169.7	125.9
1956	162	188.4	111.1	184.7	129.9
1957	179	207.9	116.1	191.3	141.5
1958	189	224.9	120.8	214.2	159.8

Year					
1959	199	242.4	116.2	244.9	181.7
1960	208	263.1	120.6	243.4	200.4
1961	224	290.9	136.2	253.1	228.3
1962	229	316.0	113.9	267.5	255.2
1963	245	332.8	126.1	278.1	268.2
1964	262	366.8	127.3	302.3	295.1
1965	280	402.9	134.0	317.7	329.3
1966	300	431.1	139.8	345.9	349.1
1967	317	462.0	137.5	387.1	382.6
1968	345	505.6	149.6	423.1	427.7
1969	355	548.1	118.9	450.6	467.0
1970	374	585.3	123.5	465.5	511.6
1971	404	635.1	134.3	488.7	564.4
1972	445	701.1	140.7	576.5	670.2
1973	497	787.4	144.6	671.3	786.3

a   at constant prices

Source: *RS 1974: 2-12.*

TABLE 4.7

Physical Output Series of the Production of Coal, Steel, Cement, and Four Main Cereals in Poland, 1946-1973

	Coal[a]	Steel[a]	Cement[a]	Production Four Main Cereals[a]
1946	47.3	1.2	1.4	5.1
1947	59.1	1.6	1.5	8.1
1948	70.3	2.0	1.8	11.3
1949	74.1	2.3	2.3	11.9
1950	78.0	2.5	2.5	11.6
1951	82.0	2.8	2.7	11.0
1952	84.4	3.2	2.7	11.7
1953	88.7	3.6	3.3	10.0
1954	91.6	3.9	3.4	11.0
1955	94.5	4.4	3.8	12.7
1956	95.1	5.0	4.0	12.1
1957	94.1	5.3	4.5	13.5
1958	95.0	5.7	5.1	13.5
1959	99.1	6.2	5.3	14.1
1960	104.0	6.7	6.6	14.3
1961	107.0	7.2	7.4	15.4
1962	110.0	7.7	7.5	13.4
1963	113.0	8.0	7.7	14.5
1964	117.0	8.6	8.8	13.5
1965	119.0	9.1	9.6	15.5
1966	122.0	9.9	10.0	15.2
1967	124.0	10.5	11.1	15.7
1968	129.0	11.0	11.6	17.3
1969	135.0	11.3	11.8	17.9
1970	140.0	11.8	12.2	15.4
1971	145.0	12.7	13.1	18.9
1972	151.0	13.5	14.0	19.3
1973	157.0	14.1	15.5	20.5

a   million ton

Source: *RS 1974:* 6-10.

the quotient to transport performance on the railroad. This was done on the basis of Barkovskii and Gorizontov (1965: 70); Gumpel (1967: 68); Madeyski, Lissowska, and Marzec (1971: 80); and Tarski (1968: 229–230), all of which provide relative cost ratios per ton-kilometer between pipelines and railroad. The weight of air passenger transport was increased in line with a note by Korbonski and Wittich (1967: 36).

The transport index has been extended to 1973 using the basically unchanged weights of the Korbonski and Wittich index and using the same procedure of relying on physical performance series obtained from RS aggregated into freight and passenger indexes, respectively, on the basis of net value added. These two indexes (shown in table 4.5) were then aggregated into the index of transport performance in Poland.

Table 4.5 shows that since 1947 freight transport developed substantially faster than passenger transport — between 1956 and 1973 more than twice as fast as passenger transport. The index of aggregate transport shows a substantial rate of growth; it more than tripled between 1946 and 1956 and more than quadrupled between 1956 and 1973. World War II does not show as dramatically on the index of transport as it does on some other indexes in Poland because of the concentrated effort made in 1945–1947 to reconstruct the transport sector under the slogan of the so-called battle for transport (Mieczkowski 1975: 80, 86–87; Alton 1955: 142), although some Soviet looting of equipment took place in 1945 (Gumpel 1963: 60).

Soviet looting of transport equipment was much more disruptive in East Germany (at the time, the Soviet zone of occupation) between 1945 and 1947, added as it was to heavy wartime losses in transport, estimated at 60 percent (Elliot and Scaperlanda 1966: 46n19, 47n22). Soviet dismantling of the East German transport infrastructure was particularly heavy in railway transport and road transport and relatively light in inland waterway transport (Nettl 1951: 184–91). East German transport was further weakened by the austere Soviet reparations policy (Nettl 1951: 200–17, 231) and by the use of East German transport equipment by the occupation authorities, greatly in excess of British and American demands on West German transport. Soviet authorities used the best railroad equipment available after reparations had been made, and they made their demands peremptorily and at short notice, thus adding considerably to the effective burden of servicing them (Nettl 1951: 216–17).

It is interesting to note an acceleration of the growth of transport in Poland between 1970 and 1973 to 47.7 percent over that four-year period, whereas the two preceding four-year periods show a growth of between 34.1 and 37.5 percent over the four-year periods. It thus appears that the general acceleration of economic growth under the first years of the Gierek regime (see Mieczkowski 1975: 169–89) has led to an acceleration of the rate of growth in transport performance.

It may be noted that the relation between Polish aggregate domestic freight traffic (table 4.5, col. 1) and national income (table 4.6, col. 1) shows more similarity to the Soviet experience, in which freight transport rose relatively rapidly as national income increased, than it does to the experience in the United States (Hunter 1968: 37–43). This relation implies that a given increase in national income generates in Poland — and presumably in other East European countries also — a larger volume of transport performance than might be considered necessary in view of Western experience. This is a handicap to East European economic growth, as it is in the Soviet case, since the cost of raising national income is relatively high in terms of the resources that are engaged in additional transport. It seems that irrational transport, discussed in the last section of the following chapter, contributes to this high relation between freight transport and national income. It also seems that the emphasis on industrialization, particularly on heavy industry, with its bulky raw materials and bulky products, appreciably tends to raise that relation. Likewise, locational decisions during the early postwar industrialization drive, which aimed at building new industries in various parts of the country and made them dependent on other regions of the country in terms of input and sales relationships, could not help but increase the need for transport, at least initially — until industrial production becomes more widespread and is distributed more abundantly — out of proportion to the rise in output.

Tables 4.5, 4.8, and 4.9 show rapid development in the transport sector. The fastest growth was by Bulgaria — the least developed country out of those shown — while the slowest rate of growth was in Poland — at least until 1962. For all countries shown, particularly striking are the fast early postwar growth of transport and the slow-down around 1952. As mentioned in the example of Poland, the communist governments early realized the crucial importance of transport and declared a "battle for transport" in order to break that obstacle to rapid growth in the immediate postwar period.

Table 4.9 gives independent estimates for the development of transport and partly of the joint sector of transport and communications in Eastern Europe for the 1965–1975 period. As stated in the preceding

TABLE 4.8

Independently Calculated Indexes of Transport Performance in Czechoslovakia, Hungary, and Bulgaria

	Czechoslovakia: Output of transport	Czechoslovakia: Net value added in transport	Hungary: Aggregate transport	Bulgaria: Aggregate transport
1937	29.3	29.0	29.5 [a]	23.6 [b]
1946	33.9	32.6	27.7	..
1947	40.8	39.4	38.0	..
1948	46.9	46.2	48.5	52.5
1949	52.1	51.6	53.3	61.1
1950	55.2	54.9	63.3	64.0
1951	65.7	65.5	81.2	69.6
1952	74.7	74.5	89.3	72.7
1953	78.0	77.8	96.0	81.6
1954	84.6	84.4	97.3	85.5
1955	92.6	92.6	100.0	93.8
1956	100.0	100.0	92.3	100.0
1957	110.3	110.4	105.0	109.2
1958	123.3	122.8	117.2	122.3
1959	135.3	134.5	129.4	148.9
1960	156.0	154.6	145.9	179.1
1961	170.2	168.7	151.5	198.3
1962	178.3	175.2	160.4	218.4
1963	..	180.7	167.4	243.3
1964	..	192.3	181.4	277.7
1965	..	199.5	184.5	295.8

a   1938   b   1939

Sources: Lazarcik 1965: 6-9; Czirjak 1965: 3-5; Lazarcik and Wynnyczuk 1968: 12; Lazarcik 1969: 9; Bandor, Czirjak, and Pall 1970: 4.

TABLE 4.9

Independent Estimates of the Growth of Sectoral Contribution of Transport to GNPS of East European Countries, 1965-1975

(indexes; weights are 1968 percentages of total GNP at adjusted factor cost)

	Poland[a]	East Germany[a]	Czechoslovakia	Hungary	Romania[a]	Bulgaria
Weights	8.72	7.07	8.64	7.38	6.36	6.71
1965	100.0	100.0	100.0	100.0	100.0	100.0
1966	108.5	103.6	102.8	103.8	111.7	111.6
1967	113.8	106.0	102.5	108.3	124.5	127.9
1968	123.1	111.7	105.9	109.4	138.7	143.9
1969	128.8	114.5	106.7	112.1	150.3	161.2
1970	135.9	123.9	113.3	118.3	164.3	180.7
1971	152.2	132.0	118.9	121.0	176.3	194.6
1972	171.2	134.3	124.8	123.4	186.2	208.2
1973	186.6	138.8	126.6	130.9	199.6	226.0
1974	216.6	143.9	134.1	138.4	216.9	257.0
1975	243.5	150.7	137.9	144.8	240.6	292.5

a   transport and communications

Source: Alton et al. 1976: 6-11. Cf. Alton et al. 1975: 52-57.

section, transport made up 85 to 95 percent of the net value added of that joint sector, and consequently changes in it can be taken, by and large, to reflect changes in the value added by the transport sector. The sectoral contributions to GNP by the transport or the transport and communications sector (shown in table 4.9) have been calculated at 1968 adjusted factor cost with 1968 taken as 100. The table also shows the 1968 proportional contribution to GNP by transport or by transport and communications in terms of adjusted factor cost in that year, which contribution was then used by the authors of the index in aggregating changes in individual sectors into changes in GNPs.

Over the whole 1965-1975 period, the highest rate of growth in the transport or the joint transport and communications sector was shown by Bulgaria, Poland, and Romania (in that order), while East Germany (for which additional 1936-1958 data are found in Stolper 1960: 393-95), Hungary, and Czechoslovakia showed a markedly slower rate of growth. If growth of transport and communications for only 1970-1975 is taken into account (1970 taken as a base), however, then Poland shows the highest growth — 79.2 percent — followed by Bulgaria with 61.9 percent and Romania with 46.4 percent; Hungary, Czechoslovakia, and East Germany again showed markedly lower growth of between 22.4 and 21.6 percent. These comparisons again provide a measure of the acceleration of the overall economic growth rate in Poland that followed acceptance of new economic policies by the Gierek regime early in 1971 (see Mieczkowski 1975: 169-189).

Tables 4.10 and 4.11 show (using the example of Poland) the indexes for individual modes according to ownership for freight and passenger transport, respectively. Individual indexes for other countries of Eastern Europe (not as comprehensive as for Poland) are found in sources cited in table 4.8. Only one example is provided here in order to economize on space (for comparative statistics see Günther 1965: passim; Kneafsey 1975: 118, 212-13; United Nations, *Annual Bulletin of Transport Statistics for Europe;* International Union of Railways, *International Railway Statistics*). The developments shown here may be considered representative for other East European countries as well. The indexes in tables 4.10 and 4.11 were used to calculate the indexes in table 4.5.

The main observations that can be made from tables 4.10 and 4.11 are as follows:

1. Freight transport as a whole shows approximately twice as high a rate of growth as does passenger transport during the postwar period.

2. The fastest growth in freight transport has been (in decreasing

TABLE 4.10
Indexes of Freight Transport Performance in Poland by Sectors and Modes, 1937-1973

	State sector: Railroads[a]	Road transport[b]	Air transport	Inland waterways	Maritime transport	Ports	Cooperative sector: Road transport[c]	Private sector: Freight transport[d]	Aggregate freight index
1937	42.4	..	52.8	..	38.4	104.4	..	..	40.0
1946	37.4	2.3	8.1	8.9	10.0	50.1	..	..	30.8
1947	41.0	1.4	13.2	11.1	17.0	67.1	..	..	34.7
1948	54.3	1.9	22.3	36.1	34.9	102.0	..	..	48.3
1949	62.8	6.8	31.0	53.2	37.1	108.4	14.1	..	56.8
1950	67.4	10.8	31.5	42.0	52.3	98.6	28.2	..	62.2
1951	73.8	19.5	34.0	54.3	107.6	98.6	62.0	184.4	75.6
1952	77.4	26.8	38.6	89.0	98.5	88.2	62.0	220.3	82.8
1953	85.6	37.6	51.3	95.1	94.7	90.5	90.1	214.1	90.3
1954	92.6	50.2	64.5	91.9	71.8	102.2	100.0	108.6	84.9
1955	99.8	81.4	81.2	123.4	90.9	109.9	101.4	50.4	91.2
1956	100.0	100.0	100.0	100.0	100.0	100.0	100.0	100.0	100.0
1957	106.1	91.4	126.9	112.7	113.1	91.6	101.4	112.1	103.3

1958	109.8	95.8	114.2	110.8	128.4	109.1	184.5	108.4	111.4
1959	118.4	103.8	132.5	101.8	158.3	116.2	142.2	109.2	117.1
1960	127.7	111.4	156.9	143.9	188.0	140.8	143.7	103.0	126.5
1961	133.8	123.7	187.3	136.1	244.9	143.1	139.4	96.0	134.1
1962	139.5	142.3	231.5	130.9	266.6	158.4	190.1	92.6	144.9
1963	142.8	163.9	244.2	163.4	286.7	150.0	240.8	94.7	155.5
1964	152.6	180.4	289.8	198.7	316.9	172.5	269.0	91.9	159.8
1965	157.0	197.4	336.0	224.4	324.2	171.4	309.8	90.0	168.8
1966	165.2	223.1	490.0	280.6	365.7	173.4	901.4	95.5	212.6
1967	172.0	254.5	560.6	299.5	429.5	180.8	1,018.3	103.2	233.0
1968	180.6	304.0	667.1	321.8	563.1	208.4	1,240.8	103.2	268.1
1969	185.5	357.3	843.4	229.6	572.1	211.6	1,476.1	103.2	292.7
1970	193.9	424.4	1,014.8	365.4	613.1	234.1	1,726.8	103.2	330.9
1971	203.8	485.1	1,126.1	342.4	738.7	240.3	2,229.6	97.5	380.8
1972	214.8	562.1	1,623.8	402.1	868.8	263.8	3,249.3	94.6	465.2
1973	228.2	656.4	1,746.8	309.7	856.4	293.1	3,623.9	93.2	509.9
Weights	3,018.6	1,268.8	15.8	145.7	300.3	263.4	303.5	635.0	

a   standard and narrow gauge; pipelines added in 1:4 ratio from 1964 on   b   PKS and "branch"

c   all cooperatives   d   number of "standard teamster enterprises"

Sources: Korbonski and Wittich 1967: 29-32; *RS 1974*: 385, 398, 110, 382

TABLE 4.11

Indexes of Passenger Transport Performance in Poland by Sectors and Modes, 1937-1973

	State sector:						Cooperative sector:	Private sector:	Aggregate passenger index
	Railroads	Road transport	Air transport	Inland waterways	Maritime transport	Urban transport			
1937	18.5	18.0	12.0	..	..	15.3	..	93.0	22.1
1946	42.7	6.7	19.5	21.2	23.8	28.0	..	..	36.7
1947	49.1	12.5	20.8	24.8	213.6	36.3	..	..	43.8
1948	54.3	20.7	26.1	48.9	284.1	48.3	113.6	..	51.0
1949	57.3	28.3	24.6	56.2	247.7	54.9	67.0	..	54.5
1950	72.1	45.9	34.4	55.6	107.1	61.2	75.0	..	66.9
1951	83.9	61.4	43.7	62.0	59.7	67.6	83.0	57.1	77.6
1952	101.4	66.8	48.2	60.7	85.5	73.9	91.5	70.3	91.7
1953	97.0	74.9	45.9	77.9	79.2	80.3	85.2	76.4	90.9
1954	96.4	82.7	60.2	81.9	90.5	85.6	84.1	88.1	92.7
1955	98.4	89.7	74.4	87.8	109.1	94.2	88.6	95.8	96.6
1956	100.0	100.0	100.0	100.0	100.0	100.0	100.0	100.0	100.0
1957	101.8	117.6	114.4	107.2	50.1	109.6	121.0	133.8	106.0

Year									
1958	101.3	139.2	84.5	100.2	98.9	117.7	139.2	151.9	109.4
1959	92.8	170.2	105.9	113.6	106.7	127.2	165.3	169.0	108.7
1960	82.3	206.8	123.4	111.8	105.0	136.8	173.3	175.5	106.0
1961	82.1	249.3	148.1	121.2	101.1	150.0	193.2	181.1	111.5
1962	83.1	295.7	179.2	128.1	108.9	159.8	212.5	198.8	118.2
1963	85.5	349.5	183.1	133.4	145.3	166.4	206.8	220.4	125.9
1964	88.5	425.8	236.1	145.8	139.2	178.5	219.9	252.9	138.7
1965	91.3	489.3	279.5	149.9	123.8	181.5	228.4	280.3	147.6
1966	92.8	561.5	377.9	170.3	125.3	189.4	232.4	313.1	158.6
1967	94.3	627.5	511.7	170.0	136.3	181.6	226.1	343.1	166.8
1968	95.4	701.2	538.8	177.2	131.0	166.3	232.4	369.9	172.0
1969	98.5	764.0	604.4	174.3	178.2	171.5	247.2	409.7	182.6
1970	98.1	815.0	688.8	173.8	162.6	178.1	238.6	463.4	191.1
1971	99.0	907.4	834.1	172.6	193.5	185.6	230.7	518.5	204.7
1972	103.2	1,032.2	1,078.2	175.8	213.3	195.5	222.7	576.9	225.0
1973	105.5	1,150.8	1,397.0	160.1	197.2	207.2	234.1	625.4	244.4
Weights	2,248.0	216.6	62.5	68.6	10.0	533.8	20.3	184.6	

Sources: Korbonski and Wittich 1967: 37–39; RS 1974: 386, 497, 496; RS 1971: 452; RS 1972: 430; RS 1966: 571; RS 1970: 576, 396.

perative road transport (favored for political reasons), air
chnological reasons), maritime transport (technological
ic reasons), state road transport (mainly for economic
inland waterway transport. Railroad transport, the most
ode of transport in Eastern Europe, showed the least
growth, but it started from a high level of development and importance. Private freight transport belongs to a separate category, and its
stagnation is due entirely to political reasons.

3. The fastest growth in passenger transport has been (in decreasing
order) in air transport (technological reasons), state road transport
(owing to the deepening of capital in that sector, both in terms of
highway construction and in terms of rolling stock), urban transport
(because of urbanization), and inland waterway transport (as the
result of improvement of facilities). Maritime transport experienced
substantial fluctuations, induced apparently by political vicissitudes.
Cooperative transport has recently leveled off after a period of rather
uncertain development, mainly between 1955 and 1962. Private transport has shown a surprisingly good growth, higher than average for
passenger transport. Finally railroad transport, having been most
developed and having attained a high plateau in 1952, fluctuated
subsequently around that level. Thus, increases in passenger transport
performance have been caused mainly by the growth of air transport,
state road transport, and private transport.

4. The political bias against the private sector in communist countries, while it extended to private freight transport, did not extend fully
to private passenger transport (cf. RFER: SR, March 12, 1976: 3–4).

5. Maritime operations (maritime transport and the work of ports)
have revealed substantial growth, except in passenger operations,
which under conditions of strict political controls were the least
influenced by economic factors.

6. The general picture presented by the sectional indexes of transport is that of a growing and developing economy with increasingly
more modern transport, a progressively more urbanized society, an
improving standard of living, and with a dynamic exchange of goods
including — through maritime transport — the exchange of goods
with foreign countries.

7. The indexes are influenced by, but do not show directly, various
technological improvements in transport, as, for instance, electrification and dieselization of railroads, paving of roads, introduction of
better buses and better bus service, and introduction, however slow, of
jet airplanes.

8. World War II was felt more strongly in freight transport than in passenger transport. In freight transport the effect of the war was particularly strong in air transport, maritime transport, and port activity. In passenger transport the effect of the war was particularly marked in road transport. The effects of World War II were quickly remedied thanks to a concerted effort in the "battle for transport."

9. Peculiar to Poland, because of its change in government leadership and economic policy at the end of 1970 (see Mieczkowski 1975: 169–75), was the acceleration of transport performance after 1970. In freight transport, acceleration was particularly strong in cooperative transport, in the performance of ports and maritime transport, and in state road transport. In passenger transport, it was marked in state road transport, air transport, and private transport. Freight indexes grew in this period in response to the spectacular rise in national income (see table 4.6), while the passenger transport indexes grew largely in response to increased real incomes of the population and as a consequence of increased employment.

Regression Analysis

Data from table 4.5, in conjunction with the independent variables shown in tables 4.6 and 4.7, were used as a basis for regression analysis. Before discussing the results of that analysis, we should point out one unsatisfactory aspect of the aggregate index of transport shown in table 4.5. It indicates that the growth of aggregate contribution of transport to Polish GNP between 1965 and 1973 was 157.1 percent. Yet the official statistics of transport and communications, in which aggregate transport constitutes more than 85 percent (Korbonski and Wittich 1967: 6), indicate for the same period a substantially slower growth of 86.6 percent (Alton et al. 1975: 56). The main reason for this discrepancy, which is obvious in view of the substantial rise in communications services, is probably the use of 1956 weights in this author's independently calculated index. By 1965–1973 these weights are likely to have become unrealistic because of changed economic conditions. However, this study used the independent index because it conveniently separated the contribution of communications and transport in official statistics and because for the purpose of correlation analysis interyear variations were more important than the overall growth of the transport sector. In Alton's approach, which employed Western research methods to concentrate on sectoral contribution to national income and on growth of the economies, the official Polish figures for transport and communications were accepted in tentative preference to calculation of an independent index (Alton et al. 1975: 109).

The regression analysis was used here only for Poland because to have done so for all countries of Eastern Europe would have taken up much space and (it is believed) would not have yielded substantially different results. The conclusions from the Polish example may be taken as representative for Eastern Europe as a whole (cf. Günther 1965: 23).

The period analyzed for Poland was that of 1947–1973.[3] As a first approximation, a linear regression model was used, given by the formula:

$$Y = A_0 + A_1X + U$$

where: Y = dependent variable taken from table 4.5 as freight, passenger, or aggregate transport. No lags were used between independent and dependent variable.

X = independent variable taken from tables 4.6 and 4.7.

U = the error term.

The equation states that variations in the growth of transport services can be explained by unlagged independent variables such as national income, production of cement, steel, and others. To measure the relationship between Y and X, we estimated the regression coefficients A_0, A_1 by using the ordinary least squares method. The results of a computer analysis of the series under investigation are shown in the following sample equations.

I. Using national income as independent variable:

A. The freight index equation (Y_1) was:

$Y_1 = -62.4 + 1.025X$

    (14.4)   (0.56)

s = 34.0

$\overline{R}^2 = 0.93$

D.W. = 0.16

B. The passenger index equation (Y_2) was:

$Y_2 = 24.5 + 0.441X$

    (2.8)   (0.11)

s = 6.6

$\overline{R}^2 = 0.98$

D.W. = 0.48

C. The aggregate index of transport equation (Y) was:

$Y = -31.1 + 0.815X$

    (9.6)   (0.04)

s = 22.6

$$\overline{R}^2 = 0.95$$
$$D.W. = 0.17$$

As usual, $\overline{R}^2$ is the coefficient of determination adjusted for degree of freedom, s is the standard error of the equation, D.W. is the Durbin-Watson statistics. Below each estimated parameter, in parentheses, is the standard error of the coefficient. This gives us a measure of statistical reliability. In addition, each behavioral equation is assumed to have a set of mutually independent disturbances. The Durbin-Watson statistic for each estimated equation shows the presence or absence of serial correlation in the residuals.

Then the constant terms in each equation (i.e., -62.4, 24.5, and -31.1) represent the average effects on Y_1, Y_2, and Y by other independent variables not included in equations A, B, and C. The correlation shown is very high. Thus, 93 percent of the variations in the growth of freight transport, 98 percent of the variations in the growth of passenger transport, and 95 percent of the variations in the growth of aggregate transport can be explained by changes in national income. In other words, the rapid growth of transport in Poland during the period 1947-1973 can be attributed primarily to the growth of national income in the same period. This close correlation is helpful in projecting future transport needs on the basis of multi-year plans for the development of national economies, as shown in chapter 3.

Similar correlation studies were done for freight, passenger, and aggregate indexes of transport with the indexes of the net value added in industry, net value added in agriculture, construction, foreign trade turnover, production of coal, production of steel, production of cement, and production of cereals as independent variables. The R^2 coefficients were between 0.85 and 0.99, except for correlations with net value added in agriculture, where they were between 0.52 and 0.70, and with cereal production, where they were between 0.76 and 0.84. On the whole, the high values of $\overline{R}^2$ in our results may be partly an indication of a causative relationship, but they may have been caused partly by the independent variables being dependent on those factors that are also an important cause of changes in transport; in particular, they may be dependent on changes in national income. We must keep in mind that regression analysis does not postulate necessary direct causation. The Durbin-Watson statistics were quite low, suggesting the presence of serial correlation (cf. Kneafsey 1975: 369-71 on auto-correlation).

The average effect of factors not included in the equation was high when the independent variable X was chosen to be represented by the index of value added in agriculture, the index of coal production, and the index of the production of cereals. The standard error was unduly high when the independent variable X was represented by the index of net value added in agriculture and by the index of the production of cereals. The coefficient of determination was low when the independent variable X was represented by the net value added in agriculture and medium high when it was represented by the index of production of cereals. The best results were obtained when the independent variable X was represented by indexes of national income, net value added in industry, construction, foreign trade turnover, production of steel, and production of cement. The correlation was strong enough in most of the cases we analyzed to allow an assertion of, if not causality, then at least strong common influences. We may then say that freight, passenger, and aggregate transport develop in conjunction with the development of most of the basic economic factors considered above, especially in conjunction with the development of national income. Planners of transport have to take that relationship into account when they decide on the actual future growth of transport services. Since national income represents the aggregate of economic influences on transport, it seems reasonable to regard the correlation between it and transport as the most economically meaningful; but it seems that for particular purposes, the planners might guide themselves by their planned indexes of the net value added in industry, construction, foreign trade turnover, and the production of steel and cement.

In practice, however, the planners in Eastern Europe do not seem to devote resources to transport services on a par with the planned growth of national income. The results of such neglect are perennial shortages of transport equipment, excessive needs for human labor used to substitute for inadequate capitalization, delays of shipments and a tendency to retard production in other sectors, and the well-known overcrowding on passenger trains and buses. For example, the main point on the agenda of a recent Politburo meeting in Poland was concerned with continuing transport difficulties: the gap between transport capacity and demand for transport had dangerously widened. On an annual basis it amounted on the railroad in the middle of 1975 to about 5 percent of the amount of goods transported by rail (RFER: SR, July 18, 1975: 4). Such a shortfall in the transport of goods obviously results in bottlenecks, build-up of inventories, and loss of production. A review of the Polish performance in the socio-economic plan for 1975 concluded that despite some improvements railway transportation was still the stumbling block of the Polish economy because of the insufficiency of stationary and rolling stock, their obsolescence, and the shortcomings in management and organization of work (RFER: SR, Feb. 6, 1976: 8). The Polish press reported discussions on the disruptive effect on the country's economy of the nonfulfillment of transport targets (RFER: SR, Sept. 5, 1975: 9), as a result of which an official estimate was that about 20 percent of the labor force in the transport sector was technologically redundant (Stefanowski 1976: 3), while employment in the transport sector was still considered inadequate (RFER: SR, Sept. 5, 1975: 5). Because of such neglect of the relationship between the growth of national income and the growth of transport, I considered it necessary, in the preceding paragraph, to restate that relationship.

Concentrating on the relation between the independent variables of national income, net value added in industry, construction, foreign trade turnover, steel and cement, and the dependent variable, we may note that freight transport grows slightly more than proportionately to national income, while aggregate transport — due to the influence of passenger transport — grows more slowly than national income. In all relevant equations the freight index grows faster as a function of the independent variable than does the passenger index; consequently, it also grows faster than the aggregate index of transport. In the final analysis, planners may best use the aggregate planned indexes of national income, net value added in industry, construction, and foreign trade turnover as guidelines for their planned growth of transport. It should be noted, however, that changes in foreign trade are not the easiest to plan, particularly in the centrally planned economies of Eastern Europe. Thus, regression analysis reveals both the past observed relationship between transport and some important indexes of economic activity, and points to a tool for extrapolating future needs for transport services. The relationships indicated here may well change in the future as the result of inventions, changes in locational policy, and changes in consumer preferences. But since the correlation is as close as shown above, it can serve as an important tool in the arsenal of planners in Eastern Europe.

If causative relationship is imputed to our analysis, we may conclude that the growth of national income and of its component parts of industry, construction, and foreign trade exerted a dominant influence on the demand for transport services. A country that plans to grow economically has to develop its transport, or else it will face crippling bottlenecks. In conscious planning directed at balanced growth of various sectors of the economy, transport can theoretically be made to develop together with the expansion of the whole economy. This is not necessarily the case, however. The Polish Minister of Transport, Mieczyslaw Zajfryd (1975), pointed out in an interview that the unexpectedly steep rise of the economic indicators in Poland during 1971–1975 had led to an inability of transport to cope with all the demands made on it and to widespread discontent with transport. The faster-than-planned growth of national income and of the main economic indicators put transport for several years under a strain that did not allow it to satisfy all the demands imposed upon it. Thus, unforeseen developments may severely test the planning process as it affects transport. A future quantitative analysis of the 1970s in Poland may well reveal the intersectoral strains caused by the unplanned surge in national income. Prognostic studies by Polish transportation economists indicate an expectation, or hope, that the ratio of transport performance to national income will decline from 0.154 in 1970 and 0.143 in 1975 to 0.116 by 1990 (Madeyski, Lissowska, and Morawski 1975a: 109).

Since the Durbin-Watson statistics obtained in the first regression analysis were very low (which suggests that the estimated residuals are correlated), the second analysis used the first-order Hildreth-Lu iterative technique to correct them (cf. Lee 1975: 32–33; Hildreth and Lu 1960). (If we have omitted from the equation some variables that move in phase or if we make consistent measurement errors, then we will have serial correlation.) Our second regression analysis used double-logarithmic equations because of their generally superior fit and ease of interpretation as compared with the linear form of regression also used. The new results show appreciably higher Durbin-Watson statistics, thus decreasing the likelihood of serial correlation. Of the results of our calculations, the best were expressed in the following equations:

A. The freight index equation was:

$$\ln Y_1 = -0.639 + 0.462 \ln NI + 0.586 \ln FTT$$
$$ (-1.22) \quad (1.42) \qquad (2.30)$$

$\overline{R}^2 = 0.947$

$s = 0.063$

$D.W. = 1.74$

$\rho = 0.826$

where: $\ln$ = logarithm

NI = index of national income

FTT = index of foreign trade turnover

ρ = autocorrelation coefficient rho

B. The passenger index equation was:
$$\ln Y_2 = 0.564 + 0.790 \ln NI$$
$$ (1.95) \quad (14.68)$$
$$\overline{R}^2 = 0.971$$
$$s = 0.048$$
$$D.W. = 1.35$$
$$\rho = 0.777$$

C. The aggregate index of transport equation was:
$$\ln Y = -0.330 + 0.613 \ln NI + 0.369 \ln FTT$$
$$ (-0.69) \quad (2.18) \quad\quad (1.67)$$
$$\overline{R}^2 = 0.957$$
$$s = 0.053$$
$$D.W. = 1.44$$
$$\rho = 0.868$$

Similar equations were obtained for the other independent variables, but the fits were worse. (The lagged dependent variable was tried and dropped because it yielded unsatisfactory results. The regression of transport on coal and steel was the best among the regressions not shown here. The nonlogarithmic linear form of regression was also used, but the results were not satisfactory.) The equations shown above can be explained as yielding the demand elasticities for freight, passenger, and aggregate transport with respect to national income or foreign trade turnover. In the freight equation, for example, an increase of 1 percent in the national income will, other things being equal, bring about an increase of 0.462 percent in freight transport. Similarly, if foreign trade turnover is increased by 1 percent then, other things being equal, freight transport will increase by about 0.586 percent. Foreign trade, including transit, accounts directly for over 25 percent of railroad transport in Poland (*PKP* 1974: 3) (and for 100 percent of sea transport) and for more if indirect effects of foreign trade are taken into account, such as the multiplier effect on national income that results from an increase in exports, and the incentive effect on labor and hence on production and national income that results from an increase in imports. This explains the relatively high correlation between foreign trade turnover and freight transport. On the other hand, there is only a tenuous connection between foreign trade turnover and passenger transport; consequently, the passenger transport equation does not yield satisfactory results if foreign trade turnover is taken into account. However, foreign trade turnover appears important in determining aggregate transport, as shown in the last equation. This is so because of the high weight of freight transport (almost two-thirds) in aggregate transport (see table 4.5).

On the whole, the double-logarithmic regression seems preferable to the first approximation of a linear equation; the relation between transport and other economic magnitudes tends to be multiple and interconnected, and it cannot be singlemindedly cut up into separate, disjointed correlations. This observation is perhaps the most fitting conclusion to our regression analysis.

The Cost of Transport in Eastern Europe

The Cost of Transport to the East European Economies

In order to perform its functions, the transport sector employs a part of the nation's productive resources and uses up some materials produced in other sectors of the economy. The use of productive resources may be expressed in terms of the proportion of the labor force employed in transport, the percentage of total capital employed in transport, or the contribution those factors make to help the economy produce a certain national income. These relationships are shown for Eastern Europe in table 5.1. It may be seen from this table that the proportion of the labor force employed in transport has grown in Poland, East Germany, Hungary, Romania, and Bulgaria (presumably largely as the result of a relative increase in truck transport), and it has declined only in Yugoslavia from an unaccountably high level in 1952, later revised to 2.0 (see table 4.1), which produced a rise in the proportion in question (cf. above, pp. 000-00). It may also be seen that the proportion of capital engaged in transport is higher in Poland, East Germany, Hungary, and Bulgaria than the proportion of the labor force indicating a more capital-intensive sector than the average for the economy. Finally, it is seen that the share of transport in "material costs" in Poland is low but shows a tendency to grow and that the share of transport in national income has been growing in Poland, Czechoslovakia, Bulgaria, and Yugoslavia.

The share of aggregate capital engaged in transport is a highly relative indicator (compare table 4.2 above). Its denominator, the aggregate capital, does not cover all capital in existence in the country, and then it covers capital without the use of market prices, which for the most part do not exist in communist countries, but at cost, which is influenced by the subsidies mushrooming in Eastern Europe and by unrealistic depreciation allowances. The numerator of the indicator is open to "many doubts" even on the part of East European economists (cf. Madeyski, Lissowska, and Marzec 1971: 110). On the Polish railroad, for instance, depreciation allowances barely cover the costs of

TABLE 5.1
Indicators of the Relative Cost of Transport Services in Eastern Europe
(percentages)

	Share of employment in transport as percent of the labor force				Share of capital invested in the transport sector as percent of aggregate capital			Share of transport in the "material costs" of gross product		Share of transport in national income			
	1950	1960	1970	1973	1955	1960	1970	1960-65	1973	1950	1960	1970	1973
Poland	3.9	5.3	6.1	6.1	..	9.5[d]	9.5	2.8-3.0	3.3	..	4.9	5.4	5.6
East Germany	4.7	5.1	5.5	5.7[a]	22.7[c]	20.4[c]	16.5[c]	..	..	6.7	4.5	4.4	4.5[a]
Czechoslovakia	4.2	4.8	4.4	4.3	..	..	..	..	..	..	3.2	3.7	3.9
Hungary	4.0[e]	6.0[e]	7.2[e]	7.6[e]	..	19.1[e]	16.9[e]	..	..	..	5.8[eh]	6.1[ei]	6.6[e]
Romania	2.0	2.5	3.6	3.9	..	..	..	..	..	..	..	..	..
Bulgaria	1.2[b]	3.5	4.9	..	19.7[c]	16.7	13.0	..	..	5.0[f]	4.0	6.0	..
Yugoslavia	11.0[c]	6.6	5.9	5.9	..	..	..	..	..	5.4[g]	6.6	6.8	6.8

a 1972   b 1948   c 1952   d author's estimate   e transport and communications   f 1955   g 1954   h 1961-65   i 1966-70

Sources: Calculated on the basis of: *RS 1974*: 109, 126, 127, 194, 382; *SJ 1956*: 148, 354, 451; *SJ 1962*: 169; *SJ 1972*: 48, 53, 276; *SJ 1973*: 53, 40, 254-6; *SPBH 1967*: 137; *SPBH 1973*: 259; *SPBH 1974*: 74, 86, 245; *AS 1974*: 61; *SEzh 1971*: 38, 51, 57; *SG 1954*: 96; *SG 1967*: 93; *SG 1974*: 117, 118; Madeyski, Lissowska and Marzec 1971: 106.

major repairs, and a similar situation obtains in road transport (Malek, Grzywacz, and Zymela 1973: 105). This was alleviated in 1974 by the introduction of accelerated depreciation allowances (Renik 1974: 14–18).

The contribution of transport to national income, as shown in table 5.1, is underestimated because the "Marxist" calculation of national income excludes services, among them some transport services (cf. table 4.4). Table 5.3 endeavors to make up for that omission. The contribution of transport to national income is lower after 1960 in all countries (except Bulgaria) than the share of employment in transport in the aggregate labor force, thus indicating lower-than-average productivity of labor employed in transport (cf. above p. 95).

Within the transport sector, the cost of individual transport modes differs radically. Table 5.2 measures this cost in terms of the value of services rendered by the transport sector in Poland in 1968; this value departs from cost, as will be shown below. Table 5.2 can be compared with tables 3.2 to 3.7, where shares by transport modes are expressed in physical terms. It still shows the preponderance of the railroad, although to a lesser extent than the other tables, thus indicating higher value added and higher cost of road transport.

Table 5.2 is incomplete because some transport costs are not recorded for statistical purposes. Table 5.3, therefore, incorporates additional estimates made in Poland concerning the value of unrecorded transport services. Those services exist also in other East European countries, although their contribution may vary substantially. Their elements are: (1) the possession of their own transport by economic units, also called unorganized transport — this kind of transport is performed within economic enterprises and with their own means of transport; (2) urban transport; (3) cost of maintenance of public vehicular roads and streets; (4) cost of loading, unloading, and transloading in Poland, divided in 1968 equally between mechanized and manual loading operations; (5) cost of agricultural horse-drawn transport outside of farms and other horse-drawn transport; and (6) cost of exploitation of individual, private means of transport. Although not all these costs enter into national income as it is calculated in Eastern Europe, it may be useful to point out that their estimated total in current prices amounted to 120.1 billion zlotys in 1968, while the national income produced was in the same year equal to 668.8 billion zlotys (Madeyski, Lissowska, and Marzec 1971: 109; *RS 1970:* 80). The relation of all costs of transport, including those not included in national income, to national income was equal to 18 percent, which is a very high proportion.

TABLE 5.2
Estimated Shares of the Value of Transport Services in Poland in 1968
(percentages)

	Freight	Passenger	Aggregate
Railroad	47.6	49.3	47.9
Road transport	36.0	42.3	37.5
Air transport[a]	.2	7.0	1.7
Inland waterways	1.5	.7	1.3
Public forwarding	3.4	–	2.6
Sea transport and ports	10.3	.7	8.2
Pipelines	1.0	–	.8
Total	100.0	100.0	100.0
Structure	77.7	22.3	100.0

a   including subsidies in kind

Source: Madeyski, Lissowska, and Marzec 1971: 107.

TABLE 5.3
Estimated Shares of the Value of Additional
Transport Services in Poland in 1968
(percentages)

	Freight	Passenger	Aggregate
Total from table 5.2	58.4	47.5	53.0
Own transport	11.8	–	8.3
Urban transport	–	15.7	3.9
Maintenance cost:			
roads	..	..	3.9
streets	..	..	.7
Loading, etc.	18.0	–	12.7
Horse-drawn			
transport	11.8	..	8.3
Private transport	–	36.8	9.2
Total	100.0	100.0	100.0

Source: Calculated on the basis of Madeyski, Lissowska, and Marzec 1971: 109.

However, even such an amplification of the costs of transport does not materially advance the answer to the problem of estimating all social costs of transport in Eastern Europe. According to several Polish experts, "such a calculation is, as shown by numerous efforts, impossible" (Madeyski, Lissowska, and Marzec 1971: 110). The financial systems in East Europe are cumbrously burdened with a residue of fiscal devices that nearly obliterate the ultimate reaction of prices and official values to social costs. They consist of a system of subsidies given in various forms (e.g., as outright grants, coverage of losses incurred, provision of cost-free capital, wage-reducing subsidies to some forms of consumption — especially to housing) and of a system of taxes (e.g., positive budget differences, differential form of the turn-over tax imposed especially on consumer goods). Both subsidies and taxes are so deeply imbedded in the economic systems in Eastern Europe that their effects can be traced only approximately (cf. Alton et al. 1965: 67–85; Mieczkowski 1975: 43–45, 161–62).

Two main cost concepts are used in Eastern Europe with regard to transport. The primary one is the effective (explicit) cost of transport, that is, cost to the user. This concept will be developed in the next section. The second concept is that of alternative cost of transport. This is much less comprehensive than the Western concept of opportunity cost; it, and the effective cost, add up to the global, or aggregate, cost of transport.

The alternative cost of transport (cf. Tarski 1968: 242–48) burdens the user or the economy at large. It includes the following cost elements: lowering the quality of consignment and/or its shrinkage owing to transport, transloading, or storage; lowering of the quality of consignment and/or its shrinkage owing to a lengthening of the period of transport; tying up of capital in goods in transit (which in the West would be considered as opportunity cost of loss of interest); additional costs arising from the choice of a given mode of transport or a given way of transporting the goods, including costs of special packaging; losses or additional costs that arise as the result of delays in the delivery of materials, both in the realm of manufacturing and invest-ments; decline in the quality of products owing to delayed deliveries, e.g., in the case of late delivery of fertilizers to agriculture; cost of insurance; other losses resulting from the selection of a less efficient mode or way of transportation, e.g., too small or too large trucks; market losses caused by delays in deliveries, including penalties im-posed by international contracts for such delayed deliveries; in pas-senger transport, losses to individuals and their employers owing to selection of a given mode of transport.

Alternative costs are particularly important for decision making in transport connected with foreign trade, since the scarcity of foreign exchange and the consequent need to economize on it are a perennial problem in Eastern Europe. Foreign exchange costs of transport comprise (as do the domestic ones) effective costs and alternative costs. But in contrast to the case of domestic transport, the latter costs become now more explicit; they are payable in foreign exchange out of the country's reserves, and the pressure to minimize them consequently becomes greater. The foreign exchange price received for a shipment may vary according to the mode of transport used: domestic travelers may spend more or less foreign exchange in a foreign country depending on what mode of transport they use, foreign exchange insurance costs may vary, etc. The most important aspect of alternative cost involves spending foreign exchange rather than domestic currency. Thus, decisions may be made in favor of, say, a more expensive sea transport than rail shipment or in favor of travel abroad in a domestic bus rather than by train if such actions save foreign exchange.

An additional complication comes from differentiation between freely convertible currencies (which are more desirable from the point of view of the East European countries; the costs payable in them appear less desirable and thus are more likely to be minimized) and currencies under exchange control, in which case clearing agreements may make alternative costs seem less important.

The Effective Cost of Transport

Apart from its macroeconomic sense, the cost of transport can be looked upon from the microeconomic view, namely, as it affects the transporting enterprise or the users of transport. In this latter sense, we consider the so-called effective costs of transport. The effective cost depends on the length of transport and on costs that are independent of mileage covered. This is expressed in the following formulas (adapted from Tarski 1968: 206):

$$E_t = E_{od} + E_m \cdot l$$
$$E_{t/km} = E_{od}/l + E_m$$

where: E_t = cost of moving one ton for a distance l
  E_{od} = cost of operations at the points of origin (loading) and of destination (unloading)
  E_m = cost of moving one ton for a distance of one km
  l = distance covered
  $E_{t/km}$ = cost of a unit of transport performance

The first equation yields aggregate effective cost of transport, the second equation the cost per unit of distance, or unit cost. Since, as shown below, unit cost depends on distance covered, the aggregate cost may be a more meaningful measure (cf. Tarski 1968: 207).

The unit cost of transport tends to decline with the distance traveled, because the costs of loading, unloading, and of holding up transport units at the points of origin and destination become distributed over a larger number of units of distance. This is shown in table 5.4 for the Soviet Union. The cost of transporting one ton for a distance of ten kilometers is taken as 100, and the table demonstrates how dramatically this cost declines for most modes, except for transport by truck. The largest decline was achieved — not surprisingly — with increasing distance in sea transport; the smallest and rather negligible decline was registered by truck transport.

Similar calculations made in Poland yielded similar results for the railroad, but showed substantial (when compared with the USSR) reductions in unit costs of transport by truck up to a distance of about 110 kilometers — after which there was very little reduction in unit cost. The Polish cost conditions are summarized in table 5.5. Unit cost reduction over distance in truck transport in Poland is, however, still much smaller than on the railroad. Polish cost conditions are likely to be more representative of Eastern Europe than Soviet cost conditions are.

As seen in table 5.4, the decline in unit cost of transport is not equal for different modes of transport. This leads to the phenomenon — known also in the West — that a relatively costly mode such as sea transport becomes relatively cheap beyond a certain critical distance, while a relatively inexpensive mode such as transport by truck becomes relatively costly beyond a certain critical distance at which the unit cost curves for different modes intersect. In Poland, the critical distance in comparing the costs of transport by truck and by rail is accepted as between 50 and 100 kilometers, depending on the distance of shipment points from railway stations at both ends and depending on the kind of goods being transported (Tarski 1968: 219–20; cf. Kneafsey 1975: 245 for U.S. comparative cost data).

In the USSR, the critical distance between railroad and road transport has been calculated as follows — depending on the kind of goods: for coal and ores, 55–100 km; for metals, 75–155 km; for scrap metal, peat, cement, and sugar beets, 95–190 km; for cereals and sugar, 90–200 km; and for textiles, over 200 km (Livyant, Tikhonyuk, and Erlich 1963: 80–81, after Tarski 1968: 220). Beyond those critical

TABLE 5.4

Dependence of Unit Cost of Transport on Distance of Transport in the USSR

(1 ton per 10 kilometers = 100)

	Distance in kilometers:								
	10	20	50	100	200	500	800	1000
Railroad	100	53.4	25.6	16.4	11.6	7.7	6.9	6.7
Inland waterways	100	50.8	21.1	11.1	6.4	3.4	2.7	2.4
Sea transport	100	50.2	20.6	10.8	5.8	2.9	2.1	1.9
Truck transport	100	97.8	96.5	96.0	95.8	95.7	95.6	95.6

Source: Tarski 1968: 220. See also Malek, Grzywacz, and Zymela 1973: 333.

TABLE 5.5

Dependence of Unit Cost of Transport on Distance of Transport in Poland in 1961

(1 ton per 10 kilometers = 100)

	Distance in kilometers:							
	10	20	50	110	200	500	600
Railroad	100	55.1	20.8	18.3	14.7	12.0	11.7
Trucks: 4 ton	100	77.5	64.2	59.2	57.3	56.0	55.8
8 ton and over	100	73.1	57.0	51.1	48.9	47.3	47.1

Source: Malek, Grzywacz, and Zymela 1973: 333.

distances, railroad transport becomes less costly than road transport, and below it road transport is cheaper than rail transport. This phenomenon of intermodal substitutability is discussed for the United States in Kneafsey (1975: 246–50).

The critical distance for passenger transport tends to be less definite than for freight transport. In Poland the normal bus tariff is lower than the normal railroad tariff for distances up to 30–45 kilometers, and it is approximately equal to the rail tariff up to 150 kilometers. Beyond that the railroad tariff is lower; it has a degression element incorporated into it, and the bus tariff is almost devoid of degression. The existence of many special reductions in ticket price, especially on the railroad, tends to complicate that relationship, but since railroad tariff reductions are much more common, their effect is to introduce a strong element of cost advantage to many users in favor of the railroad on short distances also (Malek, Grzywacz, and Zymela 1973: 365–66).

It appears, therefore, that the critical distance cannot be determined precisely just as in the case of the U.S. (Kneafsey 1975: 246–54) because costs vary for the same mode of transport depending on circumstances. Thus, in railroad transport, the unit costs increase rapidly with the decline in the volume of traffic for both freight and passenger transport, as shown in table 5.6. The quality of transport units (i.e., of railroad cars, trucks, etc.), the composition of trains, the organization of transport enterprises, the composition of freight — all these and other factors influence unit costs. For instance, in road transport in Poland, the unit costs differ depending on the transporting organization and differ as between years, as shown in table 5.7.

Despite these diverse tendencies and differentiation, and in order to obtain a picture of the average unit cost of different modes of transport, economists in Eastern Europe have calculated it for those modes. Table 5.8 shows the results of such calculations for the Soviet Union. The passenger cost of sea transport, as shown in this table, is increased by the cost of food and by higher standards of comfort than on other modes of transport. Particularly striking is the high cost of freight transport by road.

In Poland the average unit cost of transport is shown in table 5.9. The second line in this table does cover a part of the cost of road through the gasoline taxes imposed on the users of the roads, but it is felt by some economists in Eastern Europe that such coverage is inadequate, which explains the addition of the third line in the table. Costs of roadway maintenance on the railroad are included in the first line, but they cover only the so-called basic repairs, as the result of

TABLE 5.6

Unit Costs in Freight and Passenger Transport on Polish Railroad as a Function of the Volume of Traffic

(zlotys)

| | Cost of transport to the railroad per: | |
	passenger/kilometer	ton/kilometer
On main lines	.16	.17
On secondary lines	.70	.80

Source: Madeyski, Lissowska, and Marzec 1971: 111.

TABLE 5.7

Unit Costs in Polish Sectoral Truck Transport

Transport organization	Unit	Unit cost (zlotys)		Average distance of transport (km)	
		1968	1969	1968	1969
Construction and construction materials	t/km	2.27	2.17	11.4	12.9
Voyvodship cooperatives for rural transport	t/km	2.52	3.37	10.8	22.2
Enterprise for transport in domestic trade	tons	89.75	91.10	19.0	20.0

Source: Madeyski, Lissowska, and Marzec 1971: 112.

TABLE 5.8
Cost of Transport in the USSR in 1957
(rubles)

	Mode of transport:					
	Railroad	Sea	Inland waterways	Road	Air	Pipelines
1 ton/kilometer	.0316	.0228	.0276	.6966		.0132
1 passenger/kilometer	.060	.1731	.1098	.081	.30	—
1 conventional t/km[a]	.0348	.0248	.0313	..	..	—

a   sum of t/km and pass/km, where 1 t/km = 1 pass/km

Source: Khachaturov 1959: 158.

TABLE 5.9

Estimated Average Unit Cost and Marginal Absorption of Capital in Transport in Poland in 1964

(zlotys)

	Average cost per t/km	Marginal absorption of capital per t/km[b]
Railroad	.20	2.43
Road transport	1.48	..
Road transport (including cost of roadway)	1.88	4.54
Inland waterways	.30	.45
Pipeline	.04-.05[a]	.45

a   author's estimate   b   1965-70 estimates

Sources: Madeyski, Lissowska, and Marzec 1971: 114; Tarski 1968: 229; Malek, Grzywacz, and Zymela 1973: 116.

which the figure in the first line is an underestimation of full cost including prorated depreciation (cf. Madeyski, Lissowska, and Marzec 1971: 113).[1]

Table 5.9 also shows that on the average road transport required the largest outlay of capital per each additional unit of transport performance, while inland waterways and pipelines, devoted to bulk transport, required the least capital per additional ton-kilometer transported.

In increasing order of cost, the modes of transport are pipelines, sea transport, inland waterways, railroads, roads, and air transport. Inland waterways apparently may have, as in Poland, higher costs on the average than the railroad, but this result obviously depends on the mixes of products carried and connections served.

In comparison with Western intermodal cost ratios, and taking railroad unit costs as a base, relative costs of road transport, as shown in table 5.9, were very high in Poland (seven times higher than the railroad costs, compared to four and a half times higher in the West), as were the relative costs of waterways transport (50 percent higher than the railroad costs, compared to less than one-third of the railroad costs in the West). Relative costs of transport by pipeline were roughly comparable in Poland to those in the West, but they were possibly higher because in the West they varied from one-fourth to one-eighth of the railroad costs. In the West the cost of transport by air, not given for Poland, was 16.3 times higher than that by rail (Keller 1963: 53, based apparently on U.S. experience, where traffic exceeded 500,000 tons annually; Burke 1963: 81, based on 30–36 inch pipeline, with distances ranging from 50 to 1,600 miles; see also Owen 1964: 98, 107; Kneafsey 1975: 242).

Cost of Transport to Its Users:
The Transport Tariff

The economic cost of transport to society (the so-called factor cost) and to transport enterprises differs from the prices charged to its users, mainly because of the underestimation of depreciation allowances but also because of various subsidies, including subsidies for social consumption of which transport enterprises are the beneficiaries. Prices of transport services do not reflect their cost, therefore, and since the differences between the two are not proportional, the resultant prices do not inform transport users about the most economic alternatives from society's point of view. Herein lies the dilemma of planners: either to make prices reflect their own preferences and help direct users to those transport modes preferred by planners as part and parcel of transport planning (discussed in chapter 3), or to make prices reflect true social costs and lead to economically optimal use of transport services. The dilemma has been traditionally solved in favor of planners' preferences, but the recent ascendancy of intellectual inquiry in Eastern Europe has made this less the case (cf. Madeyski, Lissowska, and Morawski 1975a: 211; Steplowski 1975: 58–64). Even so, the basic dichotomy of prices in a planned economy persists in Eastern Europe: are they determined by planners, who choose the politically desirable proportions of transport services to be used, or are they determined by conditions of demand and supply? Do they lead both the users and the providers of transport services to the socially least-cost solution?

Within the priorities determined by planners (which are shown in the existing price system), users of transport can decide what mode of transport to use for what consignments. However, they are obliged to specify their choices a year in advance by entering into transport contracts (see chapter 3, section 5), which allows planners to make some short-run adjustments in the supply of transport services. The planners' own ideas about what transport should be like and how transport performances should be distributed among transport modes prompt them to make longer-run adjustments basically by means of investment policy. But these ideas may prove costy to the economy, just as Lazar Kaganovich's idea of primacy of steam power on Soviet railroads proved costly to Soviet transport in the 1950s (cf. Hunter 1968: 52).

The prices charged to users of transport are embodied in the transport tariff. Tariffs are usually determined for each transport mode separately, and only research analyses give the explicit relationships between tariffs for various transport modes. Our discussion of transport tariffs in Eastern Europe will concentrate on the example of East Germany, following the detailed description in the West German study by Horst Demmler (1967: 172–228).

Railroad tariff. The economic goal of the East German railway tariff introduced in 1958 is to encourage the user of road transport on short distances and rail transport on intermediate and long distances (cf. Kopitz and Kutta 1958: 16–18). The railroad tariff is divided into ten classes, the highest of which requires payment of 0.10 mark per ton/kilometer and the lowest of which is 0.01 mark.[2] The classes differentiate between goods according to their value and economic importance, and individual goods can be shifted between classes according to need.

The part of the freight charge determined by distance is calculated by multiplying the class charge by the number of gross tons of the consignment and by the tariff distance. The latter is the shortest distance using the given transport mode — in this case the railroad — between the point of shipment and the point of delivery (not the actual distance traveled); this allows the railroad to determine routes according to its own convenience (cf. Williams 1962: 35). (Such tariff distances are, incidentally, the ones reported in East European statistics of transport performance, and transport performance in Eastern Europe thus shows the theoretically shortest haulage of freight rather than the actual performance.) The weight factor in the calculation has a minimum floor of five tons and more, depending on the capacity of railroad cars used (Demmler 1967: 175–76); this discourages frivolous use of capacity. Where the load is unspecified, the freight car capacity is used to calculate the freight charge, which again tends to discourage wasteful use of capacity. The only exceptions to this rule are where low sidewalls of cars prevent full loading or where limitations of weight apply to the roadway used (Demmler 1967: 176; Kopitz and Kutta 1958: 41–42).

The second part of the freight charge consists of a payment per axle — equal to twenty marks per axle. This part does not change with distance or with the category of merchandise shipped. The purpose behind this payment is apparently to bring the railroad tariff nearer to the cost basis (cf. Demmler 1967: 176–77) and to introduce a fairly large fixed cost element for the user to discourage short-haul shipments (to the advantage of road traffic) by making them relatively expensive. As a result, freight charges per average kilometer tend to regress at a decreasing rate as with the normal average cost curve when a fixed cost curve is present. In addition, the axle charge introduces an element of quantity discount: the capacity of railroad cars increases more than in proportion to the number of axles, and cars with six axles require a payment for only four axles, which tends to produce substantial quantity discounts (of over 20 percent in an example cited by Demmler 1967: 178; however, eight-axle cars entail an axle charge for all eight axles, as stated by Kopitz and Kutta 1958: 40).

Reductions are made in the axle charge for full trains sent by one sender to one recipient and for consignments using twenty or more axles; both reductions increase with the increase in the number of axles involved. These reductions are given, among others, to military and Soviet transport (Kopitz and Kutta 1958: 34). The result of such reduction is to bring the tariff closer to the cost basis, since large consignments involve less handling cost per unit. The reductions are made smaller if no proper notification of intended consignment is given to the railroad (Kopitz and Kutta 1958: 63).

Even without this last discount element, however, the axle charge materially reduces the difference between charges levied for different classes of freight. While the basic class structure itself involves a ratio of 1:10 between the first and the tenth class, the axle charge decreases this difference: in an example involving twenty tons transported for a distance of 110 kilometers in a two-axle car, it was reduced to about 2-1/2:10 (Kopitz and Kutta 1958: 25–26; Demmler 1967: 179). Thus price discrimination is reduced in order to foster a policy of making short-distance railroad shipments relatively costly.

Express car shipments normally pay double freight charge, and when the freight car is hitched to a passenger train, there is a triple charge (Demmler 1967: 180). Special tariff calculations are made also in the case of broken shipments (one carload sent in the same direction to two different points), making them profitable to the sender (Demmler 1967: 180–82). There is also an incentive to combine smaller loads (less than carloads) into full carloads. Consignments of less than twenty kilograms weight are generally cheaper when sent by mail. In these ways, the railroad tariff tends to encourage utilization of economies of scale.

An evaluation of the East German railroad tariff brings out the following points:

1. Inadequate allowance is made for the reduction of unit costs in large-quantity shipments.

2. No allowance is made for the reduction in cost in shipments over main lines, as compared with secondary lines (as shown in table 5.5; cf. Demmler 1967: 213–14).

3. A relatively small degression of unit cost is allowed for large quantities of freight transported over longer distances; the opposite is true for smaller quantities of freight, which entails another departure from the cost-pricing principle.

4. On the whole, the part of the railroad tariff that is graded by distance is oriented toward costs (Demmler 1967: 205–06).

5. That part of the freight charge that is based on quantity of freight, i.e., the charge per axle, contains partly a random element; that is, the railroad is not obliged to provide freight cars of the most suitable capacity and kind (Demmler 1967: 212), although some tariff concessions may then be granted (Kopitz and Kutta 1958: 49–51).

6. The quantity-based part of the freight charge results in a relatively larger increase in the unit cost of low-tariff freight when the weight of that freight is reduced than is the case with high-tariff freight (Demmler 1967: 207). It also results in a larger relative increase in unit cost of freight transported over short distances when the weight is reduced than is the case with freight transported over longer distances (Demmler 1967: 208). Finally, it results in a substantial increase in unit freight charges for quantities less than twenty tons, especially for quantities less than ten tons (Demmler 1967: 210–11). In all these considerations, the East German railroad tariff departs from the cost-basis principle on which it professedly rests.

7. The division of freight into classes, each of which has a different rate per ton/kilometer, is a clear violation of the cost principle of pricing in transport. Such division exists neither in the USSR nor in Czechoslovakia (cf. Demmler 1967: 214–17), but it exists in Poland (Tarski 1967: 152, 166–68).

8. Even though consignments of less than one carload take up on the average some 26 percent of the available covered freight cars, they make up on the average only 4 percent of the weight carried in full-load consignments. At the same time, planners found it possible to plan only the aggregate amount of less-than-carload consignments, instead of planning its individual components. Consequently the tendency in East Germany is to discourage such consignments by means of higher prices. However, despite a raise in these prices in 1968, prices cover only a part of the costs of less-than-carload traffic. An earlier uneconomic attempt to compete with highway trucks in forwarding such smaller consignments has been abandoned. Thus a move, however incomplete, toward greater overall cost-price efficiency has been made (Demmler 1967: 217–21).

Road tariff. The economic goal of the East German road tariff, introduced together with the railroad tariff in 1958, is to use the price system to direct all long-distance consignments (with the exception of easily perishable goods) to the railroad. Instead of the earlier equivalence between railroad and road tariffs, the current road tariff has a fourfold division of goods transported by road into: (1) perishable goods, the shipment of which is by and large not more expensive than shipment by rail; (2) goods shipped to and from foreign countries, the tariff for which is subsidized to achieve a level lower than that on the railroad; (3) all other goods, the basic tariff for which is equal to the highest railroad tariff group (number 10) and consists of a constant and a variable element, the latter a function of transport distance. For distances over 100 kilometers, extra charges are imposed in order to discourage such shipments; (4) consignments that can be added to others, or consignments that are taken on return, or other otherwise empty, runs. Lower incentive tariff pertains to this category in order to help utilize the existing transport capacity (cf. Kopitz and Kutta 1958: 65–69).

The tariff distance used to calculate the freight charge in road transport is the same as used on the railroad except when the difference between road and rail distance is over 30 percent. The tariff weight is obtained by rounding actual weight up to the nearest 100 kilograms, and it has to be at least equal to 80 percent of the capacity of the truck and not less than five metric tons. An effort is made, obviously, to encourage economical use of truck capacity.

In the case of broken journeys, the sum of sectional distances constitutes the tariff distance, while the tariff weight is equal to the highest weight transported over any segment of the journey (Demmler 1967: 186–90).

The following observations can be made on the basis of an analysis of the East German road tariff:

1. The costs of transport by truck as compared with transport by rail are higher in intercity traffic, even for relatively short distances (i.e., a little over 100 kilometers).

2. The volume of freight transported by truck in intercity transport is insignificant compared to that transported by rail.

3. Departures from the cost-pricing principle in railroad transport make it difficult rationally to pursue that principle in highway transport, particularly in view of the quantitative importance of the railroad.

4. Consequently, the tariff for truck transport has become a tool of the planners, an extension of their administrative power, to direct intercity traffic to the mode they prefer. Intracity transport is, of course, substantially more efficient by truck and hence has been allowed to remain less costly for that mode of transport (Demmler 1967: 222–26).

As a result of these factors, the typical journey by truck in Eastern Europe is quite short. A 1962 survey in Poland found that 45.1 percent of the tonnage transported by truck traveled less than 5 kilometers, 19.2 percent traveled 5–10 kilometers, 22.5 percent traveled 11–30 kilometers, 6.2 percent traveled 31–50 kilometers, 4.6 percent traveled 51–100 kilometers, and 2.4 percent traveled more than 100 kilometers (Malek, Grzywacz, and Zymela 1973: 21, 178–81). Thus almost two-thirds of the tonnage trucked in Poland moved not more than 10 kilometers. Similarly, in passenger transport by bus, as many as 81 percent of the passengers traveled for a distance of up to 50 kilometers (Malek, Grzywacz, and Zymela 1973: 178). It may be added here, parenthetically, that passenger tariffs in Eastern Europe embody a higher margin of profit than do the freight tariffs and thus cost the passengers relatively more (Malek, Grzywacz, and Zymela 1973: 364).

Tariff for inland waterways. In place of an earlier tariff that was equal to the railroad tariff less 5 percent, a new tariff for inland waterways was introduced in East Germany in 1964; instead of following the principle of cost pricing, it took over the division of freight into the ten classes used by the railroad and added two more classes. The freight charge is calculated as the sum of a volume charge and a distance charge. The former shows a two-step differentiation between the kinds of freight, is imposed on the basis of tonnage, and is less than the axle charge on the railroad. The distance charge has a smaller range between classes than does the railroad tariff, yielding a 1:2-1/2 ratio instead of the 1:10 ratio on the railroad. The distance charge in inland waterway transport varies from equality with the railroad charge to one-half of it. Thus, basically, the tariff yields charges from slightly to substantially lower than those on the railroad. In contrast to the similarities between railroad and road transport, however, the tariff distance in inland waterway transport is different from that of the railroad; it represents the actual distance by water between the point of loading and the point of destination. Since transport by water may be longer, the result is to decrease the cost advantage of inland waterways.

However, one offsetting factor tends to preserve the price competitiveness of inland waterways. When the route is by necessity broken between railroad and waterway, i.e., when either the shipper or the receiver of the merchandise does not have direct access to inland waterways, the part of the distance covered by rail bears the same unit charge as does the waterborne part. Since the distance unit charge by water is lower, this decreases the aggregate freight charge to be paid (Demmler 1967: 190–94; cf. Kopitz and Kutta 1958: 70–74).

The following observations can be made on the basis of an analysis of East German tariff for inland waterways:

1. The tariff for inland waterways is still modeled on that for the railroad. As the latter departs from the principle of cost pricing, the former is similarly affected.

2. A further distortion is introduced by departures of the cost of inland waterway transport from those of the railroad.

3. A third disadvantage of the existing tariff is its obliviousness to cost differences between various water transport links owing to depth of water, differences in the number and size of locks, and differences between the barges used.

4. The inland waterways tariff is therefore not adequately related to cost (Gumpel 1967: 226–28).

The character of the transport tariffs in Eastern Europe and their flagrant violations of the cost principle have led one West German writer, Werner Gumpel (1967), to leave this aspect of transport policy completely out of his study on East European transport; the implied reason is that the tariff is only an extension of the administrative direction exercised by the planners (cf. Gumpel 1963: 102–14). Therefore, a mere discussion of planners' preferences (see chapter 3) may suffice to show how traffic is directed. While this is not in our opinion a correct view, it is indicative of the secondary and subservient importance accorded to transport pricing in Eastern Europe.[3] In fact, until 1960 (in Yugoslavia until 1952) "transport costs were often omitted from calculations because equalized pricing for the whole national product market encouraged decision-makers to believe that transport costs were inconsequential." (Hamilton 1972: 196) One of the results of the planners' disregard of transport costs was to encourage arbitrary location choices. Another was that social costs of transport tended to rise above the level that was necessary. According to an East European opinion, the most effective tariff systems, those that guide users toward optimal use of capacity, are found in Hungary, Bulgaria, and the USSR (Podwysocki 1976a: 21).

Abstracting from the economic importance or unimportance of the transport tariff, one has to observe that its contradictory character is in part a direct consequence of the central planning system. The transport tariff, as it is, is important to guide the users of transport facilities to the Pareto optimum and leaves the economy in a suboptimal position from which the economy could move to a better position, one characterized by a more economical utilization of existing resources. Consequently, the transport tariff, while serving as a guidance mechanism, does not fulfill its role of bringing different markets into the most efficient equilibrium. The East European transport systems (as shown in the example of East Germany) could have functioned better than they did. This remark does not detract, obviously, from the substantial achievements in transport (see chapter 4), but it indicates that those achievements could have been made at a lower cost to the societies of Eastern Europe. The social costs of different transport modes are not adequately reflected in their prices; the transport tariffs and the use of those modes tend, therefore, to be directed by considerations other than minimization of social cost. Those considerations may be ultimately valid from a political or developmental point of view, but they run contrary to considerations of static efficiency in the economy, i.e., to considerations of the optimal use of currently available resources. Thus, even though the tariff systems of Eastern Europe may theoretically help meet some political aims or may speed up the development process, this is done at a higher cost than would have been necessary if resources had been used optimally.

A more fundamental question may also be asked, namely, whether any transport price system, however rational in and of itself it seems, will direct the user of transport to the socially least-cost combination of services if any financial losses of the enterprise that uses the transport facilities are covered by the state and if any profits accumulated by the enterprise go largely to the state. In such a system, which by and large still obtains in Eastern Europe, the financial incentives exerted upon the transport-using enterprises by the price system are considerably weakened. The role of the price system in transport may then be impaired substantially, making it even less important than it otherwise could have been.

Finally, the role of prices, or tariffs, in changing the demand for transport should be noted. Operation of transport at full capacity, as is prevalent in Eastern Europe, with demand barely satisfied and dependent mostly on the growth of the economies in question, makes price considerations insignificant in evaluating the reasons for changes in demand. Consequently, except for the case of the air transport in Eastern Europe, price elasticity of demand does not seem to be a concept that can be applied fruitfully to contemporary transport in Eastern Europe.

Irrational Transport and Its Costs

Greater cost consciousness in Eastern Europe has stimulated inquiries into the problem of unnecessary transport and its attendant costs. Of all possible unnecessary transport, the concept of irrational transport has been evolved; it is defined as transport that causes the spatial, chronological, or economic length of the journey to be greater than the minimum for no good economic reason (Tarski 1967: 286–87), or as transport that could be wholly or partially avoided without damage to the fulfillment of production tasks or to the satisfaction of social and economic needs (Blotko 1972: 5). Irrational transport may be caused by flaws in the tariff system discussed above, but it may also be caused by faulty locational policy, a faulty administrative incentive system, or bad organization of transport resulting in unnecessary empty runs (cf. Malek, Grzywacz, and Zymela 1973: 93–96).

Soviet estimates put irrational transport at 5–8 percent of all transport, while estimates for Poland vary from 3 percent (which apparently excludes irrational transport caused by wrong locational policy) to 20 percent (Tarski 1967: 287–88; cf. Malek, Grzywacz, and Zymela 1973: 31–32). Irrational transport may be caused by the use of a mode of transport that is more costly than necessary, and our analysis of the East German transport tariff leads to the conclusion that such may often be the case. Irrational transport may also be caused by absence of adequate direct transport links, as in a Polish example, where lack of hard surface on a route link of only twelve kilometers necessitated road transport of sugar beets over fifty-six kilometers, thus indicating the irrational transport of a substantial quantity of bulky sugar beets over forty-four kilometers (Tarski 1967: 299).

Under irrational transport, one may include also the difference between actual distance covered and the tariff distance. On Polish railroads, the percentage relation between those two distances was 104.6 percent in 1961, indicating the existence of some irrational transport and some potential savings (Tarski 1967: 300), although some such difference exists in response to the economic needs of forming trainloads from individual freight cars, some of which may in consequence travel longer than the shortest distance between the points of origin and destination.

There are also indications that some widely distributed goods participate in an unduly large proportion in interregional trade and movement of freight instead of being largely locally produced and locally used. A calculation made for Poland for 1965 showed that 71.4 percent of railroad shipments of stones and rocks were interregional (in the narrow sense of voyvodships), 44.7 percent of sand and gravel, 48.2 percent of bricks, 74.6 percent of cement, 66.8 percent of chemicals, 62.4 percent of potatoes, and 57.6 percent of wood and wood products. Out of all railroad shipments in 1965, 67.2 percent were interregional (which is a substantial proportion, even taken into account that the figure concerns only rail shipments of standard gauge [Tarski 1967: 305–06]). Truly local shipments are made by trucks to the extent that 95.9 percent of the tonnage shipped by truck in Poland in 1962 was in intraregional (i.e., intra-voyvodship) transport; almost two-thirds of the tonnage trucked moved not more than ten kilometers (Malek, Grzywacz, and Zymela 1973: 21). Even so, in 1974, Polish Railways moved 45 million tons of freight over distances of fifty kilometers or less (RFER: SR, July 18, 1975: 4).

Irrational transport on the railroad was recently criticized by a Polish economic commentator in an ideological weekly; he ascribed such transport to its users who do not take trouble to order their supplies from the nearest source. Thus rocks, gravel, and sand — found as they are almost everywhere — are carried by rail for an average distance of over 200 kilometers, and are shipped in large quantities — over 44 million tons annually. Although cement plants are widely distributed, railways carry 12 million tons of cement for an average distance of over 300 kilometers. Instances of cross-trips of cement can be found. Other goods are similarly irrationally transported.

According to Polish estimates, every fifth railroad freight car travels unnecessarily. Lack of adequate incentives to limit the use of transport services contributes to irrational transport. For instance, one Polish enterprise in Olsztyn, whenever it found it difficult to unload a car, customarily sent it back to the sender in order to receive it again after several days, at which time unloading might be more convenient. In this wasteful way, the enterprise in question avoided penalty payments (demurrage) for keeping freight cars at the dock above the limit allowed (ZG 1976, no. 9: 16).

Some administrative directives actually cause irrational transport, such as those that forbid transport by rail over distances less than 50, 80, or 100 km as the case may be. As a result, goods are sometimes still transported by rail instead of by truck, but they are transported over longer than the minimum indicated distances and consequently are not ordered from the closest supplier (Zbierajewski 1976: 10).

Two additional causes of irrational transport are probably not included in the East European estimates of unnecessary transport costs. One of them is connected with loading and transloading operations, in which the East European tardiness in introducing containerization and modern loading equipment (in Poland only about 30 percent of transloading is mechanized [Brdulak and Fronczak 1976: 10]) undoubtedly increases the costs of transport over and above their achievable minimum under present-day technology. The second cause of irrational transport is the partly autarkic policy of the communist countries in international trade — which may have the net effect of actually reducing transport and which thus may put its economic costs beyond the sphere of transport and into the sphere of general sub-optimization of the economic system — and partly an inability of those countries to direct their international trade clearly according to the principle of comparative advantage. In either case, there is an opportunity cost measured in terms of foregone economic opportunities. Some transport that would have benefited the economy does not take place; some other transport that has less beneficial results undoubtedly takes its place. The difference between the two is the cost of irrational transport — measured in terms of economic opportunity cost, i.e., the cost of a more desirable, but foregone, opportunity. The costs of such foregone opportunities are actually broader than the costs of irrational transport, but they also involve an element of transport costs. By and large, they may be more properly discussed in the following chapter as part of international transport in Eastern Europe.

Irrational crosshauling of freight in interregional flows exists also in the Soviet Union. There the problem of Union ministries supplying their own enterprises in other republics despite the existence of local sources of supply is apparently a continuing contributory factor. This situation persists in the Soviet Union since the only planning of inter-regional flows is done by the ministries themselves, and no central balancing of interrepublican flows is carried on (cf. Gillula 1975; Tolstov 1969: 8).

One of the results of irrational transport is to keep the ratio of the volume of freight to the volume of production unnecessarily high, thus inflating the cost of production of a given amount of goods. Efforts to reduce that ratio started in Poland even in the 1950s (Pawlak 1962), but even so inefficiencies are constantly being brought to light. For instance, it was discovered recently that just one Polish enterprise, Centrozlom, unnecessarily transports 3–4 million tons of scrap iron every year (ZG 1976, no. 17: 16). It has been estimated that, partly as the result of such practices, while total physical production in Poland in 1973 was about 500 million tons of goods, the amount of freight transported by all modes of transport was at the same time 1.8 billion tons. Thus on the average each ton was transported almost four times in the process of production (Szeliga 1975: 4). Consequently, it may be proper to make a distinction between high transport performance in the communist countries of Eastern Europe and rational transport performance.

Just as in other countries — for instance, in Great Britain in the

Beeching Plan of 1961 (Aldcroft 1968: 185–200; Thompson and Hunter 1973: 135–40; Pearson 1964: 101–10) — the East European countries are discovering that some railroad lines carry freight at a cost that warrants their being closed down. For instance, in Poland it was calculated that if the average cost of transport per ton/kilometer equals 100, then that cost is 55 on main lines, 109 on primary lines, 186 on secondary lines, and 590 on local lines — or over ten times the cost per ton/kilometer on main lines (Zbierajewski 1976: 10). Some consolidation of railway lines may, consequently, be expected in the future.

In short, appreciable waste of resources exists in East European transport but is not reflected in the statistics on the transport performance of that region. That waste effectively reduces the benefit obtained from a given volume of actual transport performance below what it would have been had no irrational transport taken place.

VI

International Aspects of Transport in Eastern Europe

When transport moves goods and people across national borders, it becomes an element of international trade and exchange and serves to tie countries together economically, militarily, and culturally. The more developed the transport connections between countries are, the lower the cost and greater the opportunity to exchange goods. Since international trade is in many respects beneficial to countries taking part in it, transport itself may be regarded as beneficial. Briefly, while transport costs by themselves decrease the area of comparative advantage and thus tend to limit trade, efficient and developing transport tends to decrease such costs and to expand the area of trading according to the principle of comparative advantage. Increased efficiency and reduced cost of transportation tend also to improve the terms of trade (Lewis 1963: 115). Transport provides strategic links between countries that are much more efficient and stronger now than they ever were. Transport brings countries closer together through tourism and an opportunity to get to know one another. It also brings them closer together through the realization that benefits from trade are mutual and that economic interdependence is a consequence. An important reason for the establishment of the (West) European Common Market was the desire to tie Germany economically to the other members of the Common Market so as to make, by virtue of that interdependence, a new European war impossible. Thus, paradoxically, transport can serve both war and peace.

Transport serves also to establish cultural exchange and thus to promote international development and international understanding. Even though it is, on the face of it, a passive vehicle of international exchange, transport influences it simply by being available, by lowering the cost of such exchange, and by compelling countries to cooperate in the planning and management of transport on the operative as well as on the policy level.

The international aspects of transport in Eastern Europe can be discussed in three separate settings: cooperation in transport within Comecon; cooperation within Comecon in making of common transport investments, in standardizing of equipment, and the like; and cooperation with the rest of the world.

Cooperation in Transport Within Comecon

Transport costs are a rather small proportion of the value of goods exchanged in foreign trade within Comecon. Table 6.1 shows that share by main commodity groups. Even such small relative costs are important, however, to the territorial extension of markets. In order to reduce costs and assure a steady flow of goods among the East European countries, transport must be coordinated. Immediately after World War II, such coordination was administered by the Soviet Union in the interest of its army and on behalf of the reparations administration. Later, coordination seems to have been established on a case-by-case basis. Comecon was established in 1949, but its impact on transport was institutionalized as late as 1957, when a working team for transportation was set up. In June 1958, the team was reorganized into a standing commission (Gumpel 1967: 73–79; see below, point [15]; Gumpel 1963: 13–20). As late as 1954, an expert on transport in East Europe observed that while transport planning formed part of the overall national plans in Eastern Europe, there was no direct evidence of a common transport plan. Individual countries cooperated closely in matters concerned with transport and presented a common pattern of organization in transport (Rudzki 1954a: 3).

The pattern of organization of transport involves its distribution as between different modes of transport. Table 6.2 shows such distribution for 1960 and 1965 and the changes that took place between those years. It is apparent that the substantial relative decline in the importance of railroads was caused at that time mainly by the start of shipments of oil from the Soviet Union through the new "Friendship" pipeline, which was opened in 1964 and subsequently extended. To a lesser extent, it was due to a relative increase in the importance of sea transport and, to a much lesser extent, inland waterway and road transport. These tendencies were expected to continue. Nevertheless, railroads still carry most of the foreign trade between the Comecon countries.

Coordination of transport in Eastern Europe was made easier right after World War II because the area was occupied by Soviet troops, that is, by a single unifying force. Since by far the most important mode of transport was the railroad, the Russian broad gauge was

TABLE 6.1

The Share of Transportation Costs in the Value of Goods Exchanged in Foreign Trade Within Comecon

(calculated in foreign exchange rubles; percentages)

Construction materials	23.8
Fuels, mineral raw materials, metals	19.4
Raw materials for foodstuffs	8.9
Chemical products, fertilizers, rubber	6.4
Raw materials of vegetable and animal origin (except food)	4.3
Foodstuffs	2.6
Machinery and equipment	.9
Industrial consumer goods	.4
Average for all goods	7.6

Source: Barkovskii and Gorizontov 1965: 68.

TABLE 6.2

Share of Different Modes of Transport in the Trade Between Comecon Countries

(percentages based on tons of the volume of freight)

	1960	1965	Change in percentage points
Railroad	87.9	72.6	-15.3
Sea transport	7.5	10.5	3.0
Inland waterways	4.5	4.7	.2
Road motor transport	.1	.2	.1
Pipelines	—	12.0	12.0

Source: Tarski 1968: 396.

introduced into Eastern Europe by the Soviet armies. A 1945 agreement between Poland and the Soviet Union left the line from the Soviet border through Przemyśl-Kraków-Katowice to Wrocław as broad gauge, with the Soviet Union providing the rolling stock and receiving a rental payment for it (Jezierski 1971: 51). The broad gauge was almost wholly converted back to standard gauge by 1947 (Rudzki 1954a: 21), except for the subsequently constructed Cop-Kosice line in Czechoslovakia (Tarski 1968: 398). Soviet armies were careful to keep control over their main supply routes. The Soviet peace treaties with Hungary and Romania allowed Soviet troops to remain in those countries for the avowed purpose of guarding transportation lines between the Soviet Union and Austria, where Soviet occupation troops were stationed. Later, the signing of the Warsaw Pact (May 14, 1955) permitted stationing of these troops in Romania and Hungary even after the Soviet troops left Austria (Korbonski 1969: 10, 23).

Coordination of transport in the early postwar years was based on formal intergovernmental agreements between individual countries (bilateral) or blocs of countries (multilateral). Several cooperation agreements were signed for transport in the early postwar period:

1. Hungarian-Polish trade agreement of November 4, 1948, contained a Polish proposal for use of the Polish port of Szczecin by Hungary.

2. Polish-Romanian Economic Convention of September 10, 1948, involved mutual cooperation in the transport of each country's exports.

3. Polish-Czechoslovak transportation agreement of July 4, 1947, coordinated transit passage through both countries and created a Polish-Czechoslovak Transportation Commission whose task was to coordinate and maximize common transport. A particularly valuable part of that agreement dealt with Czechoslovakia's use of the port of Szczecin.

4. Two East European and Soviet conventions signed in November 1951 in Warsaw regulated passenger and express parcel traffic and freight traffic, respectively (cf. Rudzki 1954a: 15-19); the latter was called International Freight Transport (Tarski 1968: 398).

Later a more organized cooperative effort emerged within Comecon:

5. Since 1954 transport has been regulated by two updated treaties: the Agreement on International Freight Transport and the Agreement on International Passenger Transport. The agreements do not en-

visage direct, unbroken international railroad tariffs (thus penalizing international traffic by breaking the usual regression of tariff rates with distance) but for transport in transit provide tariffs other than those used domestically (thus offsetting part of the penalty inherent in breaking of transport distances). A uniform transit tariff was introduced, one that does not include costs of origin and destination operations, in order to compensate for the frontier-caused break in the regression of the tariff with regard to the length of journey (Tarski 1968: 398). The cost of rail transport to or from the Soviet Union is raised by the necessity to convert from or to the broad gauge. Western European frontier arrangements seem to be more advanced (Bayliss 1965: 148–54).

6. Since 1957 general problems of railroad transport have been handled by the Organization for Collaboration of Railroads — the governing body of which is a Council of Ministers scheduled to meet annually. The administrative committee of the Organization has its seat in Warsaw. Different commissions handle individual fields of international cooperation.

The Organization for Collaboration of Railroads is concerned with economic and technical problems of transport by rail, coordination of plans for transport and for technical development of railroad, and exchange of experiences. Coordination of transport plans includes amounts transported, rational distribution of freight, and provision of freight cars. Other decisions concern raising of efficiency in international passenger transport, coordination of timetables, and the uniform international passenger tariff that has been in operation since 1963. Work has been done on making the nomenclature of consignments more uniform, on introducing uniformity in the calculation of quantitative and qualitative indicators of railroad performance, in calculating costs, and in calculating aggregate costs when freight is transported over the territory of more than one country. The Organization for Collaboration of Railroads cooperates closely with the International Union of Railroads, which brings together railroads of 37 countries and is concerned with European railroad transport, and with the Comecon Transport Commission (Tarski 1968: 399).

7. Since 1963, the Comecon countries have established a Common Pool of Freight Cars to offset shortages of transport capacity through better utilization of existing equipment and through a reduction in the movement of empty wagons. The Office of Exploitation of the Common Pool of Freight Cars is in Prague. Its Council meets periodically. The goal of the pool is to decrease empty runs of cars in international

traffic, to increase efficiency at border stations, and to make better use of the capacity of existing railroad lines (cf. Rolow 1975: 13). It has been calculated that in East Germany's rail movement with Poland and Czechoslovakia, empty runs of cars decreased by about 10 percent in only the three first years after the pool was set up (Tarski 1968: 400–401).

Jozef Wilczynski praised the success of the Common Pool: the scheme drastically reduced empty international runs, improved the quality of cars used in international transport, and raised their availability from 93,000 in 1964 to 230,000 in 1972. There is no charge to member countries for the use of the Pool cars, but fines are imposed for their use above the quota contributed by a member country (Wilczynski 1974: 228–29). A recent East European review of the activity of the Common Pool of Freight Cars indicated good performance and increasing activity of the Pool (Szukiel and Szymaniuk 1975: 3–5; Pogonowska-Szuszkiewicz 1976: 51).

Cooperation in container handling has begun. The principles on which the Comecon container transport system is based were laid down on December 3, 1971, when an agreement on a uniform container transport system was concluded among Comecon members. The contracting parties agreed on a program for introducing a uniform container transport system. The program covered the following points: (1) container routes between the Comecon countries, including deadlines for making them operational; (2) the manner in which these routes are to be linked with those of third countries; (3) a list of terminals to be opened by individual Comecon countries, and the deadlines for doing so; (4) necessary organizational, commercial, and legal measures. It was also agreed that the container transport system would be operated in all contracting states by a single enterprise, which would also coordinate the system's operations on the territories of the contracting states.

In 1971 a regular weekly run of container trains was inaugurated between Decin in Czechoslovakia and Berlin-Rostock in East Germany. In 1973 a regular rail container service was opened up between Kosice in eastern Czechoslovakia and the Soviet Union, initially on a twice-a-month basis (*RFER*, Czechoslovakia, March 13, 1974: 13). Also in 1973, a Berlin-Warsaw container railroad route was inaugurated, and preparations were later made for a more comprehensive route that was to link Sofia via Bucharest, Budapest, Bratislava, Prague, and Berlin with the East German port of Rostock. Accompanying those preparations were also preparations for opening up

East European container routes by road (Kolaczkowski 1974: 14–15).

Later, a uniform system for container use and transport was approved by the Permanent Transport Commission of Comecon (Bras 1975: 13–17), with container capacity (basically ten, twenty, and thirty tons) and sizes agreed upon by the International Standards Organization. The main type of container is to be the twenty-ton container, but containers with capacity of two and a half, five, and forty tons were also allowed (Brdulak and Fronczak 1976: 10).

The exchange of containers within Comecon started as early as 1965. In 1973 130,000 containers were exchanged, and in 1975 between 75 and 85 million tons of freight were moved within Comecon. By early 1976 there were 1,400 container handling points in Comecon, and there were plans for a considerable expansion in the use of containers (Brdulak and Fronczak 1976: 10). Figure 6.1 shows a map of the East European container routes. East European planners expect that by 1980 the East European container transport system will be fully developed (Gesiarz 1974: 48; see also 47–63).

8. Most of the trade within Comecon is in bulky raw materials that are not usually transported by road. Hence the relative importance of road transport in the international trade within Comecon is small; yet it deserves a separate section for motor transport within the Permanent Transport Commission of Comecon (described in point 15 below). Among others, this section deals with the problems of organization of motor transport, with legal and current management problems of freight and passenger transport, and with international tariffs (Tarski 1968: 405–06).

9. As has been pointed out in chapter 2, East European geography has made inland waterways important as transport links within, as well as between, countries. Some links are still missing, notably the perennially postponed canal between the Oder and Danube rivers. The Comecon countries have made cooperative agreements on inland waterways in order to increase the efficiency of use of barges, ships, and ports, and to unify tariffs. An agreement concluded in Sofia concerned broken transport by water (on the Danube) and by rail (Tarski 1968: 404–05).

10. The third most important mode of transport among Comecon countries, after railroad and pipelines, is sea transport. Within Comecon the largest volume of shipping services for other member countries is rendered by Poland. In order to make better use of shipping tonnage, joint services have been established in several directions to the outside world, e.g., between East Germany and Poland on the one

FIGURE 6.1
East European Container Routes

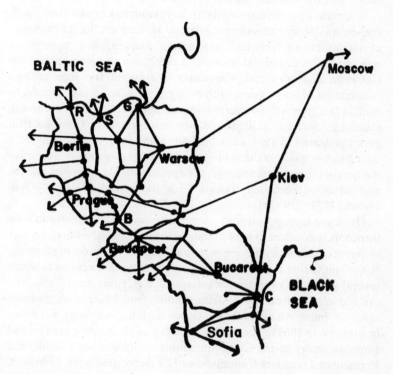

B Bratislava
C Constanta
G Gdansk
R Rostock
S Szczecin

Source: adapted from Brdulak and Fronczak 1976: 10.

hand, and both East and West Africa on the other; the "Baltamerica" line between the USSR and Poland, and South America. In addition, cooperation within Comecon extends to other problems of transport, such as cooperation between shipping lines, unification of shipping lines, unification of shipping documentation (a model charter, called "Novyi 1964," has been worked out), provision of ships with needed spare parts, problems of freights, and transit rights to the ports in the Baltic and the Danube regions (Tarski 1968: 401–02).

Wilczynski summed up the latest developments in maritime cooperation by stressing existence of bilateral agreements "on the exchange of scientific and technical information and on joint research on selected topics of mutual interest." In 1970 ten shipping lines of the Comecon countries and Yugoslavia established the International Association of Shipowners, with its head office in Gdynia, in order to protect their interests in international shipping and to solve technical, economic, operational, legal and other problems. The Complex Program, proposed in 1971, embodied a broader form of cooperation by laying down "tasks in the field of shipbuilding, ship repairs, the introduction of the latest technology, the application of computers and the unification of container transport for the period 1971–85." (Wilczynski 1974: 239, 241)

11. A separate problem of cooperation within the Comecon's sea transport is an effort to exploit monopsonistic power *vis-à-vis* foreign shipping chartered by its members so as to lower the prices of shipping. It was found that there are some thirty shipping connections in which several Comecon countries are interested, e.g., sugar from Cuba, iron ore and apatites from West Africa, apatites from Murmansk, and iron ore from India. An office for the Coordination of Shipping was set up in Moscow in 1963 to coordinate the work of all shipping brokers and shipping fitters of the Comecon countries. This office is under the Permanent Transport Commission of Comecon (see point 15 below). Its functions are threefold: operative, informational, and coordination of planning. In the operative functions, the principle of exclusiveness was adopted wherever possible: one single broker would deal with all the freight of member countries going in a specified direction and would then charter shipping space for it. In this way, a strong monopsonistic element has been created with strong pressure on shippers to lower their charges when presented with the all-or-nothing clause by the unified East European customers. Additionally, the Office for the Coordination of Shipping works toward unification of the forms of documents, as in the model charter, "Novyi 1964."

The informational function of the office is to pass on to other member countries information on changes in charges of shipping lines and shipping conferences and information on expected future tendencies in sea transport. The coordinating function consists in trying through preparation of annual plans to make better use of the existing shipping tonnage of the Comecon countries on both a bilateral and a multilateral basis (Tarski 1968: 402-04). The OECD seems concerned about Soviet maritime competition (OECD 1976: 11-13).

12. Cooperation in air transport began in 1957, when the airlines of Poland, East Germany, Czechoslovakia, Hungary, Romania, and Bulgaria entered into an agreement in Budapest under the name of the Pool of Six, the role of which was cooperation rather than pooling of resources. In 1962 a new Section of Air Transport was created in the Permanent Transport Commission; it replaced a working group that heretofore was supposed to perform the task of coordination. In 1965 a new agreement, involving the Soviet Union and Mongolia as well, was signed in Berlin replacing former agreements. Under the new agreement, cooperation in air transport includes mutual agency representation, mutual servicing of aircraft, technical and organizational aid, mutual information, legal and organizational matters, and especially cooperation in international flights with respect to scheduling and capacity. Pools are used only on some lines and under special agreements (Tarski 1968: 406). In 1975 the Soviet Union proposed the establishment of a Permanent Standing Commission on Commercial Air Transport in the Air Transport Section of the Comecon (Trend 1975: 5).

13. A common oil pipeline "Friendship," constructed with two main branches, the first of which, the southern branch, was completed in 1962, while the second, to Poland, was completed in 1963 and subsequently extended (cf. Bozyk 1974: 120-21), makes it necessary for countries on whose territory the pipeline is located to cooperate, viz., the USSR, Poland, Czechoslovakia, Hungary, and East Germany. A similar need will arise upon the completion of the gas pipeline from the Soviet Union to Eastern Europe; it is currently under construction.

Another pipeline is planned as an extension of the Rijeka (Yugoslavia)-Vienna pipeline, which is to be constructed from Vienna through Czechoslovakia to Poland (Tarski 1975: 84). The first phase of the Rijeka-Vienna pipeline will go through Hungary and Czechoslovakia and will be completed in 1978 (Antic 1975a: 2). A shorter gas pipeline has been completed between the Ukraine and Bulgaria

(RFER: Bulgaria, Sept. 6, 1974). A large new gas pipeline is being built, with completion date scheduled for 1978, from Orenburg (east of the Volga river) to Eastern Europe and from there with proposed extensions to Western Europe. Seven Comecon countries participate in the project, namely, the Soviet Union, Poland, East Germany, Czechoslovakia, Hungary, Romania, and Bulgaria (Trend 1975b; Heneghan 1975: 25). Figure 6.2 shows the giant Soviet network of gas pipelines, of which the Orenburg pipeline will be a part.

14. In 1963 transmission lines for electric power were brought under a unified system for Poland, East Germany, Czechoslovakia, Hungary, and Bulgaria. In 1964 the USSR and Romania were included. The system, under the name "Peace," has its Central Disposition in Prague.

East European cooperation in transmission of electricity resulted in construction of power lines to link adjoining regions of different Comecon countries in order to reduce line loss in transmission, to take advantage of different peak hours, and to utilize generating capacity more economically. In 1970 there were fifteen such link lines between seven European members of Comecon, resulting in the case of Poland in a decrease of needed reserve capacity from 8–12 to 3 percent of total capacity. The "Peace" grid connected by early 1970s power stations with a combined capacity of 60,000 MW. It reduced the likelihood of massive power failures and increased the possibility of an East-West European energy cooperation (Wilczynski 1974: 64–65; cf. RFER: Hungary, March 19, 1974: 2–3). In 1975 Yugoslavia and Bulgaria agreed upon construction of a common electric power grid between southern Yugoslavia and Bulgaria (Antic 1974c: 4).

15. Reference has already been made to the Permanent Transport Commission of Comecon. Created in 1958 with its headquarters in Warsaw, it replaced the working groups that functioned earlier. It has five sections: planning and economic, railroad, water, highway, and air. The task of the sections is to prepare materials for the Commission. In 1975 the sections of the Permanent Transport Commission were regrouped as follows: coordination of long-range economic plans and complex transport problems, railroad transportation, water, motor vehicle transportation and highways, and container transportation. The old fifth section on air transport was converted into a Permanent Commission on Civil Aviation (Trend 1975a: 13, 17; see also Kaser 1967: 260, 82–83).

The functions of the Permanent Transport Commission are: (1) coordination of multi-year and long-range plans of transport; (2) or-

FIGURE 6.2

The Comecon Transcontinental Natural Gas Pipeline Network

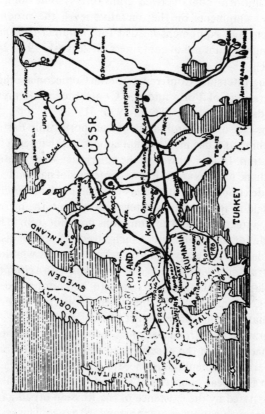

Source: Trend 1975b: 3, adapted from *Vneshnaya Torgovlya*, December 1973.

ganization of international freight and passenger transport; (3) rational utilization of the means of transport; (4) the most effective utilization of investments in the transport sector; (5) coordination of research and development; and (6) unification of norms and parameters in the field of transport (Tarski 1968: 407–09).

The Permanent Transport Commission recently began to deal with cooperation in the field of containers. A special Working Group for Containerization has been created within the Commission to introduce a uniform containerized transport system, joint planning of container shipments on the operative level, the production of the machinery and equipment needed for container transport and handling, and the joint use of containers (Wilczynski 1974: 249–50; Trend 1975: 11).

Among Interstate Conferences of the Comecon are the Conference on Operations of Ports and the Conference of Representatives of Railroads and Customs (Trend 1975: 7).

On the face of it, coordination of transport within Eastern Europe is far-reaching and has institutional conditions that seem to favor close cooperation. In fact, however, the emergence — or continuance — of nationalistic feelings and the vested interests of national planners seem to impede cooperation. It is likely that there will be closer cooperation in the field of transport in Eastern Europe, but the mere existence of treaties, agreements, and commissions does not seem to be a sufficient condition for the fulfillment of such a trend. A note of disappointment was evident in the assessment by a Polish expert who found integration of transport within Comecon by assumption a comprehensive one since plans for all transport were to be coordinated. In practice, however, the majority of achievements concern cooperation among individual branches of transport (Tarski 1968: 332).

Integration of railroad transport encounters an additional difficulty in connection with the necessary conversion of cars[1] or, more commonly, transshipment to another freight car at the Soviet border with the East European countries of Poland, Hungary, and Romania. This is necessitated by the existence of the Russian broad gauge while the East European countries use the standard gauge. This results in bottlenecks at the border, and the delays are compounded by an uneven flow of shipments and by an apparent Soviet unwillingness to cooperate (RFER: Hungary, July 30, 1975: 3–4).

The degree of participation by the East European countries in international transport can be measured in terms of the two modes used predominantly for international shipments, namely, ocean shipping and air transport. Table 6.3 shows the tonnage of seagoing vessels owned by the East European countries and the USSR and the turnover in their ports. Among the East European countries, Poland is the largest maritime nation followed by Yugoslavia and East Germany. Poland is also by far the dominant participant in freight turnover through ports, partly because it handles much of Czechoslovakia's transit trade. Ship movement in Eastern Europe is quite small when compared with West European ship movement, and the Polish merchant marine transports only about 0.7 percent of world freight (Tarski 1975: 99–100). Czechoslovakia and Hungary, being landlocked, do not have sea transport through their own ports.

Table 6.4 shows the 1971 international air transport of the East European countries, with the Soviet Union added for comparative purposes. In contrast to sea traffic (table 6.3), Poland finds itself in the last place with respect to aggregate air freight transport performance, although it is second only to East Germany in intra-Comecon air freight. Similarly, in aggregate international passenger transport performance, Czechoslovakia, Romania, East Germany, and Bulgaria had precedence over Poland, and only Hungary showed a slightly lower performance. In intra-Comecon passenger air transport performance, Poland found itself again in next-to-last place, with Romania in last place and East Germany in first place. Poland's relatively poor performance is probably explained by its relatively high accessibility from the West and the East by sea, rail, and road transport. In 1971 Poland accounted for less than 0.1 percent of world air transport performance (Tarski 1975: 100).

The last two columns of table 6.4, which the present author calculated from the preceding four columns, show the relative dependence of the East European countries on air transport in terms of its performance within Comecon. Not surprisingly, and for several reasons (e.g., industrial leadership within Eastern Europe, politics, dependence on the Soviet Union), East Germany shows the highest such dependence, with Poland, Czechoslovakia, and Bulgaria in tow. The lowest relative dependence on freight and passenger air transport performance within Comecon is shown by the political maverick of Eastern Europe, Romania. Political factors probably play a dominant role in limiting the share of East European international transport in the world transport.

The development of transport in Eastern Europe is hampered by the autarkic tendencies of all countries in that region. A foremost British expert on Comecon made in 1967 an observation that is still eminently

TABLE 6.3
Tonnage of Ships and Turnover in Ports in Eastern Europe

	Seagoing ships (thousand BRT)[a]	Turnover in ports (thousand tons)[b]	Ship movement in ports (million NRT) incoming[c]	outgoing[c]
USSR	18,176	127,655[cd]	...	...
Poland	2,292	51,848[ef]	8.3	13.1
East Germany	1,224	16,320	...	...
Czechoslovakia	116	—	—	—
Hungary	...	—	—	—
Romania	611	9,111[g]	...	...
Bulgaria	865	17,025[c]	15.0	...
Yugoslavia	1,224	18,864	9.3	5.7

a July 1, 1974   b 1974   c 1972   d without transit   e including bunker
f including transloading from ship to ship   g 1970

Sources: *RS 1975*: 616, 617; Tarski 1975: 95.

TABLE 6.4
International Air Transport in Eastern Europe in 1971

	Freight transport performance (million t/km)		Passenger transport (million passenger/km)		Proportion of air transport within Comecon (percentages)	
	All international	Within Comecon	All international	Within Comecon	Freight	Passenger
USSR	130.5	30.6	3,267	880	23.4	26.9
Poland	8.9	2.6	475	123	29.2	25.9
East Germany	13.3	5.8	1,029	806	43.6	78.3
Czechoslovakia	17.5	1.8	1,074	454	10.3	42.3
Hungary	9.9	.6	408	134	6.1	32.8
Romania	22.1	1.0	1,060	83	4.5	7.8
Bulgaria	17.5	2.2	937	304	12.6	32.4
Yugoslavia	63.2	..	..	..	..	..

Source: Tarski 1975: 96, 101.

valid. Comecon's history shows that a rapid growth of its aggregate production has not been accompanied by a relative increase in the international division of labor, either internally within Comecon or externally with other countries (Kaser 1967: 16). This experience contrasts sharply with the experience in the West. A relatively slow growth of the division of labor and exchange, characteristic of Comecon, reduces the relative need for transport. Consequently, a relatively inefficient or not well-developed intra-Comecon transport system may just suffice in view of the comparatively sluggish growth of the demand for its services.

Finally, the Comecon countries also cooperate in transit trade. The largest volume of transit in Eastern Europe flows through Poland: 3.8 percent of its railroad transport, compared to 74.6 percent of purely domestic traffic and 21.6 percent of traffic resulting from exports or imports (*PKP* 1974: 3). The aggregate transit services in Poland in 1973 were divided into the following components: railroad transport — 49.1 percent; transport by sea — 3.3 percent; transport by inland waterways — 0.7 percent; transloading at river ports — 0.6 percent; pipelines — 33.1 percent; and road transport — 0.1 percent (Socha 1976: 26). Railroads and pipelines are thus the most important modes for transit. The international service of the Polish railways has suffered from some persistent problems, such as fluctuation in traffic, shortage of railroad cars, shortage of adequate storage facilities, shortage of road transport to service the ports, and some bottlenecks on the railroad (Pajak 1975: 16–18). Rail passenger transit also showed a higher increase than the aggregate increase in railroad passenger transport, just as the aggregate international passenger transport grew faster than the total railroad passenger transport during the period 1966–1974 (Pankow 1976: 7). Transit transport is certain to increase greatly in importance in Eastern Europe, and it is likely to increase its relative importance within the aggregate volume of transport in that area. Such transit transport is often in competition with transit to Western Europe (Gumpel 1963: 123–26).

The 1976–1990 Comecon investment plans in the area of transport, agreed upon in 1976, will concentrate on the reconstruction of nineteen major railway routes (and probably increasing the handling capacity at border stations); the integration and reconstruction of thirty-nine trunk highways; the extension, reconstruction, and modernization of twenty-two seaports; the construction of three new seaports; the development of ten inland waterways ports on the Danube and five on the Elbe river; the expansion of twenty-six existing airports, and the construction of one new airport (Trend 1976: 7).

Cooperation Within Comecon in Investments for the Transport Sector, Including Transport Equipment

According to the socialists, international coordination of the market for transport services in the planned socialist economies entails international planning of the demand for transport services on the one hand, and planning of the supply of transport services on the other. Consequently, international coordination of transport pertains to long-range plans for the development of transport made on the basis of the long-range plans of the development of the demand for transport. International cooperation is thus based on domestic long-range plans. Their full coordination is possible within the framework of integration of socialist countries owing to socialization of the means of production and state monopoly of foreign trade (Tarski 1968: 342, 394). The socialists are critical, however, of the actual integration of transport within Comecon, as shown at the end of the preceding section, although they also assert that Comecon countries have integrated their transport more than the West European economic community (Tarski 1968: 395; Tarski 1975: 86).

International cooperation, particularly in the long range, involves investment decisions that determine the future supply of transport services. In 1964 the Permanent Economic Commission of Comecon adopted a temporary method of comparing the economic effectiveness of investments with different parameters for individual economic sectors. For transport the time limit on amortization of investments was fixed at 8–10 years, and the coefficient of tying up of investment funds was fixed at 0.15.

A related indicator for foreign-exchange effectiveness of investments in transport was as follows (adapted from Tarski 1968: 396–97):

$$E_d = (C + E_o . I + U)/D$$

where: E_d = foreign exchange effectiveness of investments

C = annual costs

E_o = a normative coefficient of comparative effectiveness of investment = $1/T$ (see chapter 3, pp. 80ff.)

I = investment outlays

U = costs of transport and of conducting foreign trade, both connected with exports.

use of this formula, different investments can be compared
relative impact on foreign exchange returns and thus on a
balance of payments. This is certainly not the only criterion
d in determining investments in transport, but it may help
ser together the marginal efficiencies of investments in transport in various Comecon countries.

Cooperation in investment in various branches of transport includes railroads, where a joint effort helped construct the broad-gauge
line from the Soviet border into Czechoslovakia, the Cop-Kosice line,
and where joint endeavor is made to increase the number of railway
wagons, to make them more uniform as between models, to electrify
and dieselize the motive power, to strengthen the roadbed, and
generally to modernize the equipment (Tarski 1968: 398). Poland
specializes in the production of railroad cars, passenger as well as
freight, and exports them, especially to the USSR (Bozyk 1974: 118).

The motor traffic section within the Permanent Transport Commission deals with construction of main highway arteries, the technology of highway construction and maintenance, standardization of
roads and motor vehicles, spare parts provision, repair workshops and
specialization in the production of trucks as between member countries (Tarski 1968: 405). Research is coordinated among others through
the Organization for Cooperation in the Ball-Bearings Industry,
which was set up about 1960 and includes the USSR, Poland, East
Germany, Czechoslovakia, Hungary, and Bulgaria; through Intrans-
mash, a Bulgarian-Hungarian center for the design and improvement
of machines used in transport between enterprise plants, established in
Sofia in 1965; and through the Bureau for Tractor Research and
Development, joining Polish and Czechoslovak R & D established in
Brno about 1965 (Wilczynski 1972: 255).

In the production of buses Hungary is the second largest Comecon
producer. Manufacture of its Ikarus buses is a good example of intra-
Comecon industrial cooperation and specialization, supported by
loans from the Comecon International Investment Bank and based on
formal agreements (Wilczynski 1974: 230–31).

In the production of passenger cars, every Comecon country in
practice seems basically to fend for itself. In the early 1970s the
Comecon countries produced eighteen makes of passenger cars with
over sixty different models (cf. Wilczynski 1974: 235n21). Poland and
the Soviet Union did enter, nevertheless, into a cooperative production agreement in 1968 and 1970 concerning production in both
countries of a licensed Fiat: the Soviet Union delivers windows, brake

linings, clutch discs, insulation, and spark plugs to Poland, and Poland delivers shock absorbers, headlights and taillights, circuit breakers for directional lights, interior lights, and cooling system and fuel tank sensors to the Soviet Union (Bozyk 1974: 119–20). In 1975 Poland and the Soviet Union signed an agreement on cooperation in the production of trucks during 1976–1980, with Poland to receive the big Soviet trucks "Kamaz" (*Kultura* 1975: no. 6, p. 144). Cooperation in the production of cars has been extended to Czechoslovakia, East Germany, and Poland (see Trend 1973: 37–41). It includes provision of parts by one country for cars produced in another, and cross-sales of cars and buses between these three countries.

Cooperation in investment plans in road transport extends also to priorities accorded to different highway construction projects. Thus, for instance, an "absolute priority" was given during the 1976–1980 Five-Year Plan in Poland to the great East-West transit superhighways leading through Poland from the Soviet border at Terespol to the East German border at Słubice via Warsaw-Poznań, and via Przemyśl-Kraków-Katowice-Wrocław-Zgorzelec. In contrast with this, apparently strategic, priority, Poland's own national interests emphasize the importance of the north-south routes that connect its important industrial areas with the Baltic coast ports (RFER: Poland, August 20, 1975: 5). East European countries also emphasize the construction of highways with international European connections. Some of them serve to link them among themselves and with Western Europe, but some, inevitably, link them more closely with the Soviet Union (Froelich 1975: 8; RFER: Situation Report, August 20, 1975: 5; Bejm 1976: 81). A map of proposed international road connections — with 1939 borders — was provided by the European Conference of Ministers of Transport 1965.

In inland waterways Romania and Yugoslavia successfully undertook the construction of the Iron Gate hydroelectric and regulation project on the Danube river; it increases the capacity and safety of navigation on the Danube. The project was started in 1964 and was completed in 1972 (Antic 1975b: 6). A canal between the Danube and Oder rivers has long been in the planning stage. Comecon countries have also standardized barges into two main groups: those for use on the Danube and those for use on smaller rivers.

In sea transport joint efforts concern construction and expansion of port facilities (Gumpel 1963: 63, 74–75), investments in bases for ship refitting, and standardization of ships as well as international division of labor in their construction (Harbron 1962: 9–23). Poland is by far the largest seller of ships to other Comecon countries, mainly to the Soviet Union. In 1973 Poland entered into cooperative agreements on ship engines and ships with Czechoslovakia and Romania (Bozyk 1974: 120). In 1975 a larger agreement was entered into by Poland and the USSR: during 1976–1980 Poland will deliver 75 modern ships of 900 thousand DWT, and the USSR will deliver 157 ships, including 22 passenger ships (*Kultura* 1975: no. 6, p. 143). In 1974 Poland and East Germany began a joint operation, Interport, which is designed to coordinate the development and use of a number of Baltic ports belonging to those two countries. The organization is based in Szczecin and is expected to create possibilities for further development of Czechoslovak, Hungarian, and Yugoslav transit through Polish and East German ports (Kolaczkowski 1974: 2–17).

In air transport, the production of passenger planes is concentrated in the Soviet Union, although other countries produce smaller planes for special uses (e.g., crop spraying, first aid), as well as some military planes and helicopters.

The "Friendship" oil pipeline links all the East European countries from East Germany to Bulgaria with the Soviet Volga-Ural oilfields (total length 5,500 km). Its construction required coordination of investments in the pipeline by all the countries through which the pipeline runs. In 1974 construction was started on a new gas pipeline from Orenburg with a total length of 2,500 km to reach Poland, Romania, and Hungary. Its construction was divided into five sections, the first of which (560 km) is to be constructed by Poland, the rest by the other countries. In return, the Soviet Union will supply to the investing countries natural gas for over ten years, 2.8 billion cubic meters to each investor every year until their investments are paid off. It was calculated that such amounts will cover 40 percent of the gas requirements in Poland. Gas deliveries are scheduled to start in 1978 (*Kultura* 1975: no. 3, p. 143).

Coordination of investments is also inherent in the existence of the "Peace" electric grid. In 1970 the Comecon countries produced nearly one billion MWh of electricity, or over 20 percent of the world production, which was nearly twice as much as the output of the original six members of the European Common Market (Wilczynski 1974: 61). Apart from the "Peace" grid, transmission lines now link adjoining regions of different Comecon countries.

In a related field, the USSR, Poland, East Germany, and Bulgaria established the International Laboratory for Strong Magnetic Fields and Low Temperatures in Wroclaw, Poland, in 1970 to conduct joint research in low-temperature physics (Wilczynski 1974: 64). Scientific cooperation in the field of transport includes exchange of technical documentation for the development of transport. Until 1955 such documents came to East Europe mainly from the Soviet Union, but that flow has since largely abated.

Figure 6.3 shows the main joint fuel, power, and raw materials projects of the Comecon countries, including pipelines. The raw materials projects give rise to a substantial need for transport capacity, during both construction and exploitation, the latter due to the bulkiness of most raw materials.

Cooperation in Transport with the Rest of the World

Eastern Europe has been moving further and further away from Stalinism, both internally and in international relations. The number of international agreements concluded between Eastern Europe and the rest of the world in the field of transport has been growing. East European countries feel the need to coordinate their transport policies with those outside their area and to utilize foreign experience and innovations in the field of transport. Consequently East Europe finds itself progressively more represented on various international bodies in the area of transport. The possible ideological objection that most of these international bodies are dominated by capitalist countries seems to carry little, if any, weight. This new trend toward greater participation is, obviously, connected also with the expanding trade between East Europe and the nonsocialist world, and — especially in the case of Yugoslavia — with expanding tourism from capitalist countries.

It seems that cooperation with noncommunist countries is favorable to all parties concerned, but especially to the East European countries. Participation in the worldwide process of standardization, free access to the latest information including that on foreign research and development, some free or low-cost publicity, increased accessibility of one's countries, lower cost of handling of goods including processing at frontier customs offices — all these are benefits of a quite tangible character. Since East European countries have been less advanced in technological development (cf. Wilczynski 1974; Gomulka 1975: 11), in administrative organization, and in research, their gains tend to be larger.

Membership in international transport organizations is either by governments (as in the case of the Inter-Governmental Maritime

FIGURE 6.3

Joint Fuel, Power, and Raw Materials Projects of the Comecon Countries

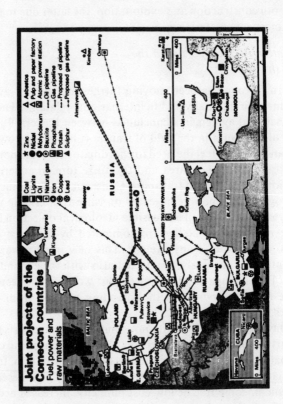

Source: *The Economist*, Jan. 17, 1976: 79. (Reprinted by permission of *The Economist*, London)

Consultative Organization), by socialized enterprises (as in the case of airlines in the International Air Transport Association), or by individuals who, in their private capacity, represent their countries, as in the case of International Automobile Federation. The founding date of an international organization does not simply that the original charter or agreement is still valid, e.g., the Central Office for International Railway Transport was founded in 1890, but the applicable conventions were agreed upon in 1961 and in subsequent years. There is no distinct pattern of membership as far as Eastern Europe is concerned. Yugoslavia tends to be the most active "joiner," East Germany the least active except for Albania.[2] The membership roster, however, tends to grow and, in time, differences in membership between individual East European countries may tend to disappear. The most comprehensive information on international organizations is found in the Union of International Associations (annual; the 1974 issue was used here). Other sources on East European membership and on international transport organizations are the United Nations (1971: 231–33), Wilczynski (1970: 189–195), and Tarski (1968: 362–76).

Below is a list of international transport associations. Their history and activities can be found in specialized sources, especially in the Union of International Associations. We give only the name of the organization, its founding date, location of the head office (as a rule in capitalist countries), its aims, and the East European countries that were members in 1974. Information was necessarily abbreviated, and we divided it according to the main fields related to transport.

Participation in international organization does not necessarily indicate constructive cooperation.[3] It does seem, however, to indicate a conciliatory and interested (for whatever reason) attitude. No verdict on the performance of East European countries in the international organizations will be given; no such verdict can be arrived at without a thorough study, which would take us far afield and might yield controversial results. Our information is, therefore, solely on the fact of membership in a given organization.

I. East European countries participated in the following rail transport organizations:

1. *Central Office for International Railway Transport,* founded in 1890, headquarters in Berne. Its aims are to facilitate and ensure application of the conventions, to codify international transport laws completely with respect to carriage of goods, passengers, and luggage by rail. Membership includes Poland, Czechoslovakia, Hungary, Romania, Bulgaria, and Yugoslavia.

2. *Intercontainer — International Company for the Transport by Transcontainers,* founded 1967, headquarters in Basel. To coordinate and develop container traffic by rail. East Germany, Czechoslovakia, Hungary, Bulgaria, and Yugoslavia.

3. *European Goods Trans Timetable Conference,* founded 1924, headquarters in Prague. To organize the international movement of trains scheduled for freight traffic, including the routing of parcels in full wagons; to accelerate movement of wagons, particularly at frontier stations; to facilitate the exchange of experience acquired in the field of freight transport. Poland, East Germany, Czechoslovakia, Hungary, Romania, Bulgaria, and Yugoslavia.

4. *European Passenger Time-Table Conference,* founded 1923, headquarters in Berne. To endeavor to obtain from competent authorities the simplification of passport control and police inspection at frontier stations. USSR, Poland, East Germany, Czechoslovakia, Hungary, Romania, Bulgaria, and Yugoslavia.

5. *International Carriage and Van Union,* founded 1921, headquarters in Berne. To regulate the reciprocal use of carriages (passenger cars), vans (baggage cars), and postal vans in international railroad traffic. Poland, East Germany, Czechoslovakia, Romania, Bulgaria, and Yugoslavia.

6. *International Federation of Railwaymen's Travel Associations,* founded 1947, headquarters in Paris. To develop international touring for members of railwaymen's travel associations and their families. Poland, Czechoslovakia, and Yugoslavia.

7. *International Rail Transport Committee,* founded 1902, headquarters in Berne. The development of international law relating to rail transport on the basis of the Berne conventions, the adoption of standard rules on other questions of international transport law. Poland, East Germany, Czechoslovakia, Hungary, Romania, Bulgaria, and Yugoslavia.

8. *International Railway Congress Association,* founded 1884, headquarters in Brussels. To promote the exchange of acquired experience and knowledge among members by holding congresses, to disseminate information by publishing technical reviews. USSR, Poland, Czechoslovakia, Hungary, Romania, Bulgaria, and Yugoslavia.

9. *International Railway Film Bureau,* founded 1961, headquarters in Paris. Promotion of international collaboration among railway film specialists. Poland, East Germany, Czechoslovakia, Romania, and Yugoslavia.

10. *International Railway Wagon Union,* founded 1921, head-

quarters in Berne. To ensure application of the Rigolamento Internazionale Veicoli (RIV) for the reciprocal use of railway freight wagons in international traffic. Poland, East Germany, Czechoslovakia, Hungary, Romania, Bulgaria, and Yugoslavia.

11. *International Union of Railways,* founded 1922, headquarters in Paris. To unify and improve conditions relating to construction and operation of railways engaged in international traffic; to coordinate and standardize the general action of the international organizations that, for this purpose, concluded a special agreement among themselves; to ensure the outside representation of railway administrations for the study of questions of common interest. Poland, Czechoslovakia, Hungary, Romania, Bulgaria, and Yugoslavia.

12. *International Union of Railway Medical Services,* founded 1949, headquarters in Brussels. To promote progress of medical science in its application to all aspects of railway operation. Poland, East Germany, Czechoslovakia, Hungary, and Yugoslavia.

13. *Office for Research and Experiments,* founded 1950, headquarters in Utrecht, the Netherlands. The pooling of results of research carried out by the various railway administrations; the carrying out of certain investigations on joint account; the undertaking of studies with a view to reducing cost price; the rationalization of means of construction and division of industry among the different countries. Poland, Czechoslovakia, Hungary, Romania, Bulgaria, and Yugoslavia.

14. *Union of European Railways Road Services,* founded 1950, headquarters in Vienna. To represent and defend at the international level the road services of European railways for passenger and goods transport; to represent the railways within international organizations concerned with international road traffic; to organize and run the Europabus international railway road services. Hungary.

II. East European countries participated in the following road transport organizations:

1. *International Automobile Federation,* founded 1904, headquarters in Paris. To establish a union between its members, chiefly in order to promote the development of international motor traffic and touring; provide for regulations governing automobile sport; encourage reinforcement and improvement of facilities and services of members; ensure the unity of the automobile movement and safeguard the interest — material and moral — of automobilism in all countries. Membership includes the USSR, Poland, Czechoslovakia, Hungary, Romania, Bulgaria, and Yugoslavia.

2. *International Prevention of Road Accidents,* founded 1957, headquarters in Monthlhery, France. To study problems of accident prevention, stimulate an exchange of ideas and information, and organize collective action. Hungary and Yugoslavia.

3. *International Road Federation,* founded 1948, headquarters in Washington, D.C. To encourage and support the planning and execution by governments of sound programs for improvement and extension of road systems throughout the world; to develop the training of road technicians; to collect and disseminate statistical, technical, economic, educational, and other material pertaining to the betterment of road systems; to publicize the social and economic benefits to be derived from adequate road systems. Czechoslovakia, Hungary, and Yugoslavia.

4. *International Road Transport Union,* founded 1947, headquarters in Geneva. To study and solve all questions raised in road transport; promote unification and simplification of regulations and customs relating to such transport; coordinate and support efforts made in different countries with a view to developing transport of passengers and goods by road. Poland, East Germany, Czechoslovakia, Hungary, Romania, Bulgaria, Albania, and Yugoslavia. Transport International Routier (TIR) carnets for customs clearing were distributed through this Union, among others, to Poland and Yugoslavia (Bayliss 1965: 146-47).

5. *Permanent International Association of Road Congresses,* founded 1909, headquarters in Paris. To foster progress in the construction, improvement, maintenance, use, and economic development of roads and encourage the growth of road systems throughout the world by the organization of congresses and publication of documents; to collect and disseminate results obtained. USSR, Poland, East Germany, Czechoslovakia, Hungary, Romania, Bulgaria, and Yugoslavia.

6. *Transfrigoroute Europe — Central Organization for Road Transport at Controlled Temperatures,* founded 1955, headquarters in Basel. To promote coordination and exchange of experiences; to study all problems of road transport at controlled temperatures and its development. Yugoslavia.

7. *International Motorcycle Federation,* founded 1912, reconstituted 1949, headquarters in Geneva. To assure the unity of the motorcycle movement. USSR, Poland, East Germany, Czechoslovakia, Hungary, Romania, Bulgaria, and Yugoslavia.

III. East European countries participated in the following inland waterway organizations:

1. *Danube Commission,* founded 1948, headquarters in Budapest. Its aims are to draw up overall plans for large-scale projects to ensure and improve navigational conditions; consultation and recommendations on hydrotechnical installations; exchange of information; establishment of uniform system of navigation, control, customs, health regulations, hydro-meteorological services, statistics. USSR, Czechoslovakia, Hungary, Romania, Bulgaria, and Yugoslavia. This seems to be the only international organization in the field of transport that includes a nonsocialist country (Austria) and that has its headquarters in a socialist country.

2. *Permanent International Association of Navigation Congresses,* founded 1900, headquarters in Brussels. To foster progress in the design, construction, improvement, maintenance, and operation of inland and maritime waterways, ports, and coastal areas; to compile and publish information about subjects in its field; to institute research into particular problems; to organize international congresses and international committees. USSR, Poland, Czechoslovakia, Hungary, Romania, Bulgaria, and Yugoslavia.

IV. East European countries participated in the following sea transport organizations:

1. *Permanent International Association of Navigation Congresses,* mentioned above.

2. *Inter-Governmental Maritime Consultative Organization,* founded in 1948, headquarters in Geneva. To provide machinery for cooperation among governments on technical matters affecting international merchant shipping; to ensure the highest possible standards of safety at sea and of efficient navigation; to prevent pollution of the sea by the ships; to encourage removal of hindrances to international shipping; to convene international maritime conferences. See also United Nations 1971: 231-233. USSR, Poland, Czechoslovakia, Hungary, Romania, Bulgaria, and Yugoslavia.

3. *European Tugowners Association,* founded 1963. To bring together tugowners, provide information and guidance in matters of common interest. Yugoslavia.

4. *International Association of Lighthouse Authorities,* founded 1957, headquarters in Paris. To assemble lighthouse authorities for discussion of general technical interests; circulate information to encourage improvements; encourage, support, and make known re-

search and inventions useful to lighthouse authorities. USSR, Poland, and Yugoslavia.

5. *International Association of Ports and Harbors,* founded 1955, headquarters in Tokyo. To associate members in the common cause of mutual international friendship and understanding; to exchange information about port and harbor organization, administration, management, development, operation, and promotion; to encourage, develop, and promote waterborne commerce; to encourage the standardization and simplification of procedure governing imports, exports, and clearance of vessels in international trade. USSR and Yugoslavia.

6. *Baltic and International Maritime Conference,* founded 1905, headquarters in Copenhagen. To unite shipowners and other persons and organizations connected with the shipping industry in order to consider and, if expedient, take action on all matters affecting the industry; to communicate to members instances of unfair charges and claims, freight speculation and other objectionable practices, and any other useful information; to improve charter parties and other shipping documents. USSR, Poland, East Germany, Czechoslovakia, Hungary, Romania, Bulgaria, and Yugoslavia.

7. *International Maritime Committee,* founded 1897, headquarters in Antwerp. To contribute to the unification of maritime and commercial law, maritime customs, usages, and practices; to promote the establishment of National Associations of Maritime Law and cooperate with-other international associations. USSR, Poland, East Germany, Bulgaria, and Yugoslavia.

V. East European countries participated in the following air transport organizations:

1. *International Civil Aviation Organization,* founded 1947, headquarters in Montreal. Its aims are to develop the principles and techniques of international air navigation and foster the planning and development of international air transport so as to: ensure safe and orderly growth of international civil aviation throughout the world; encourage the arts of aircraft design and operation for peaceful purposes, encourage the development of airways, airports, and air navigation facilities for international civil aviation; meet the needs for safe, regular, efficient, and economical air transport; prevent economic waste caused by unreasonable competition; ensure that the rights of contracting states are fully respected and that every contracting state has a fair opportunity to operate international airlines. Membership

includes the USSR, Poland, Czechoslovakia, Hungary, Bulgaria, and Yugoslavia.

2. *International Civil Airport Association,* founded 1962, headquarters in Paris. To develop relations and collaboration among civil airports of all nationalities and legal status; to study common problems, define common positions, and present them on the international level; to promote progress of civil airports and the interests of air transport in general. Poland, East Germany, Czechoslovakia, and Yugoslavia.

3. *European Airlines Research Bureau,* founded 1952, headquarters in Brussels. The improvement and development of commercial air transport in Europe by means of studies, statistical comparison, and other research projects in collaboration with its members. Yugoslavia.

4. *Institute of Air Transport,* founded 1944, headquarters in Paris. To study economic, technical, and policy aspects of air transport and the economy of transport and tourism. Poland, Czechoslovakia, Hungary, Romania, and Yugoslavia.

5. *International Aeronautical Federation,* founded 1905, headquarters in Paris. To develop world aeronautics, particularly by encouraging progress of aerial navigation; to develop solidarity, urging authorities to remove hindrance to air traffic, stimulating aeronautical sports, tourism, and private flying. USSR, Poland, Czechoslovakia, Hungary, Romania, Bulgaria, and Yugoslavia.

6. *International Air Transport Association* (known popularly as IATA), founded 1945, headquarters in Montreal. To promote safe, regular, and economical air transport, foster air commerce, and study problems connected therewith; to provide means of collaboration among air transport enterprises engaged directly or indirectly in international air transport services; to cooperate with other international organizations. Poland, Czechoslovakia, and Yugoslavia (see also Thornton 1970: 9).

7. *International Federation of Airline Pilots Associations,* founded 1948, headquarters in London. To coordinate activities of airline pilots associations. USSR and Yugoslavia.

8. *International Federation of Air Traffic Controllers Associations,* founded 1961, headquarters in Troon Ayrshire, the United Kingdom. To promote safety, efficiency, and regularity in international air navigation. Hungary and Yugoslavia.

VI. In other fields of transportation, East European countries participated in the following organizations:

1. *International Container Bureau,* founded 1933, headquarters in Paris. To contribute toward the use of containers and other equipment for transport combined; to encourage technical research; to suggest administrative, customs, commercial, and tariff measures that might facilitate extension of container usage; to act as information and documentation center. Poland and Yugoslavia.

2. *International Organization for Transport by Rope,* founded 1959, headquarters in Rome. The progress and extension of transport by cable. Czechoslovakia.

3. *International Union of Public Transport,* founded 1885, headquarters in Brussels. To study all problems connected with urban transport; to promote its progress, both from the technical and economic standpoints and in the public interest. USSR, Poland, Czechoslovakia, Hungary, and Yugoslavia.

4. *European Conference of Ministers of Transport,* founded 1953, headquarters in Paris. To take all appropriate actions to secure the best utilization and most rational development of European inland transport, generally and regionally; to coordinate and encourage the work of international organizations concerned with internal European transport. Yugoslavia.

VII. East European countries participated in the following tourism organizations:

1. *Federation of International Youth Travel Organizations,* founded in 1950, headquarters in Salzburg. To promote educational, cultural, and social travel among young people. Yugoslavia.

2. *International Academy of Tourism,* founded 1951, headquarters in Monte Carlo. To develop the cultural and human aspects of international tourism; to undertake linguistic research in relation to tourism. USSR, Poland, and Czechoslovakia.

3. *International Association of Scientific Experts in Tourism,* founded 1951, headquarters in Berne. To maintain friendly relations among its members; to promote personal contact, provide documentation, facilitate exchange of views and experience; to support the activity of tourist institutions of a scientific nature and other centers of research and training specializing in tourism. Poland, Czechoslovakia, Hungary, Romania, Bulgaria, and Yugoslavia.

4. *International Bureau of Social Tourism,* founded 1963, headquarters in Brussels. To promote the development of social tourism on an international level; to coordinate the tourist activities of its members and inform them on all matters concerning social tourism, as

regards both cultural and social and economic consequences. USSR, Poland, Czechoslovakia, and Yugoslavia.

5. *International Touring Alliance,* founded 1898, headquarters in Geneva. To study questions relating to international touring and traffic and achieve progress and reforms as a result; to encourage the development of international touring and traffic; to bring together touring associations in order to coordinate their efforts, facilitate the execution of international work, and protect their interests; to establish an international touring documentation. USSR, Poland, Czechoslovakia, Hungary, Romania, Bulgaria, and Yugoslavia.

6. *International Union of Official Travel Organizations,* founded 1925, headquarters in Geneva. To promote the economic development of countries through tourism, enhance the social and cultural role of tourism in the life of nations, further the contribution of tourism to international trade, foster expansion of international tourist flows, supply its members with the results of permanent tourist market research, protect the interests of tourists and of the tourist industry, gain recognition of the value of tourism as a means of promoting international understanding and world peace. USSR, Poland, Czechoslovakia, Hungary, Romania, Bulgaria, and Yugoslavia.

7. *Universal Federation of Travel Agents' Associations,* founded 1966, headquarters in Brussels. To act as the negotiating instrument with principals, international governmental or nongovernmental bodies concerned with tourism, on behalf of, or for the benefit of the travel agency industry; to provide professional protection of tourist agencies and assistance to tourism. USSR, Poland, East Germany, Czechoslovakia, Hungary, Romania, Bulgaria, and Yugoslavia.

8. *International Federation of Popular Travel Organizations,* founded 1950, headquarters in Brussels. To secure cooperation among affiliated national bodies; to promote development of workers' travel associations in countries where they do not exist; to represent the interests of workers' travel associations; to promote and encourage study tours and educational visits. Poland, Czechoslovakia, Hungary, and Bulgaria.

9. *International Youth Hostel Federation,* founded 1932, headquarters in Garden City, the United Kingdom. To encourage cooperation among Youth Hostel Associations in all countries. Poland, Czechoslovakia, Hungary, Bulgaria, and Yugoslavia.

International tourist associations are among the best organized users of transport and are thus in a position to influence transport organization and procedures in individual member countries, including the East European members.

In addition to membership in international organizations, the socialist countries are signatories to miscellaneous conventions and treaties or agreements in the field of transport and have participated in various conferences, as for instance, in the 1966 and 1967 sessions of the navigation commission of the United Nations Conference for Trade and Development (UNCTAD). These activities, some of which were connected with established or new international organizations, are not listed in the present study.

Apart from participation in international organizations, the East European countries have concluded a number of bilateral transport agreements with Western countries. For instance, Yugoslavia and Poland started production under license from the Italian Fiat, Romania did the same with the French Renault, Poland obtained from France a license for the production of the Berliet autobus, and Poland bought from the British firm Leyland Motors in 1967 a license for high-compression engines for heavy trucks and construction machinery (cf. Bozyk 1974: 129–30).

Poland and Austria announced in 1975 a cooperation agreement between the Austrian automotive firm of Steyr-Daimler-Puch and the Polish state enterprise Polmot: the Austrian firm will supply equipment to build heavy trucks in Poland worth $162 million over the following five years, and Poland, starting in 1980 and continuing for ten years, will supply Steyr with engines worth $285 million. Austrian transit to Polish Baltic ports has also been increased as the result of closer economic cooperation between the two countries (RFER: SR, Sept. 19, 1975: 3). Yugoslavia has obtained aid from the European Investment Bank for the construction of a superhighway linking Austria with Greece and Turkey (Antic 1976). The Yugoslav share of the Adria oil pipeline between the Adriatic coast and Hungary has received financial help from Kuwait and Libya (Antic 1975a). Late in 1975 the General Motors Corporation announced plans to manufacture half-ton trucks in Lublin, Poland, and the Polish Ursus plant near Warsaw contracted with the Massey-Ferguson tractor manufacturers to coproduce tractors for sale in both countries and on foreign markets (Heneghan 1975: 3, 17; *The New York Times,* Sept. 30, 1975).

In his latest book Wilczynski (1976: 52–114) divided East-West economic relations into four main forms, namely, trade, licenses, industrial cooperation, and joint ventures, all divided into subcategories. In the field of transport equipment, examples include:

1. Trade — Japanese sale of ships to Poland and Yugoslavia; British sale of ships to Yugoslavia; U.S., British, and French sales of aircraft to Romania and Yugoslavia; Western purchases of ships from Poland, East Germany, and Yugoslavia.

2. Licenses — for cars from Renault to Romania and Bulgaria, from Fiat to Poland, from Fiat and Volkswagen to Yugoslavia; for buses and trucks from Berliet and British Leyland to Poland, from Daimler Benz to Yugoslavia; for helicopters from France and Great Britain to Yugoslavia; for small aircraft from Great Britain and West Germany to Poland; for marine diesel engines from Switzerland to Bulgaria.

3. Industrial cooperation — West Germany and Hungary cooperate in producing large trucks; the U.S. (International Harvester) and Poland cooperate in the manufacture of machines for laying large-diameter oil and gas pipelines; West Germany (Ford) and Yugoslavia cooperate in producing parts for passenger cars; Great Britain and Poland cooperate in producing tractors; Japan and Poland cooperate in the manufacture of electric components for cars; Sweden (Volvo) and Hungary cooperate in producing buses; and West Germany and Great Britain participate in the construction and operation of modern gas stations in Hungary.

4. Joint ventures — Citroen of France and Tomos of Yugoslavia jointly produce passenger cars in Yugoslavia; Fiat of Italy and Red Banner Automotive Works of Yugoslavia have agreed to produce jointly passenger cars in Yugoslavia; Volvo of Sweden and two Hungarian enterprises have agreed to assemble and market four-wheel-drive vehicles in Hungary.

Such bilateral and other trade agreements, whether with the West or within Comecon, help to bring foreign technology into the East European countries and to utilize economies of scale. But the search for the latter may prove, at times, the wrong strategy; this apparently happened in Poland, when in 1969–1970 an attempt was made to abandon production of small specialized airplanes (for farming, first aid, etc.). That attempt, in the view of one writer, "was not preceded by adequate analyses of its prognostic and effectiveness results" (Zacher 1974: 47n). This unsuccessful attempt at international specialization reflects not so much faulty sectoral planning (as explained in chapter 3) as inadequately rational choice of the general strategy of economic development.

When successful, however, bilateral trade agreements are an important source of economic growth and help reduce the technological gap between East and West (cf. Wilczynski 1974: 297). The substantial number of existing agreements (cf. Wilczynski 1974: 298–324) indicates how much the socialist countries appreciate this point. By and large, there is still a substantial technological gap between Eastern Europe and the West in the area of transport. There is no inherent reason, however, why this gap might not be closed in the future given adoption of rational economic policies, proper incentives, and greater attention devoted to passenger travel, particularly to individual transport.

Apart from cooperative transport relations, relations between the different East European countries may well be, at least partially, competitive, as for instance for transit and tourist transport or for the production of transport equipment, and between East European and Western countries (e.g., competition between Poland, East Germany, and West Germany for Czechoslovak transit to the sea). Economic interests are in this respect intertwined with political and possibly emotional considerations, and the result is an interesting mosaic of potential future relations. However, speculation on future developments is beyond the scope of the present study.

VII

Conclusions and Projections

A Synoptic Review

The importance of transport in Eastern Europe is a particular instance of its universal importance in every economy, most noteworthily in a modern, developed economy. In the accelerated economic development of Eastern Europe, the importance of transport is enhanced by the need to transport a rapidly rising volume of raw materials, semimanufactured goods, and finished products as well as to transport a growing number of people with growing real incomes to their places of work and leisure.

Eastern Europe is varied geographically, economically, and (even though it seems uniformly communist) politically. Its varied backgrounds and contexts have influenced current differences in the stages of economic development just as they have influenced transport development in individual countries. According to an expert on East European geography, the East European countries remain "distinct economic and social organisms that continue to carry the stamp of their own history and culture." (Osborne 1967: 5) Poland, East Germany, Czechoslovakia, and Hungary show a higher degree of development of transport than does the rest of Eastern Europe, although the higher rate of growth of the less advanced countries of Romania, Bulgaria, and Yugoslavia tends to reduce that difference and has in fact done so. It should also be realized that the political origin of transport policies in Eastern Europe influences both the direction and the volume of transport, particularly in terms of transport to and from foreign countries.

The economic backbone of the transport systems in Eastern Europe is their method and apparatus of central planning borrowed from the Soviet Union. Planning, as an explicit technique of economic management, is of crucial importance for an orderly and dynamic growth of transport, according to East European authorities on the subject. Planning within the context of East European transport is also analytically important to some Western specialists on East European transport, including the present writer. Just how efficient transport planning is, however, is evaluated differently by different experts. Exaggerated official claims are often made about the efficacy of planning in eliminating waste and raising output. However, some Western observers criticize communist planning as less productive than Western transport planning. The comprehensive character of Soviet-type centralized transport planning then raises the question of the economic usefulness of such a type of planning.

In view of the East European cocksure official confidence in the efficacy of the central planning of transport, two chastening thoughts arise from Western analysis of transport planning. First, there is the assertion that planning is becoming "less and less a matter of precise propositions . . . and more and more a matter of ideas and policies loosely assembled under constant review, within which, every now and then, some project is seen to be as ready for execution as human judgment can pronounce." (Buchanan et al. 1966, cited in Bruton 1970: 34)

Second, there is a trend away from absolutes and certainties in transport planning, a trend expressed in the laconic assertion: "There are no absolute standards by which a transportation plan can be evaluated." Transport planning is not a precise tool. Rather, "it is a rational process, which isolates all those factors which apparently influence movement demands, and attempts to present a logically argued case for estimating future movement demands."(Bruton 1970: 207, 224–25) And a textbook on transportation and economic policy concluded:

> In the present stage of intellectual development it is not possible to base the major transportation investment decisions entirely on precise scientific calculations. There may never be a time when all the political considerations and human considerations can be reduced to a single calculation with the economic. Analytic progress in developing the tools of rational decision making, however, is pushing back the frontier of knowledge and reducing the elements in these decisions that must be imponderable. [Lansing 1966: 43]

In view of these Western conclusions, transport planning in Eastern Europe may look a bit pretentious and a bit too precise. In fact, part of this results from the centrally planned economic system adopted by the countries of Eastern Europe, a system under which material balances (including their spatial movement) have to be balanced for the planned periods. Multi-year and long-range planning, however, do contain an element of spurious exactitude that may actually prove harmful to the economies in question.

Since fundamental criticism of transport planning is not allowed in Eastern Europe, there may be some advantage in assessing the role of such planning on the basis of Western experience. Yale Brozen opposed politically motivated and centrally imposed governmental regulation in the United States on the ground that the investment decisions that result under such conditions involve a staggering waste of resources whether measured in terms of alternative foregone uses of capital, or in terms of the original objectives (Brozen 1975: 115). William Jordan contended that there is accumulating evidence that regulation greatly increases operating costs. This supports "assertions that regulatory commissions have been perverted from their alleged purpose of promoting consumer benefits, and . . . frequent statements from academicians that regulation should be substantially changed, reduced, or even abolished." (Jordan 1975: 57)

Some inherent waste and perhaps several social inequities may be produced by the East European reliance on central control and planning of transport, although one should not leap to the facile conclusion that governmental planning should be abandoned. Governmental regulation of transport in the West does not seem to be resented as such by most economists, even if they advocate changes in that regulation (cf. e.g., Healy 1966: 39, 43–46; Hodges 1966: 175–81; Lansing 1966: 390–92, 395–96).

A study of Western transport economics, as, for instance, the work of Alan Hay (1973), reveals considerable similarities in concepts and methodology of planning with East European transport planning practice. In Eastern Europe, though, not enough use seems to be made of cost-benefit analysis and computer techniques. It may be doubted whether the full use of cost-benefit analysis is at all possible given the artificial price formation prevalent in Soviet-type economies. On the positive side, chapter 3 described the main transport planning methods used in Eastern Europe, categorizing them according to the chronological length of the plan period and according to the subject of the planning.

Taking into account the limitations of transport planning as discussed in the West and in particular the limitations of East European transport planning, we should acknowledge the degree of coordinating effort that is made in transport planning in that area. The least that can be said about it is that it is apparently in the hands of transport experts who try to implement some objective rules in the planning process. That their procedures are not grossly incorrect seems to be proven by the rising quantum of transport services in Eastern Europe, but the social cost at which those services adapt themselves to the volume of demand may be high. These twin problems of rising output in transport and its cost were discussed in chapters 4 and 5.

Whether in terms of official indexes or whether in terms of independent calculations, the performance of transport in Eastern Europe is quantitatively imposing. While the present study has not dealt with the quality of transport services, their statistical growth in terms of tons transported or ton/kilometers transported has been impressive. Transport in Eastern Europe has taken an increasing proportion of the labor force, has received substantial investments, has shown large productivity increases, and has vitally contributed to the growth of national incomes in the area. Transport has played an active part in the overall expansion of Eastern European economies, stimulating their growth and, in turn, being stimulated to grow — assuredly in a planned way. Not all modes of transport showed equal rates of growth, which fact is understandable and, indeed, desirable from the point of view of economic dynamics: it shows that the transport sector was able to adapt itself to varying rates of growth within the structure of the overall demand for its services (cf. Malek, Grzywacz, and Zymela 1973: 113).

Our regression analysis showed that the best fit can be obtained between transport and national income, although the indexes of net value added in industry, construction, and foreign trade turnover have also high coefficients of codetermination with transport. The use of double-logarithmic equations in the regression analysis revealed satisfactory correlation between aggregate transport on the one hand and national income and foreign trade turnover on the other hand. These relationships make it easier to adjust the planned growth of transport to the needs for it.

Transport uses up a substantial portion of national resources. This points not only to the importance of that sector but also to the considerable cost of all necessary and desirable transport services to the economy. The cost of transport to its users is not proportional to the social cost of transport as between different transport modes, thus resulting in some transport decisions that are irrational from the point of view of society. Irrational transport includes several other elements and may amount to as much as 20 percent of the total cost of transport. Obviously, substantial savings in transport may still be made in Eastern Europe even at the present stage of its technology, especially if that technology were to be raised to Western levels. The wider setting of social costs of transport will be discussed in the following section.

Finally, the important international implications of transport have been discussed. It has been shown that transport can link countries economically and culturally and facilitate the conduct of wars (cf. Czownicki 1975: 148). The East European countries have made decisive steps to link their national transport systems with those of other countries, especially with those of the Comecon group. The organizational framework of this cooperation is extensive, and it covers all relevant aspects of transport. In practice, however, it may be doubted whether actual cooperation in transport is as extensive as ideology would claim. Moreover, in international cooperation in the field of transport with countries outside of Comecon group, i.e., mainly with Western countries, the East European effort seems to be extensive rather than intensive: i.e., broad participation in many organizations, the stated aims of which in some cases seem to conflict with the actual policies of the East European countries. It is encouraging, however, to find the East European countries ready to open up channels of formal communication and formally to consider adoption of standards accepted by many Western countries. This "microconvergence" may signify existence of a broader convergence tendency, at least in a limited sense.

This is the first English-language study to give a comprehensive view of the development of transport in Eastern Europe between 1945 and 1975. That thirty-year period has been eventful, and it has indeed been necessary to fill in the information gap. A general presentation of the East European transport experience as a whole was also necessary: individual national studies have not given a general picture of what has been happening in transport in Eastern Europe and what the implications of those developments may be. The present study may become a first step in the further exploration of East European transport. Better knowledge of East European transport is that much more useful and, potentially at least, applicable in other economies — partly because transport within East European economies has become relatively much more important and partly because the international importance of Eastern Europe has grown.

The Social Cost of Transport in Eastern Europe

The statistical data supplied in chapters 3–5 prove the importance of transport in the development of Eastern Europe. Both material production and the standard of living have been significantly affected by the strong performance of transport (cf. Malek, Grzywacz, and Zymela 1973: 397–98). Its growth is bound to continue as the result of further economic development and the economic aspirations of the peoples of Eastern Europe. It is likely that in the future qualitative changes in transport will become more important than in the past and that further shifts will take place in the relative importance of various modes of transport. But the question that ought to be answered, however tentatively, on the basis of the present study is whether the growth of transport has so far been adequate to the needs of Eastern Europe.

East European transport operates with little or no excess capacity (except possibly for some strategic reserves that are kept unused), although it seems that such reserves would be minor compared to the overall transport capacity. Consequently, whenever the demand for transport services exceeds the level that planners thought likely, bottlenecks appear or intensify. This is what happened spectacularly in Poland during the 1971–1975 period of accelerated economic growth stimulated by imports from abroad (cf. Zajfryd 1975), and it is happening in Bulgaria and Hungary (RFER: Bulgaria, December 20, 1974: 2–5; Hungary, January 8, 1974: 5–7; cf. RFER: Poland, September 5, 1975: 5–10 and July 18, 1975: 4). This particular shortfall of transport services imposed severe inconveniences on the public, but by and large it does not seem to have retarded the surge in economic growth. By rigid subordination of existing transport capacity, including transloading at any time, however inconvenient, this capacity has been made to suffice, but just barely. Consequently, the system has operated without adequate flexibility on a permanent emergency basis. In the last analysis it made do, but at a cost.

That cost, mainly from the overall social point of view, becomes then the focus of our attention. The question is whether the growth of transport services has taken place at an exorbitant cost and whether the transport sector functions at too high a cost, that is, in comparison with countries in the West. One factor that raises the social cost of transport is irrational transport (chapter 5), which raises the social cost of transport by up to 20 percent. Another factor is the need to keep abnormally high inventories in order to ward off work stoppages occasioned by delays in the delivery of raw materials or parts (cf. Czownicki 1975: 134), insofar as those delays are caused by lack of transport capacity reserves. Yet another factor that raises the cost of transport in Eastern Europe is its absolute subordination to the needs of production, a subordination that requires overtime work, work at night and on holidays, work under difficult environmental conditions, and the like. While tending to make better use of existing capacity, as pointed out above, such subordination has its human costs and tends to create an unduly high proportion of inoperative equipment, equipment awaiting overhaul or repair. An indication of the real character of that cost is thus provided.

There are also several less tangible costs in a transport system that barely covers the needs. If passenger transport is less than adequate, for example, there is a loss of mobility, which lessens the availability of certain scarce human skills, increases the inconvenience of housing in locations that are less preferable but more proximate to work, and decreases the psychic satisfaction from spatial freedom. If inadequate equipment is used in freight transport, the transport itself becomes less safe than it would have been. This imposes certain social costs: the accidents that otherwise might have been avoided. When utmost pressure is exerted on full utilization of existing equipment, there is less room for experimentation — including experimentation with technologically new equipment — which has undoubtedly been an element in the relative technological backwardness of East European transport. Such pressure brings about a characteristically short-sighted attitude: concentration on existing technology, an unwillingness to change because change always implies disruption of present patterns, and a temporary loss of production and absence of incentives to learn about new methods and new techniques.

The technology and quality of transport in Eastern Europe has not been explored in the present study, but its author has discerned several general trends in this respect. First, the technology of transport in Eastern Europe was very backward in comparison to Western technology in the late 1940s; this was the result of World War II and the erection of the Iron Curtain between Eastern Europe and the West. This relative backwardness has persisted and seems to have been intensified during the forced industrialization drive and for a short time after the death of Stalin in 1953. The effects of that policy lingered on until the early 1960s. Second, after about 1965, a period of economic intensification began spreading in Eastern Europe (see Mieczkowski 1970; Wilczynski 1972: 39–44; Wilczynski 1974: 9–17; Wilczynski 1974a; RFER: Czechoslovakia, March 19, 1975: 3–7; RFER: Bulgaria, March 13, 1975: 1–3); among other things, it brought an improvement in technolgoy. Third, this phase has continued into the mid-1970s. Apparently, it has gathered force and may lead in the future (but not yet, cf. Kruczek 1975: 86) to a semi-Galbraithian new industrial state and to technocratic rule by experts. Fourth, the technological gap between Eastern Europe and the West persists, although it might have narrowed somewhat recently. Fifth, much of the modern transport technology adopted in Eastern Europe seems to have been imported from the West, including aircraft design and entire automotive plants. Sixth, transport remains an underinvested sector, it is organizationally inadequately coordinated, and it fails to fulfill its functions properly (Madeyski, Lissowska, and Morawski 1975: 11). Seventh, the quality of transport service in Eastern Europe is still considerably below that accepted in the West (cf. Jedrzejewski 1975: 59–61), at least partly because of inadequate investments and generally obsolete technology.

Thus, the strategy of intensive use of existing equipment and the general strategy of forced and centrally planned economic development have been costly in terms of modernization and in terms of quality of service. They have also had explicit and implicit costs, as mentioned earlier. It seems to follow that the costs of transport in Eastern Europe have imposed a partly unnecessary burden on the East European countries, a burden that has added to the other — by no means minor — costs of economic development. A better strategy for developing transport services would have been socially more desirable. But, again, if the socialist countries of Eastern Europe decided for ideological or any other reasons to pay the high price of securing the necessary transport services, then they certainly got them, regardless of their quality.

There is already an awareness of the social costs of excessive transport in Eastern Europe. The fact that the Polish railroad is in second place in transport in Europe and fifth in the world has created some concern: after all, Poland is sixtieth in the world by area and twentieth by population. It has been found that Poland transports by rail more than other countries in relation to its production and area and that a higher proportion of such transport is carried by rail. The causes of this have been diagnosed as: (1) location of mineral resources in the south of the country and the consequent need to distribute them through the rest of the country and to transport them to the northern ports for export; (2) a relatively high proportion of mining in the aggregate industrial production; (3) existence of substantial transit transport; (4) several "subjective" causes, such as incorrect location of industry, improper distribution of production, and an inadequate use of alternative modes of transport. It is found regrettable that the production of modern railroad equipment is barely in its incipient stages (Chelstowski 1975: 3). How much proper rationalization of transport could have achieved has been demonstrated recently in Poland in the Gdansk voyvodship, where a special central staff for transport was given special powers and was able to achieve substantial social savings (Zbierajewski 1975a: 2).

At present, transport in Eastern Europe is inferior to that in the West but not inordinately so. In Poland, East Germany, Czechoslovakia, and Hungary, it is not far behind Western Europe, although it conspicuously favors public transport — especially the railroad — and only recently has made ventures into individual transport. In Romania, Bulgaria, and Yugoslavia, transport is markedly behind West European standards, but it is improving. Some modes of transport, such as air transport and river transport, have been held back in Eastern Europe, partly because countries in that area are relatively small and partly because of unsuitable terrain (e.g., for river transport). On the whole, nevertheless, East European transport has made tremendous strides at high social cost, and its achievements should justly receive their due. However, it should again be stressed that such achievements could have been attained with greater economic efficiency and at lower social cost. It should also be realized that East European transport is still inadequate. In the opinion of a Polish expert, the Polish transport system does not satisfy the freight and passenger demand for transport, especially in rural areas. The intermodal allocation of transport work, as well as the organization of transport frequently violate macroeconomic criteria (Madeyski 1973: 8–9). Thus, in general, the economic sacrifices made in order to raise transport performance in Eastern Europe have not brought complete success, while the expectations of a rational planned system and planned performance might have inclined an observer to higher hopes.

Because of the relative backwardness of East European transportation, its modal life cycle has been different from that of the United States. The standard five stages in the life of a mode — experimentation, early extension, rapid expansion, maturity, and decadence (cf. Kneafsey 1975: 11) — are in each case in Eastern Europe technologically behind those in the U.S.,[1] that is, in the sense of saturation with infrastructure and in terms of economic utilization. This does not mean, however, that transport modes do not develop rapidly in Eastern Europe or that their relative importance does not change (chapter 3). As already pointed out, this development has high costs. On the other hand, however, transfer of transport technology from countries where transport is more advanced costs less than the original research and development, with the element of trial and error that is inherent in all pioneering activity. East European countries can also, at least theoretically, jump over intermediate technological stages, even if the very opportunity to make such jumps implies the existence of relative backwardness. In this way, although East European countries incur an appreciable economic sacrifice in raising their transport performance, they at the same time seem to achieve some cost savings by virtue of being followers rather than pathbreakers.

The Future of Transport in Eastern Europe

A study of East European transport would not be complete without some projections into the future. These projections may (continuing the argument that closed the preceding section) be expressed as the social cost of providing transport services, they may entail East European projections as to the expected transport performance in the future, and they may evaluate the probable future role of transport in Eastern Europe. These three topics will be taken up in turn in the present section.

It may then be asked whether the development of transport services in the future is likely to keep imposing a high cost on the East European countries. No unequivocal answer seems possible, but the main alternatives may be at least indicated:

Alternative 1: continuation of current reliance on extensive economic growth with some modernization and some borrowed technological change. Social costs of transport would continue at above-Western levels and would, also assuming a drive toward improved quality of life to replace the spartan ideological ideal of hard work for the sake of a utopian future, restrict the rate of economic growth.

Alternative 2: a more radical change in the strategy of economic growth: toward intensive development that relies to a large extent on technological change. This alternative would require greater investments in the transport sector than in alternative 1, but it would ultimately result in lower social costs.

Alternative 3: decentralization of economic decision making in a move away from central planning. It is believed that the results of such a development would approximate the results of alternative 2. The costs of passenger travel might then decline relative to freight costs, since passenger tariffs embody higher profit margins for transport enterprises than do the freight tariffs, thus indicating the particular preferences of central planners in Eastern Europe (cf. Malek, Grzywacz, and Zymela 1973: 364).

Alternative 4: return to the hard-line strategy of the early 1950s, however improbable it may seem. Transport would then again become a casualty of the struggle for quick industrial ment and for ideological dominance; the strain on transpo double, while its growth would be retarded. In contrast to th transport could then break down; even without such a brea ...,, however, transport would become a liability to the growth effort. A review of Polish long-range thought seems to favor alternative 2, and our subsequent remarks assume that this option will be taken.

Transport in Eastern Europe can also play a vital role in shaping the economic future of the countries it serves. Domestically, it can be a factor in raising the level of living of the population by offering fast, convenient, and perhaps personalized means of travel. Electrification of railroads, expansion of highway systems and bus services, official sponsorship of tourism, and increase in the number of private cars — all indicate that this will probably be the direction of future development of transport. Transport can also provide a cheaper future movement of freight, thus extending markets, allowing economies of scale, and saving national resources. The first steps in containerization, encouragement by tariffs for large, multi-car freight shipments, a considerable growth in the number of trucks — all point to an expanded role for freight transport.

East European transport experts, using material from long-range plans, expect further substantial increases in the demographic indicator of transportability (Madeyski, Lissowska, and Morawski 1975: 15-16); an increase in the share of services, including transport, in aggregate employment (cf. Piskozub 1975: 124); and an integration of the transport system into one economically rational whole (Goscilowicz 1975: 47-49). The assumptions made by Polish long-range planners with regard to Poland may be cited here as an example of the expectations of growth of transport in Eastern Europe. According to these planners, the total volume of transport is expected to increase sharply in the future, but at a somewhat slower rate than in the recent past. The surge in long-distance bus transport will be moderated by rapid growth of transport in passenger cars. Between 1970 and 1990, the volume of freight transported will increase by 344 percent,[2] the share of road transport in the total of tons transported will rise from about 67 percent in 1970 to about 80 percent in 1990, while the share of railroads will decline from about 29 percent to about 17 percent. In terms of transport performance, the share of railroads will decline from about 80 percent to about 60 percent. The share of pipeline transport will increase from 5.6 percent to 7.3 percent, and inland waterway transport will rise elevenfold between 1970 and 1990, increasing its share from 1.9 to 3.6 percent (cf. Glowczynski 1975: 127).

In long-distance passenger transport in Poland, there will be an increase of 219 percent between 1970 and 1990. There will be a further decline in the share of railroads and a rise in the share of road transport. A rise of 700 percent in air travel is expected, despite its relatively small advantage over the railroad (cf. Mikulski 1975: 127, 129). A rise of 285 percent in urban transport is also expected (Madeyski, Lissowska, and Morawski 1975: 15-17; cf. Piskozub 1975: 145, 213-14; Goscilowicz 1975: 46; Jedrzejewski 1975: 61).

Better location of industry in Poland is expected to bring considerable savings — in terms of ton/kilometers, 8-10 percent of aggregate transport performance (Piskozub 1975: 210-12). The number of freight transport points on the railroad is expected to decline by 1990 from 2,331 to 400, and the number of passenger transport points from 3,839 to 3,268, despite an increase in the number of suburban railway stations. More kilometers of railroad track will be closed down than constructed. On the other hand, the highway network will be increased by 77 percent. The pipeline network will be expanded, including the oil pipeline from the Adriatic (Rijeka) to Poland (Madeyski, Lissowska, and Morawski 1975: 29-32).

It is also expected that transloading operations in Poland (currently mechanized, on the average, at less than 45 percent of operations) will be substantially mechanized by 1990; this will save some labor from the labor force, which will grow much less in the 1980s than it did in the late 1960s and early 1970s (Goscilowicz 1975: 56-57). It may be added that in road transport, transloading was mechanized in 1976 only to 53 percent, but 45 percent of that was by dump trucks, leaving only 8 percent of other transloading mechanized (*ZG* 1976, no. 35: 15). The turnover in Polish ports is expected to increase between 1975 and 1990 by 364 percent, and a telling change in the structure of freight handled is expected to take place: oil and oil products will increase their share in the aggregate main bulk turnover handled by Polish ports from 7 percent in 1975 to 54 percent in 1990, while all the other main bulk commodities will decline in their relative importance. The smallest relative decline will take place in iron ore, the imports of which through ports are expected to increase considerably, implying a decrease in Polish dependence on Soviet iron ore. The tonnage of the Polish merchant fleet is expected to increase by 564 percent between 1975 and 1990 (Andruszkiewicz 1975: 109, 114). The number of tourists and vacationers using public inland waterway transport between 1970 and 1990 will increase four times over, while the aggregate number of passengers in that mode will double (Glowczynski 1975: 130). Judging by Western developments, the use of inland waterways by privately owned pleasure craft will increase greatly. Finally, the introduction of RTOL (Reduced Take-Off and Landing) and STOL (Short Take-Off and Landing) aircraft will increase the density of air transport points and may help to popularize domestic air travel (Czownicki 1975: 139–143; Czownicki 1976: 8–10).

A separate, though related, problem concerns future planning of spatial distribution of economic activity, residential districts, green belts, and the like. Increasing density of population in Eastern Europe (except for East Germany and Hungary) and progressive urbanization call for such planning (cf. Celechovsky 1972). Poland has already set up a planning unit for macroplanning of urban-industrial develop-ment up to 1990; part of the long-range planning involved is devoted to the problems of transport. The first steps in this new planning direc-tion in Poland were restricted to the southwestern belt of the country from Wroclaw to Krakow, including the highly industrialized region of Silesia (RFER: Poland, November 17, 1972: 14).

The expected increase in transport services in Poland is thus con-siderable and will require a large investment and a considerable tech-nological effort. Other countries of Eastern Europe are laying similar plans for expanding their transport, having pragmatically come to the conclusion that transport may in the future either make or break their ambitions for economic success. But their plans tend to be less ambi-tious than the Polish plans. For instance, Romanian planners assume that the volume of aggregate freight traffic in 1990 will double that of 1975. At the same time, however, they assume a very steep rise in maritime shipments (twelve to thirteen times their 1975 level) and an increase in the share of seagoing cargoes carried in Romanian vessels to 75–80 percent (RFER: Romania, August 14, 1974: 13). Romanian transport plans reveal a mercantilistic tendency (observable in all East European countries) to carry one's merchandise in one's own ships. They apparently reveal a planned shift in foreign trade to markets linked to Romania by sea and thus presumably to Western markets. The projected high rate of expansion of Romanian sea transport extrapolates the Romanian experience of the largest increase in the share of sea transport in the aggregate tonnage moved by transport between 1960 and 1971, which was by a factor of 9.3. According to a Romanian author, that increase took place as the result of Romania's "expanded economic relations with a considerable number of remote states." (Constantinescu 1973, quoted in RFER: Rumanian Press Survey, September 7, 1973: 3)

More attention is likely to be devoted in the future to greater fuel economy, better road surfaces, and to environmental problems connected with transport. These new concerns and the research done on them were revealed in a recent article by a Soviet researcher (Afanasyev 1975).

Internationally, transport may be even more important in the future reshaping of Eastern Europe than it will be domestically. It could provide a physical bridge between East and West, and it could enable greater and more far-reaching cultural, economic, and technological interchange. However, the future of this aspect of transport depends intimately on the shaping of politically determined overall policy decisions by the East European countries and, albeit to a lesser extent, by the Western countries. If the current trend is projected into the future, these decisions may bring East and West closer together. Transport would then of necessity be the tie that binds them together.

Notes

Chapter 1
Introduction

1. "The arteries of any society are its transport." *The Economist* (London) 1974: 5. This metaphor has become a cliché.
2. This seems to be true for developing countries but may not be true for highly developed ones. See Mason 1969: 7–8.
3. The current 1976–1980 Five-Year Plans try to remedy past neglect by markedly increasing investments in transport. See, for instance, Jaroszewicz 1976: 98. However, the backwardness of East European railroads is still striking. For instance, in Poland the railroad so far does not have automatic traffic control, except for a total of barely 101 kilometers; 30 percent of telephone links are manually operated; telegraph operation is not automated; cable lines cover only 20 percent of the network, the rest being aerial lines inadequate for potential computer use (Podwysocki 1976: 11). Efforts are being made to modernize the railroad. See, for instance, Karpinski 1975.

Chapter 2
Geographic and Economic Determinants of Transport in Eastern Europe

1. The interested reader may find more information in the following sources: Toschi 1959: 650–74; Deasy et al. 1959: 520–52; Petrovic 1965: 108–24; *Yugoslavia and Her Republics* 1969: 105–330; Osborne 1967: 84–86, 107–11, 143–50, 172–77, 210–16, 249–63, 305–10; Zielinski 1973: xxxv–xxxvi; Kawalec 1965; Leszczycki and Lijewski 1972; Berezowski 1962: 48–186; Hamilton 1971; Keefe 1971: 44, 159–64; Keefe 1974: 47–48, 249–65; Keefe 1972: 36–37, 275–89.
2. See the 1957 treaty between the USSR and East Germany, art. 15; the 1957 agreement between the USSR and Romania, art. 2, 12–14; the 1957 agreement between the USSR and Hungary, art. 2, 12–13. Meissner 1962: 49, 72, 127; Jain 1973: 249, 252–53, 256, 260. See also U.S. Congress, Senate 1966: 19–23.
3. In an effort to overcome their inferior endowment with cars, the East European countries increased their annual production of passenger cars between 1970 and 1974 by the following percentages: Poland — 107 percent, East Germany — 22 percent, Czechoslovakia — 18 percent, Romania — 186 percent, Bulgaria — 80 percent, the Soviet Union — 225 percent (Paradysz 1976: 208).

Chapter 3
National Planning of Transportation

1. Some less adequate definitions of planning are: (1) the practice of
resource allocation and programming of production as typified by the Soviet
Union (Meier 1965: x). (2) government action designed to secure results
different from those of the market (Lewis 1969: viii). Lewis appropriately
cautioned also that "The quality of a Plan depends on the quality of its
policies, rather than on the quality or quantity of its arithmetic" (Lewis 1966:
24). (3) A "strategic device for mobilizing and concentrating resources on
selected crucial targets, preventing their dispersion on other objectives, and
imposing the central planner's will on producers and consumers." (Feiwel
1967: 66) (4) Traditional Soviet planning "presupposes that virtually all
targets for economic units, as well as the means for attaining them, are
determined by central authorities. Directives on production, distribution, and
investment are transmitted from the center down to lower agencies, following
a set hierarchy, by means of administrative dossiers. The plan consists simply
in the aggregate of those current administrative dossiers." (Zaleski 1967: 3) A
good general definition was provided by Nicolas Spulber: "An economic
plan . . . is the product of compromises among competing goals; the reflection
of a basic strategy of how best allocate resources in order to reach these goals;
and the embodiment of certain principles of planning and methods of imple-
menting them. It is . . . a program of action, combining directives with fore-
casts concerning investment, output, and employment, and intended to
expand a country's productive capacity and to bring about a new pattern of
interdependence between sectors of the economy." "Comprehensive planning
. . . requires extensive and methodical coordination among current economic
activities and those which will arise in the future as various branches and
sectors expand at different rates of growth. This coordination requires, in
turn, the establishment of a number of plans: short-term operational plans and
long-term "perspective" or general plans. . . ." (1964: 7, 98). Cf. Kaser and
Zielinski 1970: 24–76 and *passim*. See also Bornstein 1975.
2. For standard life-spans of different kinds of railroad equipment see
Mikhaltsev 1957: 46–50.
3. For one of the uses of interest in Poland recently see Zielinski 1974: 62.
4. For an outline of planning of repairs on railroad see Michalski 1975:
96–105.

Chapter 4
Statistical Growth of Transport in Eastern Europe Since World War II

1. Compare data for Polish private sector value added in transportation in
1956 and for 1956–60 in *DN 1956:* 38, *DN 1957–58:* 45, *DN 1955–60:* 52, and
DN 1960–63: 48. See also a study embodying research by the present author in
Korbonski and Wittich 1967: 7.
2. Official statistical data because of different method of calculation of
national income do not agree with this conclusion as seen, for instance, for
East Germany in Jurek 1974: 364. Western computations are accepted here as
more comprehensive.

3. The correlation analysis was done by Dr. Po-chih Lee, senior economist at Bell Canada.

Chapter 5
The Cost of Transport in Eastern Europe

1. Several methods of calculating costs on the railroad have been devised, as described in Stawrowski 1969: 45–51. They are: substitution method, mathematic method, analytical (statistical) method, the method of outlay allocations, structural analysis of costs, and direct calculations.

2. Poland has eight classes for carload shipments. See Tarski 1967: 152. Differential increases in the tariff for all classes were introduced in 1976 with the aim of covering the cost incurred by the railroad. The top tariff is now 366 percent of the lowest tariff (Zolcinski 1975: 2–6).

3. Partly as the result of cost inflation that resulted from the worldwide price increases during the 1973–75 period, and partly to rationalize transport and introduce the principle of covering of cost by the prices charged, a reform of freight charges on the railroad and road transport was introduced in Poland at the beginning of 1976 (Zolcinski 1975; Lenartowicz 1975; Podwysocki 1976a; Podwysocki 1976b). Transport pricing encounters some difficulties also in the nationalized sector in Great Britain (Thompson and Hunter 1973: 157–81).

Chapter 6
International Aspects of Transport in Eastern Europe

1. For a technical discussion of axle width see Slezak 1963: 121–27.

2. Probably as a result of its limited international recognition during the 1960s.

3. The Bulgarian Motorists' Union has stressed ideological education of its members, possibly to counteract the influence of foreign contacts (RFER: Situation Report, 5 February 1976).

Chapter 7
Conclusions and Projections

1. In the U.S. the use of fuel for intercity freight shipments, expressed BTUs (British Thermal Units), declined between 1950 and 1971 in consequence of technological improvements and conversion from coal to diesel fuel on the railroad. That decline was achieved despite rising transport performance (Kneafsey 1975: 377–78, 118).

2. According to a different estimate, the volume of freight transported will rise by 400 percent (Goscilowicz 1975: 46). For other projections by mode, see Nowosielski 1972: 9–18; Lissowska 1972: 19–27; Bartosiewicz and Szczygiel 1973: 17–22; Ostaszewicz 1973: 23–25; Rostocki and Wieniawski 1973: 13–21; Dobromirski, Glowczynski, and Milkowski 1973: 6–14.

Bibliography

For abbreviated references, the reader.is advised to refer to the List of Abbreviations on pages x–xi.

Afansyev, L. L. 1975. "The Tendency Towards Fuel Economy and Decreasing Air Pollution in Automobile Transport of the U.S.S.R." *Transportation Research,* July (vol. 9, no. 2/3).

Aldcroft, Derek. 1968. *British Railways in Transition.* London: Macmillan.

Alton, Thad. 1955. *Polish Postwar Economy.* New York: Columbia University Press.

———. 1970. "Economic Structure and Growth in Eastern Europe." In U.S. Congress, Joint Economic Committee, *Economic Developments in Countries of Eastern Europe.* 91st Congress, 2nd Session.

———. 1974. "Economic Growth and Resource Allocation in Eastern Europe." In U.S. Congress, Joint Economic Committee, *Reorientation and Commercial Relations of the Economies of Eastern Europe.* 93rd Congress, 2nd Session.

Alton, Thad et al. 1962. *Czechoslovak National Income and Product, 1947–1948 and 1955–1956.* New York: Columbia University Press.

———. 1963. *Hungarian National Income and Product in 1955.* New York: Columbia University Press.

———. 1965. *Polish National Income and Product in 1954, 1955 and 1956.* New York: Columbia University Press.

Alton, Thad, Elizabeth Bass, Laszlo Czirjak, and Gregor Lazarcik. 1975. *Statistics on East European Economic Structure and Growth.* OP-48.

Alton, Thad et al. 1976. *Economic Growth in Eastern Europe, 1965–1975.* OP-50.

Andruszkiewicz, Witold. 1975. "Problemy rozwoju polskich portow i floty morskiej." In PAN, *Perspektywy rozwoju transportu w Polsce* (Biuletyn ño. 86).

———. 1975a. "Problemy unifikacji w procesach transportowych." *Zagadnienia transportu,* no. 1–2.

Annuarul Statistic al Republicii Socialiste România. Annual. Bucharest: Directia Centrala de Statistica.

Antic, Zdenko. 1975a. "Financing for Yugoslav-Hungarian Oil Pipeline Arranged." RFER: BR, Aug. 12.

———. 1975b. "Productive Results of Yugoslav-Rumanian Co-operation." RFER: BR, Apr. 25.

———. 1975c. "Yugoslav-Bulgarian Economic Co-operation Broadening." RFER: BR, June 6.

_____. 1976. "Yugoslavia to Build Highways With Western Aid." RFER: BR, March 12.

Bac, Jan. 1969. "Analiza porownawcza PKP z kolejami innych krajow." *PK*, no. 5.

Bandor, Frank, Laszlo Czirjak, and George Pall. 1970. *Hungary: Extension of Growth Indexes to 1967.* OP-33.

Barbov, Toma. 1969. "Rozwoj i osiagniecia transportu kolejowego w Ludowej Republice Bulgarii." *PK*, no. 12.

Barkovskii, A. and G. Gorizontov. 1965. "Puti snizenya transportnikh razkhodov v sisteme mezhdunarodnovo sotsyalisticheskovo razdelenya truda." *Planovoe khozyaistvo*, no. 11.

Bartosiewicz, Marian and Ernest Szczygiel. 1973. "Rozwoj transportu rurociagowego." *PK*, no. 2.

Bayliss, Brian. 1965. *European Transport.* London: Kenneth Mason.

Bejm, Tadeusz. 1976. "Program rozwoju transportu." *Nowe Drogi*, no. 11.

Berezowski, Stanisław. 1962. *Geografia transportu.* Warsaw: PWN.

_____. 1975. *Zarys geografii komunikacji.* Warsaw: PWN.

Beshchev, B. 1965. "Sovyetski transport pered nowymi sadachami." *Ekonomicheskaya gazeta*, no. 50.

Blotko, Kazimierz. 1972. "Zrodla przewozow nieracjonalnych." *PK*, no. 3.

Bornstein, Morris. 1975. "Introduction." In Morris Bornstein, ed., *Economic Planning East and West.* Cambridge, Mass.: Ballinger Publishing Co.

Bożyk, Paweł. 1974. *Gospodarka Polski wspolczesnej.* Warsaw: Interpress.

Braś, Władysław. 1975. "Jednolity kontenerowy system transpowy krajow RWPG." *PK*, no. 1.

Brdulak, Jacek, and Krzysztof Fronczak. 1976. "Kontenerowa szansa." *ZG*, no. 12.

Brown, Earl. 1971. "Comments." In George Hoffman, ed., *Eastern Europe: Essays in Geographical Problems.* New York: Praeger.

Brozen, Yale. 1975. "Introduction." Part Four: Evaluations of Federal Transportation Programs. In James Miller, ed., *Perspectives on Federal Transportation Policy.* Washington, D.C.: American Enterprise Institute for Public Policy Research.

Bruton, M. J. 1970. *Introduction to Transportation Planning.* London: Hutchinson Technical Education.

Buchanan, Colin et al. 1966. *South Hampshire Study.* London: Her Majesty's Stationery Office.

Brzeski, Andrzej. 1974. "Nationalism and the Comecon: A Reconsideration." *Canadian Review of Studies in Nationalism,* spring (vol. 1, no. 2).

Burke, J. L. 1963. "Movement of Commodities by Pipeline." In *STD*, vol. 5, *Transportation.*

Čelechovský, Gorazd. 1972. "Goods Transport in Etarea." *Transportation,* Aug. (vol. 1, no. 2).

Chekrezi, Constantine. 1971. *Albania Past and Present.* New York: Arno Press.

Chełstowski, Stanisław. 1975. "Transport kolejowy: potega z koniecznosci." *ZG*, no. 35.

Constantinescu, R. 1973. "Cooperation and collaboration in material production among the socialist countries." *Viata Economica,* July 3 and 13. Cited in RFER: Rumanian Press Survey, Sept. 7.

Czére, Béla. 1966. "Transport." In Zoltan Halasz, ed., *Hungary*. Budapest: Corvina Press.

Czirjak, Laszlo. 1965. *Hungary: Index of Transportation and Communication Services: 1938-1962*. OP-8.

Czownicki, Jerzy. 1975. "Lotnictwo w przestrzennym zagospodarowaniu kraju." In *Perspektywy rozwoju transportu w Polsce* (Biuletyn no. 86).

———. 1976. "Rola krajowej komunikacji lotniczej w zintegrowanym systemie transportu." *PK*, no. 9.

Deasy, George, Phyllis Griess, Willard Miller, and Earl Case. 1958. *The World's Nations: An Economic and Regional Geography*. Chicago: J. B. Lippincott Co.

Demmler, Horst. 1967. *Verkehrspolitik in der Sowjetzone Deutschlands*. Heidelberg: Quelle & Meyer.

Dobromirski, Walerian. 1973. "Zegluga srodladowa w zintegrowanym systemie transportowym." *PK*, no. 5.

Dochód narodowy. Occasional. Warsaw: GUS.

Dzięciołowski, Jerzy. 1975. "Przystanek 'Ursus'." *ZG*, no. 11.

The Economist (London). 1974. "Freight Transport." Nov. 16.

———. 1976. "Britain's Transport." Apr. 17.

Elliot, James and Anthony Scaperlanda. 1966. "East Germany's Liberman-Type Reforms." *The Quarterly Review of Economic & Business*, autumn (vol. 6, no. 3).

European Conference of Ministers of Transport. 1965. *XV Council of Ministers: Resolutions*. Lisbon and Paris.

Fabirkiewicz, Janusz. 1975. "Nie czepiac sie pociagow." *Polityka*, no. 5.

Farris, Martin and Forrest Harding. 1976. *Passenger Transportation*. Englewood Cliffs, N.J.: Prentice-Hall.

Feiwel, George. 1967. *The Soviet Quest for Economic Efficiency*. New York: Praeger.

Feld, S. 1965. "Planirovanye vazhneishikh otraslevikh i territoryalnikh proportsii obshchestvennogo vosproizvodstva." *Planovoye khoziaystvo*, no. 11.

Fiedorowicz, Kazimierz. 1974. "Racjonalnosc ukladow sieciowych infrastruktury ekonomiczno-technicznej kraju w zagospodarowaniu przestrzennym." *ZN*, no. 95. Warsaw: SGPiS.

———. 1976. "Planowanie infrastruktury gospodarczej w Polsce." *PK*, no. 5.

Fisher, Jack. 1971. "The Emergence of Regional Spatial Planning in Yugoslavia: The Slovenian Experience." In George Hoffman, ed., *Eastern Europe: Essays in Geographical Problems*. New York: Praeger.

Froelich, Lech. 1975. "Jechac droga." *ZG*, no. 29.

Gajda, Bronisław. 1975. "Wydajnosc i sprawnosc transportu." *Zagadnienia transportu*, no. 1-2.

Galitskii, A. 1950. *Planirovanye sotsyalisticheskogo transporta*. Moscow: Gosplanizdat.

———. 1956. *Die Planung im sozialistischen Transportwesen*. Berlin (East): Verlag die Wirtschaft.

Gavrilov, V. S. 1964. "Sotrudnichestvo stran-chlenov SEV v oblastii transporta." *Zheleznodorozhnyi transport*, no. 5.

Gęsiarz, Zdzisław. 1974. *Konteneryzacja*. Warsaw: PWE.

Gillula, James. 1975. "The 1966 Ukrainian Input-Output Table and an Analysis of the External Economic Relations of the Ukraine." Paper presented at the Harvard Conference "The Ukraine Within the USSR: An Economic Balance Sheet," Sept. 26-27, 1975.

Giś, Aleksander and Janina Sierakiewicz. 1973. "Komunikacja publiczna w aspekcie rozwoju motoryzacji indywidualnej." *PK*, no. 4.

Główczyński, Stefan. 1975. "Prognoza zeglugi srodladowej w ramach jednolitego systemu transportowego kraju." In *Perspektywy rozwoju transportu w Polsce* (Biuletyn no. 86).

Gomulka, Stanisław. 1975. "The New Policy for Poland's Industrialization." *Poland and Germany (East & West)*, Jan.-June (vol. 19, no. 1/2).

Gościłowicz, Czesław. 1975. "Perspektywiczne problemy transportu ladunkow." In *Perspektywy rozwoju transportu w Polsce* (Biuletyn no. 86).

Grzywacz, Waldemar. 1969. "Zatrudnienie w transporcie." *PK*, no. 7.

Gumpel, Werner. 1963. *Die Seehafen- und Schiffahrtspolitik des Comecon: Ihre Auswirkungen auf den Hafen Hamburg.* Berlin (West): Duncker & Humblot.

_____. 1967. *Das Verkehrswesen Osteuropas: Entwicklung und Gestaltung im Comecon.* Köln: Verlag Wissenschaft und Politik.

Gunston, Bill. 1972. *Transportation: Problems and Prospects.* New York: E. P. Dutton.

Günther, Joachim. 1965. *Transportstatistik.* Berlin (East): Transpress, 2nd edit.

GUS. 1958. *DN 1956.* Warsaw: 1958.

_____. 1960. *DN 1957 i 1958.* Warsaw: 1960.

Gutowski, Antoni. 1974. "Statystyka ludziom na pocieche." *Kultura* (Paris), no. 12.

Güttler, Krzysztof. 1971. "Spoleczne problemy motoryzacji indiwidualnej." *Zmiany spoleczne i postep techniczny.* Wroclaw: Ossolineum.

Hamilton, Ian. 1971. "The Location of Industry in East-Central and Southeast Europe." In George Hoffman, ed., *Eastern Europe: Essays in Geographical Problems.* New York: Praeger.

Harbeson, Robert. 1959. "Transportation: Achilles Heel of National Security." *Political Science Quarterly,* March (vol. 74, no. 1).

Harbron, John. 1962. *Communist Ships and Shipping.* London: Adlard Coles.

Hay, Alan. 1973. *Transport for the Space Economy: A Geographical Study.* London: Macmillan.

Hayek, Friedrich. 1956. "The Present State of the Debate." In Friedrich Hayek, ed., *Collectivist Economic Planning.* London: George Routledge & Sons.

Healy, Kent. 1966. "Effective Allocation of Resources." In George Mott, ed., *Transportation Century.* Baton Rouge: Louisiana State University Press.

Heneghan, Thomas. 1975. "Polish Trade and Polish Trends: Economic and Political Considerations." RFER: BR, Nov. 13.

Hildreth, Clifford and John Lu. 1960. "Demand Relations with Auto-Correlated Disturbances." *Technical Bulletin,* Nov. (no. 276). East Lansing, Mich.: Michigan State University: Agricultural Experiment Station.

Hodges, Luther. 1966. "Policy Goals Become Less Elusive." In George Fox

Mott, ed., *Transportation Century*. Baton Rouge: Louisiana State University Press.

Hoffman, George, ed. 1971. *Eastern Europe: Essays in Geographical Problems*. New York: Praeger.

Hofmann, Karl. 1960. *Die Güterbeförderung der Eisenbahn und die Grundzüge ihrer Planung*. Berlin (East): Verlag für Verkehrswesen.

Hughes, William. 1969. "Social Benefits through Improved Transport in Malaya." In Edwin Haefele, ed., *Transport and National Goals*. Washington, D.C.: The Brookings Institution.

Hunter, Holland. 1968. *Soviet Transport Experience: Its Lessons for Other Countries*. Washington, D.C.: The Brookings Institution.

Institut Kompleksnykh Transportnykh.Problem. 1968. *Perspektivnoe planirovanye transportno-ekonomichskikh svyazei v SSSR*. Moscow: Izdatelstvo "Transport".

International Union of Railways. Annual. *International Railway Statistics*. Paris: The Statistics Bureau of the U.I.C.

Jain, J. P. 1973. *Documentary Study of the Warsaw Pact*. Bombay: Asia Publishing House.

Jaroszewicz, Piotr. 1976. "Zalozenia spoleczno-gospodarczego rozwoju kraju w latach 1976-1980." *Nowe Drogi*, no. 1.

Jędrzejewski, Zygmunt. 1975. "Perspektywiczne problemy komunikacji pasazerskiej w Polsce." In PAN, *Perspektywy rozwoju transportu w Polsce* (Biuletyn no. 86).

Jezierski, Andrzej. 1971. *Historia gospodarcza Polski Ludowej, 1944-1968*. Warsaw: PWN.

Jordan, William. 1975. "If We're Going to Regulate the Airlines, Let's Do It Right." In James Miller, ed., *Perspectives on Federal Transportation Policy*. Washington, D.C.: American Enterprise Institute for Public Policy Research.

Jurek, Wacław. 1974. "Struktura i wzrost gospodarki Niemieckiej Republiki Demokratycznej." *Przegląd Zachodni*, no. 4.

Kadas, Kalman. 1970. *Technisch-ökonomische Steurung von Verkehrsablaufen mit Hilfe Kybernetischer Systeme*. In series *Vortrage und Studien aus dem Institut für Verkehrswissenschaft an der Universität Münster*, vol. 9. Götingen: Vandenhoeck und Ruprecht.

Karpiński, Alojzy. 1975. "Modernizacja sieci PKP w latach 1974 i 1975 na tle zadan przewozowych dla zwiekszenia przepustowosci kolei." *PKP*, no. 4.

Kaser, Michael. 1967. *Comecon: Integration Problems of the Planned Economies*. Oxford: Oxford University Press, 2nd ed.

Kaser, Michael and Janusz Zielinski. 1970. *Planning in East Europe: Industrial Management by the State*. London: The Bodley Head.

Kawalec, Wincenty. 1965. *Okregi przemyslowe i regiony ekonomiczne w Polsce*. Warsaw: PWE.

Keefe, Eugene et al. 1971. *Area Handbook for Albania*. Washington, D.C.: U.S. Government Printing Office.

———. 1972. *Area Handbook for Romania*. Washington, D.C.: U.S. Government Printing Office.

———. 1972a. *Area Handbook for East Germany*. Washington, D.C.: U.S. Government Printing Office.

_____. 1972b. *Area Handbook for Czechoslovakia.* Washington, D.C.: U.S. Government Printing Office.

_____. 1973. *Area Handbook for Poland.* Washington, D.C.: U.S. Government Printing Office.

_____. 1973a. *Area Handbook for Hungary.* Washington, D.C.: U.S. Government Printing Office.

_____. 1974. *Area Handbook for Bulgaria.* Washington, D.C.: U.S. Government Printing Office.

Keller, W. M. 1963. "Phase Building of Railroads and Equipment for Less Developed Countries." In *STD,* vol. 5, *Transportation.*

Khachaturov, Tigram. 1952. *Zheleznodorozhnyi transport SSSR.* Moscow: Transportnoe Zheleznodorozhnoe Izdatelstvo.

_____. 1954. *Zur Ökonomik des Eisenbahn-Transportwesens.* In series *Wirtschaftsliteratur,* no. 8. Berlin (East): Verlag die Wirtschaft.

_____. 1959. *Ekonomika transporta.* Moscow: Akademia Nauk SSSR.

_____. 1964. *Ekonomicheskaya effektivnost kapitalnykh vlozhenii.* Moscow: "Ekonomika".

_____. 1965. "The Economics of Transport." In Akademia Nauk SSSR, *Social Sciences in the USSR.* Paris: Mouton & Co.

Khanukov, Evgenii, ed. 1965. *Ekonomika zheleznodorozhnovo transporta.* Moscow: Izdatelstvo "Transport," 2nd ed.

Kneafsey, James. 1975. *Transportation Economic Analysis.* Lexington, Mass.: D. C. Heath.

Kolaczkowski, Ryszard. 1974. "Interport: A New Solution to the Long Tug of War Over Szczecin?" RFER: Poland, July 31.

Komisja Planowania przy Radzie Ministrow. 1962. *Instrukcja ogolna w sprawie metodyki badan ekonomicznej efektywnosci inwestycji.* Warsaw.

Kopitz, Gerhard, and Egon Kutta. 1958. *Güterbeforderungstarife in der Deutschen Demokratischen Republik.* Berlin (East): Verlag die Wirtschaft.

Korbonski, Andrzej. 1969. "The Warsaw Pact." *International Conciliation,* no. 573.

Korbonski, Andrzej and Claus Wittich. 1967. *Index of Polish Transport and Communications, 1937 and 1946–1965.* OP-19.

Koropeckyj, Ivan. 1977. "Regional Development in Postwar Poland." *Soviet Studies,* January (vol. 29, no. 1).

Kruczek, Adam. 1975. "W sowieckiej prasie." *Kultura* (Paris), no. 9.

Kultura (Paris). Monthly.

Kuzienkowski, Roman. 1975. "Miejsce kolei w systemie transportowym Polski." *RKP,* no. 7–8.

Lansing, John. 1966. *Transportation and Economic Policy.* New York: The Free Press.

Lazarcik, Gregor. 1965. *Output and Value Added in Czechoslovak Transportation and Communications, 1937 and 1946–1962.* OP-9.

_____. 1969. *Czechoslovak Gross National Product by Sector of Origin and by Final Use, 1937 and 1948–1965.* OP-26.

Lazarcik, Gregor and Alexej Wynnyczuk. 1968. *Bulgaria: Indexes of Construction, Investment, Housing, and Transportation and Communications, 1939 and 1948–1965.* OP-30.

Lee, Po-chih. 1975. "Income and Price Elasticities of Taiwan Import Demand." *Industry of Free China,* Febr.

Lenartowicz, Zygmunt. 1975. "Reforma towarowych taryf transportu samochodowego i spedycji." *PK*, no. 9.

Leszczycki, Stanisław and Teofil Lijewski, eds. 1972. *Geografia przemyslu Polski*. Warsaw: PWN.

Levine, Herbert. 1967. "Economics." In George Fisher, ed., *Science and Ideology in Soviet Society*. New York: Atherton Press.

Lewis, Edward. 1963. "Integration of Overseas and Domestic Transportation in Developing Countries." In *STD*, vol. 5, *Transportation*.

Lewis, William. 1966. *Development Planning: The Essentials of Economic Policy*. New York: Harper & Row.

———. 1969. *The Principles of Economic Planning*. New York: Harper Torchbooks.

Liberadzki, Bogusław. 1971. "Planowanie przewozow w przedsiebiorstwie PKP." *ZN*, no. 85. Warsaw: SGPiS.

Lindner, Werner. 1962. *Aufgaben und Probleme der komplexen Planung des sozialistschen Transportwesens der DDR*. Berlin (East): Verlag für Verkehrswesen.

Lissowska, Elżbieta. 1971a. *Ekonomika i organizacja transportu samochodowego*. Warsaw: SGPiS.

———. 1971b. "Ksztaltowanie zintegrowanego systemu transportowego." *ZN*, no. 85. Warsaw: SGPiS.

———. 1972. "Rozwoj transportu samochodowego." *PK*, no. 12.

Lissowska, Elżbieta and Romuald Bauer. 1975. "Modernizacja transportu a ksztaltowanie sie czynnikow tworczych." *Zagadnienia transportu*, no. 1–2.

Litterer-Marwege, Wanda. 1967. *Rozwoj ludnosci Polski a planowanie przestrzenne i programowanie gospodarki mieszkaniowej*. Warsaw: PWE.

Livyant, J. A., J. N. Tikhonyuk, and M. D. Erlich. 1963. *Koordinatsya roboti avtomobilnovo i zheleznodorozhnovo transporta*. Moscow: Izdatyelstvo Ministerstva Avtomobilnovo Transporta i Zheleznykh Dorog RSFSR.

Locklin, Philip. 1966. *Economics of Transportation*. Homewood, Ill.: Richard D. Irwin, 6th ed.

Madeyski, Marian. 1971. "Ogolnokrajowy system transportowy jako podstawa polityki i prognozy rozwojowej transportu." *ZN*, no. 85. Warsaw: SGPiS.

———. 1973. "Ogolnokrajowy system transportowy jako podstawa polityki transportowej i prognozy rozwoju transportu." *PK*, no. 1.

Madeyski, Marian, Elżbieta Lissowska, and Jan Marzec. 1971. *Wstep do nauki o transporcie*. Warsaw: SGPiS.

Madeyski, Marian, Elżbieta Lissowska, and Wojciech Morawski. 1975. "Perspektywy rozwoju sieci transportowych w Polsce." In PAN, *Perspektywy rozwoju transportu w Polsce* (Biuletyn no. 86).

———. 1975a. *Transport: Rozwoj i integracja*. Warsaw: WKL.

Mahuzier, Albert. 1965. *L'Albanie entrouvre ses frontières*. Paris: Presses de la Cite.

Małek, Przemysław, Waldemar Grzywacz, and Bronisław Żymeła. 1973. *Ekonomika transportu samochodowego*. Warsaw: WKL, 2nd ed.

Małek, Przemysław. 1975. "Problemy ekonomicznej efektywnosci procesow transportowych." *Zagadnienia transportu*, no. 1–2.

Maleszewska, Halina. 1976. "Polak w ruchu." *ZG*, no. 37.

Mares, Vaclav. 1957. "Transportation and Communications." In Vratislav Busek and Nicholas Spulber, eds., *Czechoslovakia.* New York: Praeger.

Marshall, Alfred. 1920. *Industry and Trade.* London: Macmillan.

Mason, Edward. 1969. "Transport and Energy in India's Development." In Edwin Haefele, ed., *Transport and National Goals.* Washington, D.C.: The Brookings Institution.

Meier, Richard. 1965. *Developmental Planning.* New York: McGraw-Hill.

Meissner, Boris. 1962. *Der Warschauer Pact.* Köln: Verlag Wissenschaft und Politik, vol. 1.

Michalski, Czesław. 1975. *Ekonomika kolei* (part 2). Warsaw: WKL.

Mieczkowski, Bogdan. 1967. "The Unstable Soviet Bloc Economies." *East Europe,* October.

_____. 1970. "The Sinews of Poland's Current Policy of Economic Intensification." *The Polish Review,* autumn.

_____. 1975. *Personal and Social Consumption in Eastern Europe.* New York: Praeger.

Mikhaltsev, Evgenii. 1957. *Sobestoimost zheleznodorozhnykh perevozok.* Moscow: Gosudarstvennoe Transportnoe Zheleznodorozhnoe Izdatelstvo.

Mikulski, Mieczysław. 1975. "Komunikacja lotnicza Gornoslaskiego Okregu Przemyslowego." In Akademia Ekonomiczna w Krakowie, *ZN,* no. 62.

Moore, Thomas. 1976. *Trucking Regulation: Lessons from Europe.* Washington, D.C.: American Enterprise Institute for Public Policy Research.

Mott, George. 1963. "Transportation in Contemporary Civilization." In Thorstein Sellin, ed., *The Annals of the American Academy of Political and Social Science.* Philadelphia: The American Academy of Political and Social Science, vol. 345.

Mrzygłód, Tadeusz. 1962. *Polityka rozmieszczenia przemyslu w Polsce, 1946-1980.* Warsaw: Ksiazka i Wiedza.

Munby, Denis. 1968. *Transport: Selected Readings.* Harmondsworth, England: Penguin Books.

Neider, Janusz. 1976. "Rola spedytorow w obsludze przewozow lotniczych." *PK,* no. 10.

Nettl, J. P. 1951. *The Eastern Zone and Soviet Policy in Germany, 1945-50.* London: Oxford University Press.

Neuberger, Egon. 1957. "Transportation." In Robert Byrnes, ed., *Yugoslavia.* New York: Praeger.

The New York Times. Daily.

Nichols, T. E., ed., *Transportation and the Changing South.* Raleigh: North Carolina State University.

Norton, Hugh. 1971. *Modern Transportation Economics.* Columbus, Ohio: Charles E. Merrill, 2nd ed.

Nowosielski, Leopold. 1972. "Rozwoj transportu kolejowego." *PK,* no. 12.

Ökonomik der Arbeit im Transportwesen der DDR. 1965. Berlin (East): VEB Verlag für Verkehrswesen.

Organization for Economic Co-operation and Development. 1976. *Maritime Transport, 1975.* Paris: OECD.

Osborne, R. H. 1967. *East-Central Europe: An Introductory Geography.* New York: Praeger.

Ostaszewicz, Jerzy. 1973. "Zagadnienia rozwoju transportu miejskiego." *PK,* no. 2.

Owen, Wilfred. 1964. *Strategy for Mobility.* Washington, D.C.: The Brookings Institution.

Pająk, Ryszard. 1975. "PKP w obsludze przewozow miedzynarodowych."
PKP, no. 10.

Panków, Mikołaj. 1976. "Pasazerskie miedzynarodowe przewozy kolejowe."
PKP, no. 2.

Paradysz, Stanisław. 1976. "Proporcje wzrostu srodkow produkcji i przed-
miotow spozycia." *Nowe Drogi*, no. 3.

Pawlak, Teofil. 1962. "Racjonalizacja przewozow kolejowych a sankcje
ekonomiczne." *PK*, no. 3.

Pearson, Arthur. 1964. *The Railways and the Nation.* London: George Allen
& Unwin.

Pegrum, Dudley. 1973. *Transportation: Economics and Public Policy.* Homewood, Ill.: Richard D. Irwin.

Petrović, Rude. 1965. *Ekonomska geografija Jugoslavijè, Evrope i nekih
izvanevrop. zemelja.* Rijeka: mimeographed.

Piskozub, Andrzej. 1975. *Ekonomika transportu: podstawy metodologiczne.*
Warsaw: WKL.

Podogrodzka, Zofia. 1977. "Kto, gdzie i jak jezdzi." *ZG*, no. 7.

Powysocki, Stanisław. 1976a. "Stopniowanie stawek taryfy towarowej PKP
w zaleznosci od ciezaru przesylek." *PKP*, no. 10.

————. 1976b. "Taryfa koordynacyjna w przewozie towarow." *PK*, no. 10.

Podwysocki, Tadeusz. 1976. "PKP na szlaku automatyzacji." *ZG*, no. 9.

Pogonowska-Szuszkiewicz, Anna. 1976. "Uzytkowanie wagonow towarowych w miedzynarodowym obrocie towarowym." *PK*, no. 7–8.

Przegląd kolejowy przewozowy, 1974. "30 lat na zelaznych szlakach PKP."
No. 7.

Rachev, Kalu. 1971. "Jednolity system transportowy w Bulgarii." *PK*, no. 10.

Racz, Gabriel. 1957. "Transportation and Communications." In Ernst Helm-
reich, ed., *Hungary.* New York: Praeger.

Radio Free Europe Research: Background Report or *Situation Report.*
Irregular.

Rajkiewicz, Antoni. 1976. "Jak sterowac ruchliwoscia spoleczna?" *ZG*, no.
44.

Rangeloff, Grigor. 1957. "Transportation and Communications." In L.A.D.
Dellin, ed., *Bulgaria.* New York: Praeger.

Renik, Bogdan. 1974. "Nowe zasady amortyzacji." *PK*, no. 1.

Renner, George, Loyal Durand, Langdon White, and Weldon Gibson. 1953.
World Economic Geography. New York: Thomas Y. Crowell.

Rocznik Statystyczny. Annual. Warsaw: GUS.

Rocznik Statystyczny Transportu. Annual. Warsaw: GUS.

Rolow, Aleksander. 1975. "Perspektywy szerokiej wspolpracy." *ZG*, no. 26.

Rostocki, Aleksander and Wladyslaw Wieniawski. 1973. "Tezy rozwoju
motoryzacji indywidualnej." *PK*, no. 4.

Rudzki, Adam. 1954a. *Organization of Transportation of Captive Europe.*
New York: Mid-European Studies Center, vol. 10.

————. 1954b. *Railroad Systems in Captive Europe.* New York: Mid-European Studies Center, vol. 13.

————. 1954c. *Roads, Waterways, and Seaports of Captive Europe.* New
York: Mid-European Studies Center, vol. 15.

_____. 1957. "Transportation." In Oscar Halecki, ed., *Poland.* New York: Praeger.

Samuelson, Paul. 1973. *Economics.* New York: McGraw-Hill, 9th ed.

Sirkin, Gerald. 1968. *The Visible Hand: The Fundamentals of Economic Planning.* New York: McGraw-Hill.

Skendi, Stavro, ed. 1956. *Albania.* New York: Praeger.

Slezak, Josef. 1963. *Breite Spur und weite Strecken.* Berlin (East): Verlag für Verkehrswesen.

Socha, Weronika. 1976. "Polska krajem tranzytu." *PK,* no. 1.

Spitzner, Osmar. 1961. "Zur Entwicklung des Vertragssystems als Teil der Planung und Leistung der Volkswirtschaft." *Staat und Recht,* no. 9.

Spulber, Nicholas. 1964. *Soviet Strategy for Economic Growth.* Bloomington: Indiana University Press.

Statistical Pocket Book of Hungary. Annual. Budapest: Statistical Publishing House.

Statisticheskii Ezhegodnik. Annual. Sofia: People's Republic of Bulgaria National Information Office.

Statisticheskii Ezhegodnik Stran-chlenov Soveta Ekonomicheskoi Vzaimo-pomoshchi. Annual. Moscow: Izdatelstvo "Statistika".

Statisticheski Godisnik na Narodna Republika Bulgaria. Annual. Sofia: Ministerstvo na Informatsiata i Suobschenyata.

Statistická Ročenka Çeskoslovenské Republiky. Annual. Prague: SNTL.

Statistički Godišnjak Jugoslavije. Annual. Belgrad: Sovezni Zavod za Statistiku.

Statistisches Jahrbuch der Deutschen Demokratischen Republik. Annual. Berlin (East): Staatsverlag der DDR.

Statistisches Jahrbuch für die Bundesrepublik Deutschland. Annual. Wiesbaden: Statistisches Bundesamt.

Statisztikai Évkönyv. Annual. Budapest: Központi Statisztikai Hivatal.

Stawrowski, Ryszard. 1969. "Metody kalkulacji kosztow kolei." *PK,* no. 2.

Stefanowski, Roman. 1976. "CC Plenum on Better Management of Resources." RFER: BR, Febr. 24.

Stęplowski, Bronisław. 1975. *Ekonomiczne czynniki racjonalizacji transportu.* Warsaw: WKL.

Stolper, Wolfgang. 1960. *The Structure of the East German Economy.* Cambridge: Harvard University Press.

Szeliga, Zygmunt. 1975. "Nie ma cudow na kolei." *Polityka,* no. 7.

Szporluk, Roman, ed. 1976. *The Influence of East Europe and the Soviet West on the USSR.* New York: Praeger.

Szukiel, Zenon and Andrzej Szymaniuk. 1975. "W dziesieciolecie dzialalnosci Wspolnego Parku Wagonow Towarowych (OPW)." *PKP,* no. 2.

Szymańska, Anna. 1976. "Ludzie na torach." *ZG,* no. 2.

Tarski, Ignacy. 1967. *Transport jako czynnik lokalizacji produkcji.* Warsaw: PWE, 2nd ed.

_____. 1968. *Koordynacja transportu.* Warsaw: PWE.

_____. 1975. "System transportowy Polski w ogolnoeuropejskim i ogolnoswiatowym systemie transportowym." In PAN, *Perspektywy rozwoju transportu w Polsce* (Biuletyn no. 86).

Thompson, A.W.J. and L.C. Hunter. 1973. *The Nationalized Transport Industries.* London: Heinemann Educational Books.

Thornton, Robert. 1970. *International Airlines and Politics: A Study in Adaptation to Change.* Ann Arbor: The University of Michigan.

Tismer, Johannes. 1963. *Die Transportentwicklung im Industrialisierungsprozess der Sowjetunion.* Berlin (West): Duncker & Humblot.

Tokarski, Jan. 1975. "Polityka racjonalnego zatrudnienia w transporcie." *PK,* no. 5.

Tolstov, V. N. 1969. "Planirovanye respublikanskovo vvoza i vyvoza promyshennoi produktsii i puti ego sovershenstvovanye (na primere Ukrainskoi SSR)." Kiev: unpublished dissertation, cited in Gillula 1975.

Toschi, Umberto. 1959. *Geografia Economica.* Torino: Unione Tipografico-Editrice.

Trend, Harry. 1973. "Economic Co-operation Among Czechoslovakia, East Germany, and Poland in the 1970s." RFER: BR, Jan. 29.

———. 1975. "Comecon's Organizational Structure." RFER: BR, July 3.

———. 1975a. "Comecon's Organizational Structure." RFER: BR, Oct. 5.

———. 1975b. "The Orenburg Gas Project." RFER: BR, Dec. 2.

———. 1976. "An Assessment of the Comecon Council 30th Session." RFER: BR, Aug. 23.

Underwood, Adam. 1972. *Let's Nationalize American Transportation Now.* Philadelphia: Dorrance & Co.

Union of International Associations. Annual. *Yearbook of International Organisations.* Brussels.

United Nations, Department of Economic and Social Affairs. Monthly. *Monthly Bulletin of Statistics.* New York: United Nations.

———, Economic Commission for Europe. Annual. *Annual Bulletin of Transport Statistics for Europe.* New York: United Nations.

———, Statistical Office. Annual. *Statistical Yearbook.* New York: United Nations.

———, Economic Commission for Asia and the Far East. 1967. *Introduction to Transport Planning.*

———. 1971. *Everyman's United Nations, 1966–1970.*

United States Congress, House Committee on Armed Services. 1959. *Adequacy of Transportation Systems in Support of the National Defense Effort in Event of Mobilization.* 86th Congress, 1st Session.

———, Senate Committee on Commerce. 1961. *National Transportation Policy.* 87th Congress, 1st Session.

———, Senate Subcommittee on National Security and International Operations. 1966. *The Warsaw Pact: Its Role in Soviet Bloc Affairs.* 89th Congress, 2nd Session.

United States DOT. 1972. *1972 National Transportation Report.* Washington, D.C.: U.S. Government Printing Office.

Westwood, J. N. 1963. *Soviet Railways Today.* London: Ian Allan.

Wilczynski, Jozef. 1970. *The Economics of Socialism.* London: Allen & Unwin.

———. 1972. *Socialist Economic Development and Reforms.* New York: Praeger.

———. 1974. *Technology in Comecon.* London: Macmillan.

———. 1974a. "Towards Greater Effectiveness of Research and Development Under Socialist Economic Planning." *Australian Economic Papers,* June.

_____. 1976. *The Multinationals and East-West Relations: Towards Trans-ideological Collaboration.* London: Macmillan.

Williams, Ernest. 1962. *Freight Transportation in the Soviet Union.* Princeton: Princeton University Press.

Wilson, Orme. 1971. "The Belgrade-Bar Railroad: An Essay in Economic and Political Geography." In George Hoffman, ed., *Eastern Europe: Essays in Geographical Problems.* New York: Praeger.

Wojterkowski, Zbigniew. 1968a. "Osiagniecia transportu w Polsce Ludowej." *PK,* no. 10.

_____. 1968b. "Rozwoj transportu w Wegierskiej Republice Ludowej." *PK,* no. 7.

Wolfe, Roy. 1963. *Transportation and Politics.* Princeton, N.J.: D. Van Nostrand Co.

Yugoslavia and Her Republics. 1969. Belgrade: Interpress.

Zacher, Lech. 1974. *Problemy strategii rozwoju gospodarczego Polski Ludo-wej.* Warsaw: Instytut Wydawniczy CRZZ.

Zajfryd, Mieczysław. 1975. "Jeszcze z mozolem, pod gorke." *Polityka,* no. 31.

Zaleski, Eugene. 1967. *Planning Reforms in the Soviet Union.* Chapel Hill: The University of North Carolina Press.

Zbierajewski, Janusz. 1975. "Przewoznik niewypelnionych nadziei." *ZG,* nos. 45 and 46.

_____. 1975a. "Sztab — to brzmi dumnie." *ZG,* no. 38.

_____. 1976. "Racjonalizowac racjonalnie." *ZG,* no. 3.

_____. 1977. "Zlom lubi podrozowac." *ZG,* no. 6.

Zielinski, Janusz. 1973. *Economic Reforms in Polish Industry.* London: Oxford University Press.

_____. 1974. *Polskie reformy gospodarcze.* London: Odnowa.

Zinam, Oleg. 1969. "The Economics of Command Economies." In Jan Prybyla, ed., *Comparative Economic Systems.* New York: Appleton-Century-Crofts.

Żółciński, Zygmunt. 1975. "Reforma taryfy towarowej Polskich Kolei Panstwowych." *PK,* no. 9.

ZG editorial. 1975. "Pomozmy kolejarzom." No. 27.

INDEX